Studies in
Modern French and
Francophone History

Inventing the modern region

Manchester University Press

Studies in
Modern French and
Francophone History

Edited by
Julie Kalman, Jennifer Sessions and Jessica Wardhaugh

This series is published in collaboration with the Society for the Study of French History (UK) and the French Colonial Historical Society. It aims to showcase innovative monographs and edited collections on the history of France, its colonies and imperial undertakings, and the francophone world more generally since *c.* 1750. Authors demonstrate how sources and interpretations are being opened to historical investigation in new and interesting ways, and how unfamiliar subjects have the capacity to tell us more about France and the French colonial empire, their relationships in the world, and their legacies in the present. The series is particularly receptive to studies that break down traditional boundaries and conventional disciplinary divisions.

To buy or to find out more about the books currently available in this series, please go to:

https://manchesteruniversitypress.co.uk/series/
studies-in-modern-french-and-francophone-history/

Inventing the modern region

Basque identity and the French nation-state

Talitha Ilacqua

MANCHESTER UNIVERSITY PRESS

Copyright © Talitha Ilacqua 2024

The right of Talitha Ilacqua to be identified as the author of this work has been asserted in accordance with the Copyright, Designs and Patents Act 1988.

Published by Manchester University Press
Oxford Road, Manchester, M13 9PL

www.manchesteruniversitypress.co.uk

British Library Cataloguing-in-Publication Data
A catalogue record for this book is available from the British Library

ISBN 978 1 5261 6925 9 hardback
ISBN 978 1 5261 9488 6 paperback

First published 2024
Paperback published 2026

The publisher has no responsibility for the persistence or accuracy of URLs for any external or third-party internet websites referred to in this book, and does not guarantee that any content on such websites is, or will remain, accurate or appropriate.

EU authorised representative for GPSR:
Easy Access System Europe – Mustamäe tee 50,
10621 Tallinn, Estonia
gpsr.requests@easproject.com

Typeset
by New Best-set Typesetters Ltd

Contents

Acknowledgements   *page* vi

Introduction: region- and nation-building in
nineteenth-century Europe   1
1 Adapting the Revolution   17
2 Basque soldiers in a French nation   40
3 Liberty, liberties and legitimism in the First Carlist War   63
4 Euskara or the spirit of the Basque nation   89
5 Inventing a Basque literary tradition   118
6 Euskara or challenges to the French nation   147
7 'The other within': ideas of progress and decline in
Basque travel writing   176
8 Reversing the 'tourist gaze'   198
Conclusion: a Basque region in a French nation   224

Bibliography   232
Index   254

Acknowledgements

Books do not only tell stories; they also have stories of their own. The story of my book began nearly ten years ago and has since lived many lives. Although the process of writing it was filled with challenges, the project was always kept alive by the remarkable people I met along the way. Niall O'Flaherty taught me how to write good essays and research applications. This whole journey started off in his office, where he patiently helped me craft my first-ever research proposal. Through innumerable conversations that produced more questions than answers, Alexis Litvine first taught me what it meant to be a historian. Michael Rowe and Jim Bjork provided a wide range of perspectives that enriched the project from the start. Sudhir Hazareesingh and Renaud Morieux offered vital suggestions and observations. To discuss my work with two such distinguished scholars was an unforgettable privilege. At various stages throughout the project, Jerome Greenfield, Richard Vinen, Eric Storm and Martin Conway took the time to read parts of my work and gave me invaluable feedback. I cannot thank them enough.

Many people along the way have asked the right questions, have encouraged me and have given me unexpected opportunities. I am grateful to Paul Betts, Michael Broers, Laura Cerasi, Will Clement, Matthew D'Auria, Timothy Garton Ash, Stéphane Gerson, Robert Gildea, Vincent Hiribarren, David Hopkin, Matteo Legrenzi, Julia Mannherz, Chris Manias, Christine Mathias, Hartmut Mayer, Isaac Nakhimovsky, Robert Priest, Judith Rainhorn, Paul Readman, David Todd, Robert Tombs and Oliver Zimmer. My students at King's College London, the London School of Economics and the University of Oxford have inspired me with their enthusiasm, curiosity and endless questions. I hope that I was able to answer some of them.

Acknowledgements

Since submitting the book manuscript to Manchester University Press, Alun Richards has been a kind, encouraging and patient editor, and Jessica Cuthbert-Smith a wonderful project manager. The two anonymous reviewers who read my work, moreover, provided thorough and detailed feedback, which greatly improved the quality of the book. I am, of course, responsible for any mistakes.

I am grateful to the AHRC's London Arts and Humanities Partnership, the Society for the Study of French History, King's College London, St Antony's College, Oxford, the Maison française d'Oxford and the Oxford Centre for European History for supporting my research. Furthermore, I am indebted to numerous archivists in Paris, Bayonne and Pau, as well as librarians in Bayonne, Paris, London, Oxford and Yale for their dedication. During the pandemic, their commitment to help researchers like me pursue our work was truly inspiring. Without them, I would not have been able to complete this book.

During my time in academia, some people have entered my life unexpectedly and have made it a happier place. Richard Vinen has kept a caring eye on me since the beginning of my doctorate and still seems to hold an unreasonably high opinion of me. Jerome Greenfield has spent an incredible amount of time reading and improving my work. I am lucky to call him my friend. Martin Conway has always given me the right advice and has never failed to remind me, once in a while, to be happy. Finally, Nick Stargardt has taught me that no distance is ever too far. For that, and everything else, thank you.

My best friend, and the best of friends, Allegra Curtopassi, has filled my days with joy, hope and lots of words since our undergraduate days. Every day I call her my friend is a happy one. I am grateful to her parents, Gioia and Giovanni, for always welcoming me to Brussels like a daughter. My insistence on visiting them has nothing to do with their new dog, Totò. Marianna Griffini always reminds me of the comic absurdity of this strange life. To Allegra and Marianna, thank you for believing in me even when I do not and for offering advice I usually do not listen to. I am also indebted to many dear friends scattered around the globe. Thank you to Mansi Bajaj, Miruna Belea, Jessica DeMarco-Jacobson, Jane Hanselman, Jana Hunter, Anastasia Kozyreva, Martina Landolfi, Martha Papaspiliou, Yuqing Qiu and Viviane Spitzhofer.

Acknowledgements

Finally, I wish to thank my many families. Alex and Ingleby Jefferson gave me a home in Britain when I most needed it. Although I do not live in London any more, they continue to be my second family. My cousin Marisa Rustico, her husband Manu and their wonderful children, Gabriel and Léa, welcomed me to Paris countless times as I was researching this book. Never have French archives felt sweeter. Laura Richling and her cat Animato gave me a new home in the United States. Mati's furry presence during the final months of writing was uniquely soothing. Lastly, this book is for my parents, Maria Chiara and Angelo, my brother Balthazar, who decided to read History at university against my best advice, and my giraffe Petronilla, who has grumpily followed me around the world since I was ten years old. None of this would be possible or worthwhile without them.

Introduction: region- and nation-building in nineteenth-century Europe

In 1925, the French weekly *La Semaine de Suzette* published *Bécassine au Pays basque*, the twelfth *bande déssinée* dedicated to the young and clumsy housemaid Bécassine, a stereotypical embodiment of the French northern region of Brittany. The story followed Bécassine and her Parisian employers in their journey through an equally folkloric and clichéd depiction of Brittany's southern counterpart, the French Basque country, where the festive *couleur locale* merged with more sombre echoes of a pre-'modern' past. There, Bécassine experienced a standard Basque *jour de fête*. She engaged in such folkloric activities as pelota, the Basques' national game, and the *corrida*, attended a traditional Basque mass, where men and women sat separately in church, and took the baths in Saint-Jean-de-Luz, where a man risked drowning in the characteristically perilous currents of the Basque coast. Her employer, Monsieur Proey-Minans, in the meantime, as director of the fictitious Académie des pays de France, settled in the invented village of Loratzean, where he performed an ethnographic study of the Basque population and their customs. In order to embrace local culture fully, he adopted the *costume basque*, wearing a short black jacket, white trousers, a red belt, a black beret and *espadrilles* as shoes.[1] The Basque country, the comic implied, was a region of France that still displayed the remains of a pre-'modern' past, where Parisians could catch a glimpse of a rural, folkloric 'authenticity' that was otherwise lost to urbanisation, industrialisation and 'modernity'.

This book contends that, albeit originating in pre-'modern' customs, the clichéd image of the French Basque country as a land of church, pelota and *espadrilles* was not the product of ancestral traditions. It was invented in the nineteenth century as part of France's process of nation-building. The invention of the French Basque region as a 'modern' cultural construct was a response to three changes that occurred in Europe in the long nineteenth century. First, it was a defence of particularism vis-à-vis the French Revolution's definition of France's new identity as *une et indivisible*. Second, it was a reaction to the emerging Europe of nations and to the hierarchy of cultures that divided the world into historical and ahistorical nations. Third, it was a revindication of a political idea of France, and to an extent western Europe, that did not conform to the values of centralisation, secularism and historicism that came to characterise the nation-state in the second half of the nineteenth century. The new age of nationalism, then, prompted local, national and international political and intellectual elites to reimagine pre-existing Basque traditions and to provide the French Basque country with a new cultural and historical repertoire that restructured pre-existing local loyalties within the new nation-centred political system. While the Basque region was intended to be complementary to the French nation, it could equally play against the interests of the nation-state.

The use of the noun 'region' to describe the French Basque country's collective cultural identity from 1789 to 1914 is improper. In Europe as a whole, the term started being used only in the late nineteenth century in conjunction with the rise of regionalist movements across the continent, and in France in particular.[2] The word, nevertheless, is useful insofar as it distinguishes the 'modern' region from the *ancien-régime* province and characterises it as a product of the European transition from absolutism to the nation-state in the long nineteenth century. As scholars have recently pointed out, the region, similarly to the political nation, was not a primordial entity nor a substitute for the nation-state. Rather, it developed in symbiosis with the 'modern' nation and shared with it some key characteristics.[3] Like the nation, the region was a constructed cultural entity, whose codification of a shared culture prompted its members to develop a collective consciousness that operated as an 'imagined community'.[4] At the core of region-building were two main elements. First was a synthesis of the principal cultural characteristics of that community. Such attributes are what Alberto Mario Banti has called 'deep images': a series of historically based virtues to which members of a cultural group attribute emotional value and believe form the foundation of their shared cultural identity.[5] In the nineteenth century, cultural practitioners reinterpreted these images as a coherent, historical metanarrative that ordinary people came to identify with the ancient core of their collective identity.[6] Second was an inevitable simplification of such features. The process of cultural stereotyping, which Susan Pitchford has defined as a 'cognitive shortcut' that enables the simplification and management of excessively numerous and complex information,[7] provided the region with a 'tertiary political identity' that strengthened its position within the political scene and helped to bridge the gap between local and national identities.[8]

Since regionalism reached its climax at the turn of the twentieth century, historians have tended to study the movement primarily in the period between 1890 and 1945.[9] Regions, nevertheless, preceded regionalism. Region-building had its roots in the age of revolution and, in particular, in the transformation of the socio-political order that the French Revolution initiated. A long-term analysis of region-formation, in this respect, is crucial for an appreciation of the origin of late nineteenth-century regionalist movements. The critical moment occurred on 4 August 1789 when, as a result of the National Assembly's abolition of privileges, language replaced fiscal liberties as the key distinctive feature of provincial France.[10] At the time, the French Basque country was formed of three distinctive *pays*: Labourd (Lapurdi), Basse-Navarre (Nafarroa Beherea) and Soule (Zuberoa). Like other fiscally independent *pays d'état* across the kingdom,[11] the three Basque provinces were jealously attached to their privileges, known as *fors* or *franchises*: local treaties that the Basques had negotiated with the French monarchy in the early modern period and that awarded them significant fiscal exemption. Despite sharing similar language and mores, under the *ancien régime* the three Basque provinces possessed no administrative, economic or historical ties, nor any self-consciousness or will of belonging together. The abolition of the *fors* transformed Basque elites' understanding of their position within the French state. Deprived of their economic particularism and facing growing state centralisation, Basque notables began to defend local exceptionalism on the basis of the three *pays*' commonalities of language, history and customs, and attributed for the first time a collective cultural identity to the Euskara-speaking territories of France. As a result of this 'inventory of the province',[12] after 1789 *les pays basques* became *le Pays basque*, singular and capitalised.

The construction of a Basque cultural identity in the nineteenth century was influenced by wider Romantic understandings of nationalism that attributed political value to the historical and cultural reserve of each nation. As western European states evaluated the 'authenticity' of the world's nations on the basis of the richness of their past, the acquisition of the correct historical and literary repertoire became imperative for the redefinition of the Basque country's cultural position within France and Europe.[13] In this sense, the transition from a pre-modern ethnic community, or *ethnie*, to a region, like the one from *ethnie* to nation,[14] was a move from culture, understood as a pre-existing series of collective customs, to metaculture, a conscious reflection on and reinvention of such habits as a response to politically changing circumstances.[15] The new significance that nineteenth-century regions and nations attributed to their pasts, in other words, played a primary role in what Eric Hobsbawm has identified as the 'modern' shift from custom to tradition.[16]

While historians have suggested that regions differed from nations insofar as the former's repertoire of mythical imagery was weaker than the latter's,[17] in the French Basque country intellectual elites elaborated a sophisticated mythos of national ethnogenesis that remained compatible with the region's political subordination to the French nation-state. This was due, to an extent, to a different understanding of nationhood compared to the centralised and nationalised model that became dominant at the end of the century. On the one hand, for much of the nineteenth century, France remained a multilingual and pluricultural country. The different regimes that were in power prior to the Third Republic preserved the centralised administrative reforms of the Revolutionary and Napoleonic years, but did not seek to achieve cultural unity. On the contrary, they celebrated local identities as a means of promoting governmental efficiency and national identity. In this respect, France shared similarities with a multinational state such as the Habsburg Empire.[18] On the other hand, the study of a nation's past was as much a national phenomenon as it was an international endeavour. As Chris Manias has shown, European scholars working in the fields of history, archaeology, philology and anthropology operated across national boundaries while all the same reinforcing national projects.[19] When the Prussian linguist Wilhelm von Humboldt travelled to the Basque country at the turn of the nineteenth century, for example, he identified the local population as a distinct nation, whose language, he hoped, would further the accurate classification of European tongues.[20] In this regard, the Basque country was not dissimilar to the case of Greece, whose national identity was, to an extent, invented by European philhellenes and, as a result, was more revealing of its European inventors than of the Greeks.[21]

Although it was common for the recovery of a nation's past to be the product of both local and international agents, in the Basque country local efforts were themselves transnational. As Basque culture extended across the boundaries of both France and Spain, French Basque scholars were influenced by and, in turn, influenced their Spanish Basque counterparts in the definition of a collective cultural identity. The Spanish Basque country was formed of four provinces, Guipúzcoa (Gipuzkoa), Vizcaya (Bizkaia), Álava (Araba) and Navarra (Nafarroa), which had been co-opted into association with the ascending power of Castile and León and, later, with the kingdom of Spain in the medieval and early modern periods. Like the French Basque *pays*, each province possessed its *fueros*, which the Spanish Basques jealously and belligerently retained until their abolition in 1876.[22] Spanish Basque intellectual elites depicted the story of the Spanish Basque country in the nineteenth century as a struggle for the protection of Basque liberties against the Spanish state's attempt to follow France's path towards administrative centralisation and cultural assimilation. As a result, although the French Basques lost their *fors* in 1789, French and Spanish Basque *savants* found common ideological ground in the construction of a Basque mythology that shielded their respective localities from state intrusion. While the key philological texts that made use of Euskara to validate claims that the divine ethnogenesis of the Basques originated in Spain, the movement for the cultivation and preservation of Basque culture first emerged in the French Basque country. Spanish *fueristas* adopted such preservationist urge at the end of the nineteenth century in their attempt to recover socio-political self-government. Paradoxically, as Europe in the long nineteenth century became increasingly defined by territorially bound nation-states, the Basque border, both territorially and culturally, became progressively more fluid and divergent from official national boundaries.[23]

Historians of the Basque country have recently warned of the risk of reading nineteenth-century Basque history teleologically as a prelude to Basque independentist nationalism, which was conceptualised by Sabino Arana y Goiri, the founder of the Basque Nationalist Party, in the final decade of the century. Such teleology was popularised by the *fueristas* in Spain and by the Basque clergy in France in the last third of the nineteenth century in order to construct a Basque metahistory that legitimised Basque autonomy vis-à-vis Spain and France, and it was later adopted by Basque nationalists and influenced the classic historiography as well.[24] While Basque tradition was indeed, to an extent, a nineteenth-century invention, however, Basque elites did not craft it with the aim of political independence. Rather, their goal was the achievement of a privileged position for their regions within France and Spain. Demands for self-government, federalism and decentralisation, then, laid the foundation for a regionalism that was both defensive of local rights and conducive to the strengthening of a French or Spanish national identity.[25] As a result, French and Spanish Basque literature had a transnational element as well as a strong national one. In this regard, the French Basque literary production was not, as it is often treated,[26] a mere appendix to the Spanish Basque one, but an independent body of work that sought to respond to French-specific political, socio-economic and cultural circumstances.

Two groups of intellectuals were primarily involved in the crafting of a Basque cultural identity in the nineteenth century: local *savants* and European scholars. These cultural practitioners worked closely together to document the cultural heritage of the Basque country and operated in the fields of language, literature, material and immaterial culture.[27] While it was a common Romantic belief that language represented the soul of a nation,[28] the Basque tongue held a peculiar place because its antiquity and mysterious origin awarded Euskara unique importance within the linguistic map of Europe. Basque and European comparative philologists, then, contended that the study of the Basque language was important not only for Basque identity but also for the division of the world into linguistic genealogical formations and the European quest for the recovery of the lost, original Indo-European language.[29] Closely related to language was literature, the quality of which revealed the strength of a nation's idiom, its literary capability and, ultimately, its status as a cultural community.[30] As in much of Europe at the time, scholars in the Basque country studied, collected and at times forged national epics, folkloric tales and bardic songs, which they believed represented the remnants of the oldest and purest form of Basque culture.[31] Since the Basque country did not possess a rich written literary production, scholars focused on the recovery of its oral tradition, in both written and spoken form. On top of collecting local songs and tales in folkloric volumes, from the 1850s onwards local elites raised the prestige of improvised sung poetry, or *bertsolaritza*, advertising it as a specific Basque poetic genre and popularising it at the newly invented Basque floral games. For the *savants*, the *poésie populaire* not only represented the debris of a pre-modern Basque culture within 'modern' France but elevated the Basque peasantry to a symbol of the purity of the French nation. As Anne-Marie Thiesse has pointed out, the idealised peasant was the antithesis of the corrupted urban worker and served as a reassurance that, in the midst of a changing society, the essence of the nation remained unchanged.[32]

While Basque and European cultural practitioners shared a preservationist goal, they also acted according to different, contingent interests. European scholars regarded the study of the Basque country primarily as an intellectual endeavour. Local *savants*, on the contrary, possessed civic concerns too, insofar as they researched their region's past in order to recover its ethos in the present and improve the wellbeing of local communities.[33] In this regard, the region, like the nation, was both a modernist phenomenon, which scholars have dated back to the French Revolution's introduction of the notions of sovereignty of the people and cultural uniformity,[34] and an ethno-symbolic one, which Anthony D. Smith has defined as the intelligentsia's reinterpretation of pre-existing myths, traditions, symbols and memories. In the nineteenth century, the two phenomena went hand in hand because 'political archaeologists' regarded the past as a living entity whose quintessence needed to be recovered in order to build a 'modern' region or nation.[35] Their understanding of a 'living past' was closer to what Pierre Nora has defined as memory, characterised as people's emotional, mythical and spontaneous understanding of the past that ties them to the 'eternal present', than to his interpretation of history, a mere 'representation of the past' that can be studied but not recovered. In this sense, nineteenth-century Basque cultural practitioners did not seek to turn the Basque country into a *lieu de mémoire*, understood as a sterile historical site of memory, but to preserve it as a *milieu de mémoire*: a memory-region where it was still possible to recover traces of a fading primordial past.[36]

The difference in intents between Basque and non-Basque intellectuals, nevertheless, should not be overemphasised as, for many European scholars, the protection of an endangered culture was a transnational phenomenon that had little to do with the militant's nationality. Such folklorists as Julien Vinson, Wentworth Webster, Pierre Loti and Antoine d'Abbadie, the inventor of the Basque floral games, for instance, were not of Basque origin or were not raised in the Basque country, yet their commitment to the protection of Basque culture exposed the blending of culture and politics. The involvement of international elites in the construction of a Basque cultural community further complicates the classic definition of France as a civic nation and of the Basque country as an emerging ethnic nation at the end of the nineteenth century.[37] While at the turn of the twentieth century Basque elites began to define 'Basqueness' in racial and cultural terms as a response to the Third Republic's aggressive secularisation and linguistic centralisation, the lines between ethnic and civic were blurred on both sides. As Stephen Harp has contended with reference to Alsace, when facing day-to-day challenges on the local ground, national ideology succumbed to pragmatism.[38]

While the characteristics of Basque region-building in the first half of the nineteenth century can be identified with Miroslav Hroch's phase A of nationalism as a time of primarily scholarly interest in the language and culture of the region, the second half of the century witnessed a transition to phases B and C, whereby the population as a whole started being involved and Basque elites began to use Basque culture for propagandistic aims.[39] The population's involvement in region-building corresponded to the arrival of tourism in the French Basque country, which was, to a large extent, the consequence of Napoleon III's choice of the seaside town of Biarritz as his summer residence during the Second Empire (1852–70). Tourists visited Basque coastal and spa towns in order to receive the water cure and to participate in polite society, but they also crucially expected to experience Basque culture. Contact with 'authentic' peasant tradition was part of the medical cure itself, as it allegedly detoxified visitors from the corruption and superficiality of urban 'modernity'. Basque hosts responded to tourists' implicit request to 'gaze' at their lives by staging their 'authenticity':[40] they produced local folkloric dances and musical performances, dressed up in traditional Basque clothes and recounted popular tales that perpetuated such stereotyped themes of Basque identity as love, contraband, desertion and pelota. The Basque population's 'staged authenticity' was significant for a number of reasons. First, it revealed the extent to which Basque tropes of identity had penetrated popular consciousness and, to an extent, had been internalised.[41] Second, it underscored the fact that, in the transition from elite to mass culture, folklore was based on a process of cultural selection whereby ordinary Basques embraced those elite-sponsored traditions that felt most familiar to them and disregarded the others.[42] Finally, 'staged authenticity' was indicative of the ways in which Basque hosts actively contributed to the process of folklorisation and stereotyping of their identity. The contribution of the local population to the process of region-building was essential because, as Thiesse has argued with reference to the nation, the region was invented yet required a 'collective adhesion to this fiction' in order to live on.[43]

The official celebration of the *petite patrie* was a political endeavour that was supported by every regime in power in the nineteenth century in order to produce their own interpretation of what constituted the French nation. In this respect, the Basque country became a laboratory of ideas of France, where new political identities could be fabricated. The restored Bourbons regarded the Basques' attachment to religion and tradition as the emblem of *ancien-régime* values, which they hoped to recover in the whole of France as a means of restoring order after the Revolutionary and Napoleonic decades. Similarly, the Bonapartist regime of Napoleon III that governed mid-century France fostered the communal spirit of France's rural villages as the cradle in which to build a depoliticised French identity.[44] The liberal, bourgeois elites who largely dominated the political scene from the 1830s onwards, moreover, equally associated the Basques with ancestral tradition but depicted the region as a vestige of French morality in a 'modern' urban world divided between aristocratic corruption and working-class depravity. At the same time, they countered the Basques' perceived 'primitiveness' with a concomitant idea of progress, which was central to the nineteenth-century notions of both history and nationhood. Historical dynamism, they believed, created a hierarchy of civilisations and, hence, of nations.⁴⁵ Historical, progressive, 'modern', European nations would ultimately earn national self-determination; ahistorical nations such as the peoples of the colonies and European remnants of an archaic past, like the Basques and the Bretons, instead, were deemed to be living museums and were doomed to become extinct. The Third Republic that came to power after the fall of the Second Empire in 1870 shared the liberal view of history as a progressive march from the French Revolution of 1789 to the consolidation of a republican identity for France. As the self-proclaimed heirs of the Revolution, republicans considered regional cultural diversity as a school of democratic values but simultaneously perpetuated such key Revolutionary ideas as national unity and secularism.

The looming threat of the *République sans Dieu* was met with defiance in the most conservative areas of the Basque country at the turn of the twentieth century. Conservative elites opposed centralisation and secularisation because they regarded them as threats to the integrity and values of the Basque region. Before the 1920s, however, conservatism never meant separatism. Basque elites were adamant that they were not against the French nation but against the republican constitutional framework of the nation-state, and they demanded administrative decentralisation and respect for an understanding of nationhood based on the principles of religion, ancestry and *terroir*. Ideologically, they did not regard the nation as the sole source of collective identity and viewed it as a pragmatic constitutional framework rather than a salvific entity.⁴⁶ Their demands echoed the claims for a federalist restructuring of France made by right-wing thinkers such as Maurice Barrès and Charles Maurras and had similarities with the regionalist movement developing in Brittany, which did not reject membership of the French nation-state yet demanded a degree of administrative decentralisation.⁴⁷ Historians have argued that the French Basques were not receptive to the separatist ideas developing in the Spanish Basque country at the time because of Sabino Arana's exclusion of the French Basque country from his writings, the incompatibility between his view of religion and the everyday reality of the French Basque region, and the French Basques' lack of acquaintance with his ideas.⁴⁸ A fourth explanation, however, is missing. The symbiotic relationship between nation- and region-building in the nineteenth century produced strong political, socio-economic and cultural ties between France and its regions, which made membership of the French nation-state both economically convenient and ideologically essential for the conceptualisation of the Basque region. Hence, the myth of France as the sum of its regions, where every element of the whole contributed to its global harmony, gave meaning to the identities of both France and its localities: the *grande patrie* found its historical essence in regional cultural diversity and the *petite patrie* gained its *raison d'être* within the bigger nation.[49]

In recent decades, scholars have debunked the republican myth according to which the Third Republic represented the culmination of a pre-determined process of French national unity.[50] Not only were local identities contributors to processes of nation-building and 'modernity',[51] but across the nineteenth century local and national identities developed in a symbiotic relationship.[52] In this respect, regions within the French nation formed a 'composition française'[53] that resembled the role that *Heimaten* played in the creation of a German national identity after 1871.[54] Since France counted eight different constitutional regimes from 1789 to 1870, though, the idea of French nation was ever evolving,[55] and the creation of the Basque region – as that of other regions across France – was not a response to one specific model only. Rather, as Elizabeth Vlossak has pointed out in her study of Alsace, the inherent fluidity of the region was essential to respond to the numerous, contradictory and contingent definitions of France from 1789.[56]

Thus, the *longue-durée* study of region-building as a process that started with the French Revolution and reached its culmination in the two decades prior to the First World War reveals the significance of the whole of the nineteenth century for the process of French nation-formation. The period between 1814 and 1870 was not, as the republican myth had it, an interlude between the French Revolution and the messianic completion of a process of French national unity during the Third Republic. Rather, as recent scholarship has claimed, the years between the fall of the two Napoleons were a crucial time in French history, when ideas of what constituted France as a nation-state were forged, discussed and negotiated.[57] In this regard, French regions did not represent ideological peripheries to Paris's centralised model of state- and nation-building. They were a crucial, effective and enduring counter-myth that exposed the strengths and weaknesses of the unitary model of French nationhood.

Notes

1 Caumery and Joseph Pinchon, *Bécassine au Pays basque* (Paris, 1925).
2 Barbara van der Leeuw has pushed the argument further and has claimed that regionalist movements in the Spanish Basque country, Frisia and Flanders developed in the first half of the nineteenth century. See Barbara van der Leeuw, 'Regionalismo y nacionalismo en el siglo XIX: la batalla de los conceptos (País Vasco, Flandes y Frisia)', *Rubrica contemporánea*, 6:11 (2017), 44–64.
3 Xosé M. Núñez Seixas and Eric Storm, 'Introduction: Region, Nation and History', in Xosé M. Núñez Seixas and Eric Storm (eds), *Regionalism and Modern Europe: Identity Construction and Movements from 1890 to the Present Day* (London, 2019), 3–4.
4 Benedict Anderson, *Imagined Communities: Reflections on the Origin and Spread of Nationalism* (London and New York, 1983).
5 Alberto Mario Banti, 'Conclusions: Performative Effects and "Deep Images" in National Discourse', in Laurence Cole (ed.), *Different Paths to the Nation: Regional and National Identities in Central Europe and Italy, 1830–1870* (London, 2007), 220–9.
6 Matthew D'Auria, *The Shaping of French National Identity: Narrating the Nation's Past, 1715–1830* (Cambridge, 2020), 4–5.
7 Susan Pitchford, *Identity Tourism: Imaging and Imagining the Nation* (Bingley, 2008), 98.
8 Katherine B. Aaslestad, *Place and Politics: Local Identity, Civic Culture, and German Nationalism in North Germany During the Revolutionary Era* (Leiden and Boston, 2005), 12.
9 Anne-Marie Thiesse, *Écrire la France. Le mouvement littéraire régionaliste de langue française entre la Belle Époque et la Libération* (Paris, 1991); Anne-Marie Thiesse, *Ils Apprenaient la France. L'exaltation des régions dans le discours patriotique* (Paris, 1997); Julian Wright, *The Regionalist Movement in France, 1890–1914: Jean Charles-Brun and French Political Thought* (Oxford, 2003); Joost Augusteijn and Eric Storm (eds), *Region and State in Nineteenth-Century Europe: Nation-Building, Regional Identities and Separatism* (London, 2012); Xosé M. Núñez Seixas and Eric Storm (eds), *Regionalism and Modern Europe: Identity Construction and Movements from 1890 to the Present Day* (London, 2019).
10 David A. Bell, *The Cult of the Nation in France: Inventing Nationalism, 1680–1800* (Cambridge, MA, 2003), 171.

11 Ancien-régime France was divided into *pays d'élection* and *pays d'état*. While the *pays d'élection* had a fiscal system controlled by the French government, in the *pays d'état* the king could not make any fiscal demands without the consent of the local estates. The three Basque provinces were *pays d'état*. See Jean-Louis Masson, *Provinces, départements, régions: l'organisation administrative de la France d'hier à demain* (Paris, 1984), 36–9.

12 François Guillet, *Naissance de la Normandie. Genèse et épanouissement d'une image régionale en France, 1750–1850* (Caen, 2000), 97: 'inventaire de la province'.

13 Astrid Swenson, *The Rise of Heritage: Preserving the Past in France, Germany and England, 1789–1914* (Cambridge, 2013), 3 and 46.

14 On the pre-modern concept of *ethnie*, see Anthony D. Smith, *The Ethnic Origins of Nations* (Hoboken, 1999).

15 Joep Leerssen, 'Introduction', in Joep Leerssen (ed.), *Encyclopedia of Romantic Nationalism in Europe*, Volume 1 (Amsterdam, 2018), 20.

16 Eric Hobsbawm, 'Introduction: Inventing Traditions', in Eric Hobsbawm and Terence Ranger (eds), *The Invention of Tradition* (Cambridge, 1983), 1–14.

17 Xosé-Manoel Núñez, 'Historiographical Approaches to Sub-National Identities in Europe: A Reappraisal and Some Suggestions', in Joost Augusteijn and Eric Storm (eds), *Region and State in Nineteenth-Century Europe: Nation-Building, Regional Identities and Separatism* (London, 2012), 21.

18 Pieter M. Judson, *The Habsburg Empire: A New History* (Cambridge, MA, 2016).

19 Chris Manias, *Race, Science, and the Nation: Reconstructing the Ancient Past in Britain, France and Germany* (New York and London, 2013), 6.

20 Tuska Benes, *In Babel's Shadow: Language, Philology, and the Nation in Nineteenth-Century Germany* (Detroit, 2008), 24.

21 K. E. Fleming, 'Philhellenism', in Christopher John Murray (ed.), *Encyclopedia of the Romantic Era, 1760–1850*, Volume 2 (New York and London, 2004), 872.

22 Paddy Woodworth, *The Basque Country: A Cultural History* (Oxford, 2008), 28.

23 On the centrality of territory for the 'modern' state, see Charles S. Maier, 'Consigning the Twentieth Century to History: Alternative Narratives for the Modern Era', *American Historical Review*, 105:3 (2000), 807–31; John Agnew, 'The Territorial Trap: The Geographical Assumptions of International Relations Theory', *Review of International Political Economy*, 1:1 (1994), 53–80. On the Basque country's acquisition of an

'open border' in the mid-nineteenth century, see Talitha Ilacqua, 'An Open Border for Two Bordered States: Basque Disputes and the Remaking of the Franco-Spanish Frontier', in Anna Ross and Christos Aliprantis (eds), *State Formation and Administration in Europe, 1830–1870* (Oxford, forthcoming).

24 On the classic historiography, see, for France, James E. Jacob, *Hills of Conflict: Basque Nationalism in France* (Reno, 1994); Igor Ahedo Gurrutxaga, *The Transformation of National Identity in the Basque Country of France, 1789–2006*, Cameron J. Watson trans. (Reno, 2008). For Spain, see Jon Juaristi, *El linaje de Aitor: La invención de la tradición vasca* (Madrid, 1987); José Luis de la Granja Sainz, 'La invención de la historia. Nación, mitos e historia en el pensamiento del fundador del nacionalismo vasco', in Justo G. Beramendi, Ramón Máiz and Xosé M. Núñez (eds), *Nationalism in Europe: Past and Present*, Volume 2 (Santiago de Compostela, 1994), 97–140; Juan Aranzadi, *Milenarismo vasco: Edad de Oro, etnia y nativismo* (Madrid, 2000); Jon Juaristi, *El bucle melancólico: historias de nacionalistas vascos* (Madrid, 2000).

25 Joseba Agirreazkuenaga, *The Making of the Basque Question: Experiencing Self-Government, 1793–1877* (Reno, 2011); Fernando Molina Aparicio, 'La disputada cronología de la nacionalidad. Fuerismo, identidad vasca y nación en el siglo XIX', *Historia contemporánea*, 30 (2005), 219–45; Fernando Molina Aparicio, 'España no era tan diferente. Regionalismo y identidad nacional en el País Vasco (1868–1898)', *Ayer*, 64 (2006), 179–200.

26 Juan Madariaga Orbea, *Anthology of Apologists and Detractors of the Basque Language* (Reno, 2006).
27 On the different cultural fields, see Leerssen, 'Introduction', 23.
28 Joep Leerssen, *National Thought in Europe: A Cultural History* (Amsterdam, 2018), 134.
29 Benes, *In Babel's Shadow*, 3.
30 Leerssen, 'Introduction', 27.
31 On such movement in France as a whole, see Thiesse, *Écrire la France*.
32 Anne-Marie Thiesse, *La Création des identités nationales. Europe XVIIIe–XXe siècle* (Paris, 1999), 159–60.
33 Odile Parsis-Barubé, *La Province antiquaire. L'invention de l'histoire locale en France (1800–1870)* (Paris, 2011), 31.
34 See, for example, Ernest Gellner, *Nations and Nationalism* (Oxford, 1983); E. J. Hobsbawm, *Nations and Nationalism Since 1780: Programme, Myth, Reality* (Cambridge, 1990).
35 Anthony D. Smith, *Myths and Memories of the Nation* (Oxford, 1999), 9 and 12.

36 Pierre Nora, 'Entre Mémoire et histoire. La problématique des lieux', in Pierre Nora (ed.), *Les Lieux de mémoire*. *La République*, Volume 1 (Paris, 1984), xviii–xix: 'présent éternel … représentation du passé'.

37 For the classic distinction between civic and ethnic nation, see Rogers Brubaker, *Citizenship and Nationhood in France and Germany* (Cambridge, MA, 1992). For a criticism, see Patrick Weil, *Être français. Les quatre piliers de la nationalité* (La Tour-d'Aigues, 2011).

38 Stephen L. Harp, *Learning to Be Loyal: Primary Schooling as Nation-Building in Alsace and Lorraine, 1850–1940* (DeKalb, 1998), 13.

39 Miroslav Hroch, *Social Preconditions of National Revival in Europe: A Comparative Analysis of the Social Composition of Patriotic Groups Among the Smaller European Nations* (New York, 2000), 22–3.

40 On the notions of 'the tourist gaze' and of 'staged authenticity', see, respectively, John Urry, *The Tourist Gaze* (Los Angeles and London, 2001) and Dean MacCannell, 'Staged Authenticity: Arrangements of Social Space in Tourist Settings', *American Journal of Sociology*, 79:3 (1973), 589–603.

41 On the process of self-internalisation of stereotypes, see Silvana Patriarca, 'Indolence and Regeneration: Tropes and Tensions of Risorgimento Nationalism', *American Historical Review*, 110:2 (2005), 380–408. For a similar process in Spain, see Xavier Andreu Miralles, *El descubrimiento de España. Mito romántico e identidad nacional* (Barcelona, 2016).

42 On the notion of acculturation as a 'selective process', see James M. Brophy, 'Which Political Nation? Soft Borders and Popular Nationhood in the Rhineland, 1800–1850', in Maarten van Ginderachter and Marnix Beyen (eds), *Nationhood from Below: Europe in the Long Nineteenth Century* (London and New York, 2012), 164.

43 Thiesse, *La Création des identités nationales*, 14: 'l'adhésion collective à cette fiction'.

44 François Ploux, *Une Mémoire de papier. Les historiens de village et le culte des petites patries rurales (1830–1930)* (Rennes, 2011), 191 and 256.

45 Eric R. Wolf, *Europe and the People Without History* (Berkeley, 1982), 5 and 12; Larry Wolff, *Inventing Eastern Europe: The Map of Civilisation on the Mind of the Enlightenment* (Stanford, 1994), 12–13.

46 Maiken Umbach, 'Nation and Region: Regionalism in Modern European Nation-States', in Timothy Baycroft and Mark Hewitson (eds), *What Is a Nation? Europe 1789–1914* (Oxford, 2006), 78–9.

47 Robert Gildea, *The Past in French History* (New Haven and London, 1994), 179–81; Caroline Ford, *Creating the Nation in Provincial France: Religion and Political Identity in Brittany* (Princeton, 1993), 199–200.

48 Jacob, *Hills of Conflict*, 57.

49 Raoul Girardet, *Mythes et mythologies politiques* (Paris, 1986), 156.
50 The classic work that follows the republican myth is Eugen Weber, *Peasants into Frenchmen: The Modernization of Rural France, 1870–1914* (Stanford, 1976). For a recent perpetuation of the same argument, see Émile Chabal, *A Divided Republic: Nation, State and Citizenship in Contemporary France* (Cambridge, 2015).
51 Ford, *Creating the Nation in Provincial France*; Peter Sahlins, *Boundaries: The Making of France and Spain in the Pyrenees* (Berkeley, 1991); Ruth Harris, *Lourdes: Body and Spirit in the Secular Age* (London, 1999).
52 Stéphane Gerson, *The Pride of Place: Local Memories and Political Culture in Nineteenth-Century France* (Ithaca, 2003); Ploux, *Une Mémoire de papier*; Francesca Zantedeschi, *The Antiquarians of the Nation: Monuments and Language in Nineteenth-Century Roussillon* (Leiden, 2019).
53 Mona Ozouf, *Composition française. Retour sur une enfance bretonne* (Paris, 2009).
54 Celia Applegate, *A Nation of Provincials: The German Idea of Heimat* (Berkeley, 1990); Alon Confino, *The Nation as a Local Metaphor: Württemberg, Imperial Germany, and National Memory, 1871–1918* (Chapel Hill, 1997).
55 Jonathan Israel, *Revolutionary Ideas: An Intellectual History of the French Revolution from* The Rights of Man *to* Robespierre (Oxford and Princeton, 2014); Jeremy Jennings, *Revolution and the Republic: A History of Political Thought in France since the Eighteenth Century* (Oxford, 2011); Lucien Jaume, *L'Individu effacé ou le paradoxe du libéralisme français* (Paris, 1997); Olivier Tort, *La Droite française. Aux origines de ses divisions (1814–1830)* (Paris, 2013); Sudhir Hazareesingh, *From Subject to Citizen: The Second Empire and the Emergence of Modern French Democracy* (Princeton, 2016); Timothy Baycroft, 'France: Ethnicity and the Revolutionary Tradition', in Timothy Baycroft and Mark Hewitson (eds), *What Is a Nation? Europe 1789–1914* (Oxford, 2006), 28–41.
56 Elizabeth Vlossak, *Marianne or Germania? Nationalizing Women in Alsace, 1870–1946* (Oxford, 2010), 19.
57 Pierre Rosanvallon, *Le Moment Guizot* (Paris, 1985); Aurelian Craiutu, *Liberalism under Siege: The Political Thought of the French Doctrinaires* (Oxford, 2003); Munro Price, *The Perilous Crown: France Between Revolutions, 1814–1848* (London, 2007); Pierre Karila-Cohen, *L'État des esprits. L'invention de l'enquête politique en France (1814–1848)* (Rennes, 2008); Benoît Yvert, *La Restauration. Les idées et les hommes* (Paris, 2013); Jerome Greenfield, *The Making of a Fiscal-Military State in Post-Revolutionary France* (Cambridge, 2022).

1

Adapting the Revolution

The French Revolution transformed 'Basqueness' from an economic to a cultural feature. Under the *ancien régime*, the local elites of Labourd, Basse-Navarre and Soule defined the exceptionalism of their respective *pays* on the basis of such distinctive attributes as their ancient history, their peculiar language and their *mœurs*, which came to form the basis of Basque cultural identity after 1789. Nevertheless, when facing the French state before the Revolution, they employed such tropes of identity almost exclusively to defend local privileges, and in particular fiscal exemption, from the increasing centralisation of the French state. As in the rest of the kingdom of France under the absolute monarchy, in the three *pays basques* privilege was central to the relationship between the king and his subjects. Upon acceding to the throne, the monarch issued an edict confirming the privileges of each province, through which he acknowledged the rights of his subjects; in turn, they recognised his legitimacy as king. In this respect, privilege in *ancien-régime* France played the role of political mediator between the sovereign and civil society.[1]

The Revolution altered the economic characterisation of 'Basqueness' insofar as it introduced a new key actor in the relationship between the French state and its provinces: the nation. As the constitution of the National Assembly on 17 June 1789 transferred sovereignty from the monarch to the third estate, Revolutionaries believed that, in order to ensure every citizen's 'equality of influence' at the local level, local privileges had to be suppressed and provincial administration was to be reorganised according to the principles of unity and uniformity.[2] Two reforms proved essential. The abolition of privileges on 4 August put an end to the demands for fiscal exemption that had permeated the relations between the Basque *pays* and the French monarchy under the *ancien régime*. Further, in January 1790, the creation of the *département* of the Basses-Pyrénées, formed of the three Basque *pays* and Gascon-speaking Béarn, united the three Basque countries administratively for the first time but, simultaneously, placed them within a bigger administrative unit in which the Basques represented only a third of the total population and were hence a linguistic and cultural minority. As a result, the Revolution's transformation of the national space prompted Basque elites, like others across France, to reimagine the position of the *pays basques* within the new administrative system of the country, redefining their sense of provincial belonging and reformulating their local identity.[3] With their liberties abolished, they began to identify cultural traits such as shared language, customs and historical ties as the Basque country's distinctive features that should protect its exceptionalism within both the French state and their *département*. Local elites' appropriation of a pre-existing Basque myth of descent, a shared culture and a sense of solidarity, and their association with a specific territory, a cultural canon and a common purpose, represented the beginning of the transition from the pre-modern *ethnie* to the 'modern' region.[4]

By debating the new administrative reforms at the National Assembly, Basque representatives contributed to the creation of an idea of France where centralisation went hand in hand with a 'deconcentration' of power at the local level.[5] While the early Revolution undoubtedly furthered the work of administrative and fiscal centralisation initiated under the late *ancien régime* that culminated in the abolition of the provinces and their historical rights,[6] the new system of administration was the product of a process of negotiation between the Assembly and provincial elites. As historians have recently argued, the creation of the *départements* was based on a mathematical obsession for symmetry, equity and unity that curtailed provincial loyalties but was also implemented with an eye to pre-existing bonds in order not to break economic and social customs too abruptly.[7] Additionally, the members of the National Assembly were overwhelmingly of provincial origin. They brought to Paris the ideas of state- and nation-building that originated in their respective localities and mediated with the chamber's radical fringes in order to protect the interests of their constituents.[8] In order to mitigate the consequences of centralisation, provincial elites responded to the new myth of national unity with local counter-myths of their own fabrication, which aimed both to reimagine the role of local communities within the new system of government and to preserve as much as possible the pre-existing status quo.[9] In this regard, in the Basque country, 1789 was the year of the invention of two myths: the myth of French national unity and the myth of Basque regional unity, which local elites conceptualised as a counter-narrative to the idea of the French nation as unitary and indivisible.[10]

Defending exceptionalism in pre-Revolutionary France

In the decades preceding the French Revolution of 1789, Basque distinctiveness within the kingdom of France bore primarily economic connotations. It consisted of protecting local privileges, fiscal autonomy and administrative exceptionalism against the growing centralising pressure of the French state. The local notability made reference to both the independent character and the constitutional tradition of the Basque lands in order to protect the rights and privileges of the three *pays*, as well as to preserve order among the lower strata of the Basque population, who, as in most of France at the end of the *ancien régime*, was prone to outbursts of violence and popular revolts.[11] Given the different administrative status of Labourd, Basse-Navarre and Soule, the three Basque *pays* lacked any sense of political unity or of a shared past. Labourd and Soule were annexed to the kingdom of France in the fifteenth century, while Basse-Navarre, alongside Béarn, was united to France by Louis XIII's Act of Union in 1620 but maintained its title of independent kingdom until 1789. The Navarrese were both proud and jealous of the fact that, until the Revolution, the monarch's official title was that of 'king of France and of Navarre'. At the end of the *ancien régime*, the Basque provinces were three of France's fourteen *pays d'état*: generalities where, unlike the *pays d'élections*, the sovereign was not allowed to make any fiscal demands without the consent of the local estates. Although similar, the three *pays* possessed different fiscal privileges and had different representative systems. Most significantly, Labourd's assembly, the Bilçar, was dominated by the third estate, while the estates of Basse-Navarre and Soule were centred around the clergy and the nobility. As a result of the absence of political, fiscal and administrative unity, the three Basque *pays* did not possess a sense of shared identity, prompting local notables to advance different claims for the present and future of each province.

In the last two decades of the *ancien régime*, discourses about the position of the three Basque *pays* within France were triggered principally by the French government's attempts at centralising and making uniform its fiscal system.[12] Like most French subjects, the Basque population, the Labourdins in particular, had an acute antipathy to taxation.[13] Towards the end of the *ancien régime*, such aversion was triggered by the increasing nationalisation of the market and international protectionism that worsened the *pays'* economic conditions. Internationally, Labourd witnessed a dramatic 40 per cent drop in exports from the port of Bayonne to Spain from 1765 to 1773 as a result of Spain's new protectionist policies that forbade the French export of cloth and silk. The position of the ports of Labourd, moreover, was unfavourable for Atlantic trade, causing a severe cut in the number of fishing boats from about seventy at the beginning of the eighteenth century to only twelve around 1775. Nationally, the Basque country was a victim of the French state's progressive establishment of a national market and of its tighter fiscal controls along the border, as well as, locally, of the lack of roads accessible for commercial purposes. As a result, the coast of Labourd suffered a dramatic population decline. Between 1764 and 1777, it dropped from 14,000 to 4,000 inhabitants in Saint-Jean-de-Luz and Ciboure and from 11,243 to 9,632 in Bayonne.[14]

Given the dramatic economic crisis in the *pays*, the rumour of the imposition of new taxes was enough to prompt the lower strata of the population to start an uprising. When, in the early 1770s, the government extended to Labourd the complete monopoly of the sale of tobacco to indirect tax collectors, the much-resented *fermiers*, the population rose in revolt. The *procureur du roi* Harriet explained the population's frustration by arguing that: 'The inhabitants of the *pays* of Labourd, deprived of their most beautiful privileges, ... thought that messieurs the *fermiers* would not pay attention to a province that they had almost destroyed. They were wrong: their ambition ... will stop only when there will be nothing left.'[15] The situation was dire, with women leading the uprising in several towns of Labourd and the mayor of Cambo being forced to fire shots in order to protect his house from the crowd.[16]

The officials sent to Labourd to mediate between the Basque population and the *fermiers* pointed at the independent character of the Basques as an explanation for the difficulties the *Ferme* was encountering in the application of the new *arrêt*. The *fermier* Dauvergne did not know 'l'esprit des Basques', wrote a state official, de L'Hôpital, in 1771, referring to the regular visits that the *fermiers* paid to the village of Sare, on the border with Spain, aiming to dissuade the local population from selling tobacco. 'The inhabitants of the *Pays* of Labourd do not know and do not accept anything that does not come from the *Intendant* or their *syndic* or a Bilçar,' he explained. 'This is the only approach that is familiar to them; all that comes in other forms is suspect to the inhabitants and excites them easily.'[17] For Harriet and the *contrôleur général des finances*, Terray, the principal issue derived from the fact that the *fermiers* had tried to impose the new *arrêt* on the population without any form of negotiation or explanation, triggering the already defensive attitude of the Basques. Women's 'fermentation' in a number of parishes, Terray wrote in 1773, was due to the fact that 'the crude people' mistook the *arrêt* for a threat. Additionally, 'the *fermiers* used incredible and extraordinary means, without anticipating the dangerous consequences that could ensue in a *pays* protective of its customs and liberty'.[18] Peasant revolts were frequent all over France under the late *ancien régime*, as a result of an increase in indirect taxation, which especially hit such products as tobacco, alcohol and salt.[19] Because of the unusual strength of the Basques' attachment to their historical 'liberties' and independence, though, state officials sent to Labourd relied on local historical dogmas in order to explain to their colleagues the reasons for the delay in and resistance to the implementation of the *arrêt*.

Historical justifications of Basque exceptionalism were popular among Basque notables, as they sought to protect the fiscal privileges of their *pays* by making reference to the historical 'liberties' that French and Spanish Basques shared. The Basques' reference to their 'liberties' was part of a long-standing French constitutionalist tradition that dated back to 1727, when Henri de Boulainvilliers had alleged that the Franks had elected their first kings and hence that the French nobility – who, it was believed, was of Frankish descent – had the right to retain all its privileges.[20] The principal product of Basque 'liberties', local literature explained, was the stipulation of local treaties, called *fors* in France and *fueros* in Spain, that the Basques had signed with their respective monarchies in the sixteenth century. The *fors*, which were in place in most Pyrenean *pays* under the *ancien régime*, permeated Basque communities' life. They regulated the organisation of their political, economic and social life, and, as local literature pointed out repeatedly in the final decades of the *ancien régime*, awarded the Basque *pays* significant fiscal privileges.[21]

When the principle of privilege, upon which early modern French society was founded, came under threat in the eighteenth century, local intellectuals popularised the early modern historical myth of the original liberty of all Basques in an attempt to defend the fiscal exceptionalism of their *pays*. The Basques, the priest Jean-Baptiste Sanadon wrote in 1785, mirroring a pre-existing manuscript written by a Basque nobleman, the Chevalier de Béla, were the first population of Spain, who had arrived there guided by Tubal, son of Japheth and grandson of Noah, after the fall of the Babel Tower, and Euskara was the original language of the Iberian Peninsula. The Basques were the only people to have resisted all conquest, including Roman domination, and hence had preserved their 'primitive liberty', which was proven by their preservation of their ancient mores and language until the eighteenth century. The product of such liberty was the *fueros* or *fors*, which, Sanadon alleged, dated historically from the early modern period but originated in the free will of the Basque people. The fact that no monarch had made an attempt on the *fors* since their stipulation, he concluded, was evidence of the Basques' original liberty, which the contemporary French government ought to commit to preserve.[22]

The myth of the original liberty of the Basques acquired further political meaning among the Navarrese elites in the final decades of the eighteenth century, as they sought to protect the fiscal and administrative independence of Basse-Navarre vis-à-vis the French state. The Navarrese's fiscal autonomy, as that of the other *pays d'état*, including Labourd and Soule, came under threat at the turn of the eighteenth century, when Louis XIV introduced two universal direct taxes, the *capitation* in 1695 and the *dixième*, later *vingtième*, in 1709–10, and substituted the *pays d'état*'s contribution to the royal budget in the form of gifts (*dons gratuits*) with *abonnements*, sums of money raised by the estates on behalf of the monarch. While the *abonnements* were still a form of privilege, they undermined the validity of claims to tax exemption and provincial 'liberties', as the gifts used to do.[23] The Navarrese opposed the French state's attempts at fiscal uniformity, affirming the allodial title of Basque land: a system of real property ownership, according to which real property was independent of any superior overlord. Allodial land was rare in feudal France before the French Revolution and was usually limited to ecclesiastical property. The Navarrese, however, argued that due to their origin antecedent to feudalism, they held their land 'in allodium' (*franc-aleu*). They opposed the state's claim that there existed no land without an owner and, consequently, that the king of France was the owner of the entirety of French land and was owed taxation from every corner of his kingdom.[24]

Étienne de Polverel, a deputy at the Estates of Navarre and one of the staunchest defenders of Navarrese autonomy in the 1780s, alleged that Basse-Navarrese land was held 'in allodium' by making reference to the history of the original liberty of Basse-Navarre. In a treaty published in 1789, he claimed that after the kingdom of Navarre was founded between 716 and 724 CE, the Navarrese first wrote their own code of law, the *fors*, and later elected their first king, who swore to respect the independence and legislation of Navarre. The fact that Navarrese law preceded the creation of the monarchy and was therefore unrelated to any political system, Polverel explained, echoing Boulainvilliers, made it apolitical or ante-political, and by extension natural, unchangeable and unchallengeable. Moreover, the fact that the king was originally elected and every king since then had had to swear an oath of allegiance to the people of Navarre meant that the monarch was only a representative of the people. As a result, Louis XVI could claim no ownership of Navarrese people's goods or land, and the latter could not be subjected to any feudal law. Finally, the king was not allowed to make any decision without the consent of the Estates. This included, among other things, that Navarrese people could only be judged by a Navarrese tribunal and, most importantly, that the king could not impose any form of taxation on the kingdom of Navarre without the consent of the Estates.[25] History, then, was crucial in the Navarrese's defence of their fiscal and judicial exceptionalism.

The status of Navarre vis-à-vis France became a source of disagreement on the occasion of Louis XVI's summoning of the Estates-General in January 1789, which prompted the Estates of Navarre to find legitimacy for their claims in Basse-Navarre's historical 'liberties' once more. The letter summoning the Navarrese representatives and the included guidelines, the Estates complained, treated Navarre as a province of France, rather than as a separate kingdom, which was historically incorrect. 'Navarre is not a Province of the Kingdom of France; it is an independent Kingdom submitted to the King of France, but distinct and independent from the Kingdom of France,' they wrote in a letter to Louis XVI asking for a redrafting of the convocation of Navarre to Versailles. Since Basse-Navarre was annexed to France in 1620, they added, every French monarch had respected its constitution because Navarrese law preceded the establishment of the monarchy. They explained:

> The constitution of the Kingdom of Navarre is such that <u>its Kings cannot promulgate any Law without the consultation, consent and will of the people of the three Estates</u>: the constitution [is] older than the monarchy of Navarre, because the Navarrese established this constitution before giving themselves a King; the constitution [was] recognised, sworn and respected by the King of Navarre for more than 900 years, from the foundation of the monarchy until 1620; [it is a] constitution that Louis XIII himself and all his successors swore to preserve and maintain unviolated; [it is a] constitution that could not be destroyed, either by multiple infringements over the long centuries, or by the silence of the Navarrese, or by any act of the absolute authority; not only because the rights of nations are inalienable, but also because it is written in the *fors* of Navarre that the Kings cannot ever contribute to their deterioration.[26]

When, in the autumn of 1789, word came that the National Assembly had decided to eliminate the title of 'king of Navarre', Polverel, as Navarrese deputy in Versailles, argued against the Assembly's decision, claiming, as the Estates had done a few months earlier, that the edict of annexation of 1620 was unlawful, as it had been enforced without the consent of the Estates.[27] A similar claim was made in Brittany by the *abbé* Maury, who argued against the abrogation of the treaty of 1532 between the duchy of Brittany and the kingdom of France that awarded the province fiscal and judicial privileges, on the basis that the Assembly could not take any decision without the consent of the Estates of Brittany.[28] The treaty, however, was unceremoniously eliminated, as was the title of 'king of Navarre' and the kingdom of Navarre itself in December 1789. The abolition of the kingdom of Navarre marked the last time that Basque elites defended their *pays'* exceptionalism on the basis of historical privilege. From January 1790, when the debate about the division of France into *départements* began, language and customs became the markers of distinction of provincial identity.

Negotiating privileges with the Revolutionary government

The National Assembly's abolition of privileges dismantled the political, economic and social foundations of the three Basque *pays* under the *ancien régime*. They lost their status as *pays d'état*, their fiscal and economic independence and their juridical institutions. Labourd and Soule also had their local assemblies eliminated and Basse-Navarre lost its independent constitution, its *parlement* and eventually its status as a separate kingdom. Finally, the three *pays*, like their Pyrenean neighbours, were deprived of their *fors* or *coutumes*, as they were known in Labourd and Soule. The abolition of privileges sent shockwaves through the Basque *pays*. As in the rest of France, Basque communities were wary of the elimination of local assemblies because, historically, they represented the defenders of provincial interests against the state's fiscal demands and 'ministerial despotism'.[29] The abrogation of the *fors*, moreover, overturned many of the traditional social structures that dictated the everyday life of local communities, such as the collective organisation of agricultural life, the inheritance law and policies of social assistance to the poor, the sick and abandoned children.[30] While some practices, such as the primogenital inheritance law, survived for much of the nineteenth century despite the reforms of the Revolutionary and Napoleonic era, others, especially those revolving around the local *curé*, struggled to regain their pre-1789 strength.[31] Like in the rest of the country, the Revolution's stripping of charitable institutions and relief programmes from the hands of the Church had dramatic consequences for the most vulnerable members of society that local communities took decades to overcome.[32]

Basque deputies in Versailles denounced the elimination of local 'liberties' as unjust, as they did not consider privilege to be in opposition to the principle of national unity. The nobility and the third estate of Labourd, for example, regarded the abolition of privileges as a response to feudalism and, as a result, they believed that it did not concern their *pays*, where feudal laws were practically non-existent.³³ Moreover, they believed in the *ancien-régime* notion that their privileges were a reward for the services the *pays* offered to the king and hoped to continue to operate similarly under the new regime. Such services were, according to their *cahiers de doléances*, the Basques' ability as seafarers and their protection of the border with Spain.³⁴ The Basques' protection of local privileges on the basis of their *pays*' different history and constitution bore similarities, again, with Brittany. Yet while the Basque nobility and the third estate formed a united front, the Bretons were internally divided. The nobility, very much like the Basques, defended the old Breton constitution on the basis of the province's peculiar history, while the members of the third estate were among the most radical in Paris and rejected the local constitution as the bearer of the inequalities of the seigneurial system.³⁵ The new French constitution rectified in Versailles similarly rejected privilege as the founding principle of society and replaced it with the ideal of a polity based on citizenship. At the local level, such a shift required a redefinition of the national space to ensure every citizen's equal access to the electoral and juridical systems.³⁶

The members of the Comité de constitution, in charge of the administrative reconfiguration of France, envisaged the *départements* as a necessary step towards the creation of a united and more equal nation, but they were also aware of the pre-existing historical, geographical and economic realities of rural France. As a result, the final draft took into account both notions of administrative centralisation and antecedent local ties.³⁷ Centralisation, then, went hand in hand with devolution of power, as the Comité believed that a degree of decentralisation was necessary to bring the new governmental and judicial systems closer to the people.³⁸ The *intendants*, the symbol of *ancien-régime* monarchical centralisation, were abolished and replaced by elected assemblies. The members of local assemblies were chosen among the male population of each *département*, which privileged local interests, and the central state exercised little control over them, allowing them to preserve a substantial level of autonomy.³⁹ Given the multiplication of local offices and the Revolutionaries' obsession with local elections, some historians have defined the moderate phase of the Revolution as an interlude of decentralisation between the *ancien régime* and Jacobin centralisation. Alan Forrest, for example, has portrayed the period as a time of 'radical decentralisation of power'.[40]

When the National Assembly announced its intention to divide France into *départements* in the autumn of 1789, Basque deputies petitioned the government to be awarded three separate *départements* whose boundaries corresponded to those of the historical *pays* of Labourd, Basse-Navarre and Soule. The *syndic* of Labourd d'Hiriart, for example, argued on 10 November: 'It seems to us that it would favour the interests of Labourd to be always alone, isolated, independent of all other counties.'[41] Such demands reflected the rivalries between the three Basque *pays* at the end of the *ancien régime*, which, as late as in the first months of 1789, could not imagine being united with any of their neighbours. In the *cahiers de doléances* of Labourd, for example, both the nobility and the clergy wrote that the *pays* should not be united with any other province, on account of '[o]ur topographic situation, our particular character, our customs, if you wish our prejudices, the organisation of our *coutume*, our idiom, our manners'.[42] On the occasion of the convocation of the Estates-General a few months earlier, moreover, Labourd had rejected the initial summoning because the Labourdins refused to participate alongside the town of Bayonne.[43] As Dominique-Joseph Garat, a representative of the Bilçar in Paris and later a proponent of the Basque *département*, wrote of the Bayonnais in January 1789: 'Their language, their mores, the *coutumes* that regulate their possessions, the way they contribute to the fiscal system, very often also their commercial interests, everything is different. These differences have triggered feelings of jealousy between the Bayonnais and the Basques, which easily degenerate into enmity.'[44] The animosity between the Labourdins and the Bayonnais was especially striking because, after the reforms of 1789–90, Bayonne became the capital of the Basque country. The Comité de constitution, however, discarded the option of awarding each Basque *pays* a separate *département*. Not only was their territory not extended enough to constitute three separate administrative units, but the Revolutionaries were committed to curtailing pre-existing provincial loyalties. As a result, they did not even name the *départements* after the historical provinces, opting instead for such natural elements as mountains and rivers.[45]

The Comité's refusal to acquiesce to the proposal of having three Basque *départements* prompted Basque notables to consider the possibility of being united with neighbouring *pays*. Such a shift produced two results. On the one hand, the notables convinced the Comité de constitution of the importance of uniting the three Basque *pays* together. This was not an obvious conclusion in 1790. Initial plans suggested uniting Basse-Navarre and Soule with Béarn, Soule's eastern neighbour, while Labourd and the town of Bayonne with the Landes, a new *département* created from dismembered parts of Guyenne and Gascony. On the other hand, Basque notables' petitions asking the Comité to take into account the special character of the Basques contributed to the development of a stronger, more self-conscious and more clearly defined awareness of the commonalities of custom between the three Basque *pays*. The tropes of identity that came to characterise the Basque region in the nineteenth century had their roots in the division of France into *départements* in 1790.

If the three Basque *pays* could not remain independent, Basque notables argued that the most logical solution was the creation of a Basque *département*. D'Hiriart, for example, wrote in the same letter on 10 November 1789 that 'it would be more advantageous for Labourd to be united with Basse-Navarre and Soule, rather than any other canton'.[46] Notables stressed the cultural and historical similarities between the three Basque *pays* and claimed that it was natural for them to be joined together. The municipality of Saint-Palais, for example, wrote to the National Assembly: 'The Basques of Navarre, Labourd and Soule all have a common origin, the same language, same mores, same taste, same customs. Nature had destined them, for their relations and their National character, as well as for their local situation, to form only one people, ruled by the principles of a common administration and by uniform laws.'[47] A similar argument of linguistic homogeneity was employed in German-speaking Lorraine, which had been split into two different *départements*. The local deputies protested against the decision on the basis of linguistic unity and proposed an alternative division that would respect the linguistic integrity of Lorraine.[48]

In January 1790, though, the Comité de constitution also rejected the Basques' demand for an independent *département* and three Basque *pays* were united with Béarn to form the *département* of the Basses-Pyrénées. Instead of weakening the sense of a shared Basque identity, nevertheless, the decision prompted Basque notables to be even more proactive in their rationalisation of the reasons why the Basques should only be united with other Basques. Their arguments for Basque exceptionalism were a mixture of *ancien-régime* rhetoric and of Revolutionary egalitarian discourse. Their initial hostility to the union with Béarn was due to their belief that the Basque country would be underrepresented because the territory of Béarn was two-thirds bigger than that of the three Basque provinces and its population was much larger too: 244,955 Béarnais to 131,248 Basques in 1791.[49] The Assembly of Ostabaret in Navarre, for example, maintained on 24 March 1790 that the fact that 'the Basques [are] a great minority in their political assemblies with the Béarnais will inevitably lead to the invalidation of their representation'.[50] The issue of representation was aggravated by differences in wealth between Basques and Béarnais and, especially, by linguistic difference. Because of the mutual incomprehension between the two populations, representatives maintained, the Basques risked lacking fair judicial representation, insofar as, in their appearances in court, they always required to be assisted by an interpreter.[51] 'If you unite people who speak one language with people who speak another language, what do you expect them to say to each other? They will end up separating, like the population of the Tower of Babel,' Garat told the National Assembly.[52] While Basque demands inevitably reflected the *ancien-régime* rhetoric that had dominated the relations between the French state and the three *pays* across the early modern period, Basque deputies did not argue for a return to the past. Rather, they wished to negotiate a favourable position for their locality within the new order.

During the Revolution, Euskara became the feature defining Basque identity vis-à-vis the French nation-state, a role that fiscal privileges had previously held.[53] Interestingly, as Chapter 6 will show, while during the Terror language became a weapon that radical Revolutionaries used to determine who belonged or did not belong to the new nation, in the first year of the Revolution it was the Basques who emphasised linguistic difference in order to protect their exceptionalism from state centralisation. Warnings about the alleged inequalities deriving from it had already emerged during the late *ancien régime* and hence were not a consequence of the Revolution. The *cahier de doléances* of the third estate of Labourd, for instance, demanded that the existing *intendants* be joined by a Basque, who could understand the language and interests of the population.[54] The Estates of Navarre, moreover, in their lengthy explanation of all that Louis XVI had misconceived in his summoning of Basse-Navarre to the Estates-General, included not having provided copies of the convocation in Euskara for the Basque-speaking portion of the population.[55] Yet, while under the *ancien régime* the 'choice of language'[56] was for the most part an unconscious process, developed as the result of tradition or convenience, in 1790 the Basques began to employ the issue of multilingualism consciously to claim a position of autonomy within the French state.

The National Assembly discussed multilingualism on 12 January 1790, on the occasion of a broader debate concerning the union of the Basque *pays* with Béarn. The arguments the Basque delegation presented to oppose the union identified Euskara as a major dividing factor between the Basque country and Béarn and, by extension, the rest of France. Linguistic difference, argued Dominique Garat during the *séance*, was 'an unsurmountable obstacle. The union that you propose is physically and morally impossible.'[57] His brother Dominique-Joseph, moreover, built on recent works of comparative philology to argue that it was impossible for non-Basques to learn Euskara, as it was not related to any other European language. 'Italian, German and English have a common origin in Latin and in the languages of the North. Euskara is the true ancient language,' he claimed.[58] They portrayed French as the language of the affluent few and Basque as the tongue of the peasant population, whose poverty denied them fair political representation. Garat, for example, told the Assembly: 'You will barely find in this county families wealthy enough to be eligible for the National Assembly.'[59] Although some members of the National Assembly were sympathetic to local languages and *patois*,[60] influential voices believed that wiping out linguistic difference was key to the regeneration of the nation; the Assembly adopted this stance.[61] Thus, the Comité de constitution rejected the request for a Basque *département*, confirming that 'linguistic difference was not a sufficient motive to forget propriety and excuse yourselves from the execution of your decrees'.[62] The union of the three Basque *pays* and Béarn became official a few days later.

That spring, each *département* was further divided into districts, which handled most administrative responsibilities, cantons – circumscriptions of six to twelve communes that held the seat of primary assemblies and of bailiwicks for justices of the peace – and communes themselves, conglomerations of villages that represented the smallest unit of the administrative hierarchy.[63] The Basque country was divided into three districts, Bayonne, Saint-Palais and Mauléon, that corresponded to the old *pays* of Labourd, Basse-Navarre and Soule, and twenty-two cantons.[64] While the classic historiography has tended to emphasise the extent of the Revolutionary reforms' rupture with the past,[65] recent studies have stressed the administrative continuities with the *ancien régime* and, hence, the malleability of the early Revolutionary regime. Patrice Gueniffey, for instance, has remarked that the new communes mirrored the role previously fulfilled by the parishes, which represented the core of local assemblies and of communities' social life under the absolute monarchy.[66] The new administrative divisions lasted until 28 *pluviôse* VIII (16 February 1800), when First Consul Napoleon Bonaparte promulgated a law that further centralised the administration of France. Together with the appointment of a prefectural system that governed each *département*, he replaced districts with less numerous *arrondissements*, each headed by a sub-prefect, who dealt with state bureaucracy.[67] In the Basses-Pyrénées, there were two *arrondissements* in the Basque country, Bayonne and Mauléon, and three in Béarn: Pau, Oloron and Orthez. Despite the new centralising reform, the Basque and Béarnais administrations within the Basses-Pyrénées remained separate. Additionally, sub-prefects were mostly local notables, familiar with the population, their needs and lifestyle, and often sympathetic to local concerns. Since the Basque notability, as in much of rural France, was limited in the nineteenth century, the role of sub-prefect, like that of mayor, was handed down across generations. The d'Andurain family, for example, served as sub-prefects of the arrondissement of Mauléon, with only a ten-year interruption, from the Restoration to the Second Empire.[68] As Pierre Karila-Cohen has pointed out, the departmental and prefectural systems set the foundations for the birth of a 'gouvernement d'opinion' after 1814.[69] From the Restoration to the Third Republic, local administrators wrote periodic reports on the *esprit public* of their *département* that were as much based on factual information as on their interpretation of local dispositions. This 'stuttering political science' often took the form of those cultural stereotypes that the Revolutionary decade charged with new political meaning and that came to define the relationship between the nation-state and its localities in the nineteenth century.[70]

As Marie-Vic Ozouf-Marignier has remarked, the departmental reform of 1790 was based on an essential contradiction between claims of national unity and the subdivision of France's territory into a multiplicity of smaller units.[71] Paradoxically, it was this dichotomy that allowed for the preservation of many Basque traditions within the new, more centralised system of French government. Although the *département* lacked executive power because every decision had to be approved by the central government, municipalities possessed extensive independence: they had jurisdiction over tax collection, the maintenance of public order, the requisition of troops and the enforcement of civil justice.[72] The *département*'s internal hierarchy was centralised enough for the state to control its activity in a homogeneous manner across France, but sufficiently decentralised for prefects and sub-prefects to govern with a degree of autonomy necessary to represent the interests of the local population.[73] Thus, the apparent contradiction between centralisation and decentralisation allowed such a culturally distinct region as the Basque country both to preserve its cultural differentness and to integrate slowly into the French nation-state in the nineteenth century.

Conclusion

In the final decades of the *ancien régime*, Basque notables employed early modern historical myths of Basque liberty and independence as arguments to protect local privileges from the increasingly centralising mission of the French state. While such mythology set the foundations for the conceptualisation of a Basque cultural identity in the nineteenth century, their use under the *ancien régime* differed in two main respects. On the one hand, such narratives lacked geographical unity. The three Basque *pays* were juridically separate from each other and proclaimed their economic and historical independence. On the other, their purpose was economic rather than cultural, as Basque elites employed them to defend their pre-existing fiscal independence in a society based on privilege.

The reforms of the early phase of the Revolution, in particular the abolition of privileges and the reconfiguration of administrative France into *départements*, prompted Basque elites to reimagine the position of the old Basque *pays* within the new model of nation-state. It transformed the meaning of Basque exceptionalism from an economic feature within the *ancien-régime* French state to a separate linguistic and cultural entity within the emerging order founded upon notions of citizenship and nationhood. In 1790, the Comité de constitution's creation of the *département* of the Basses-Pyrénées united the three Basque *pays* administratively on the basis of their common mores, language and history, which strengthened their sense of a shared identity and produced a semantic shift from *les pays basques* (the Basque *countries*), as Labourd, Soule and at times Basse-Navarre were referred to in administrative papers and cultural works under the *ancien régime*, to *le Pays basque* (the Basque *country*), one entity with a coherent set of values and traditions. The Revolutionaries' reconfiguration of France's administrative system in 1789–90, then, abolished the Basque *pays*' juridical and fiscal privileges but did not eliminate the differentness of the Basques within France. Rather, it united the three Basque *pays* together for the first time and contributed to the development of Basque elites' sense of cultural exceptionalism.

The transition from privilege to culture set the foundations for the creation of a self-conscious Basque cultural identity in the nineteenth century. It prompted local elites to expand their knowledge of local culture, studying the Basque language, crafting a Basque literary tradition and forging clichés of identity that defined the region in European popular imagination, as well as, to an extent, the Basques' own self-portrayal vis-à-vis French authorities and foreign visitors. As a result, as François Guillet has remarked with reference to Normandy, the proliferation of local cultural studies in the nineteenth century was one of the primary consequences of the Revolution.[74] Although differences between the three Basque *pays* remained, after 1789 local elites and state authorities increasingly began to regard the Basque country as a homogeneous unit with a culture distinctive from the official identity of the French nation. As the new Basque cultural identity came to be characterised in opposition to what France was not, it also became increasingly dependent on it.

Notes

1. Michael P. Fitzsimmons, 'Privilege and Polity in France, 1786–1791', *American Historical Review*, 92:2 (1987), 270.
2. Israel, *Revolutionary Ideas*, 98.
3. Guillet, *Naissance de la Normandie*, 81.
4. On the notion of *ethnie*, see Smith, *The Ethnic Origins of Nations*, 24–31. See also, on the creation of a cultural canon, Alberto Mario Banti, *La nazione del Risorgimento: parentela, santità e onore alle origini dell'Italia unita* (Turin, 2000).
5. Pierre Grémion, *Le Pouvoir périphérique. Bureaucrates et notables dans le système politique français* (Paris, 1976), 11.
6. On the notion of the Revolution as a period of unprecedented centralisation, see Isser Woloch, *The New Regime: Transformations of the French Civic Order, 1789–1820s* (New York and London, 1994). On the classic thesis that centralisation began under the *ancien régime*, see Alexis de Tocqueville, *L'Ancien Régime et la Révolution* (Paris, 1856).
7. Alan Forrest, 'Reimagining Space and Power', in Peter McPhee (ed.), *A Companion to the French Revolution* (Chichester, 2012), 94–5.
8. Peter McPhee, *Liberty or Death: The French Revolution* (New Haven, 2016), xii.
9. On the myth of national unity during the French Revolution, see Timothy Baycroft, *France* (London, 2008), 13–16.
10. Myth is understood 'not in the sense of fiction, but in the sense of a construction of the past elaborated by a political community for its own ends'. See Gildea, *The Past in French History*, 12.
11. George Rudé, 'The Crisis of 1775 and the Traditions of Popular Protest', in Isser Woloch (ed.), *The Peasantry in the Old Regime* (New York, 1970), 84–5.
12. Arnaud Decroix, *Question fiscale et réforme financière en France (1749–1789). Logique de la transparence et recherche de la confiance publique* (Aix-en-Provence, 2006), 45–8.
13. The content of the *cahiers de doléances* was revealing of the frequency of French people's demands for the equalisation of taxation, the abolition of taxes of all types and the solving of questions of public welfare. See Gilbert Shapiro, 'What Were the Grievances of France in 1789? The Most Common Demands in the *Cahiers de Doléances*', in Gilbert Shapiro and John Markoff, *Revolutionary Demands: A Content Analysis of the* Cahiers de Doléances *of 1789* (Stanford, 1998), 253–79.
14. Christian Desplat, 'Crise et projets économiques à Bayonne et en Labourd à la fin du XVIIIe siècle', *Bulletin de la Société des sciences, lettres et arts de Bayonne*, 137–8 (1981–82), 267.

15 Archives départementales des Pyrénées-Atlantiques in Pau (hereafter A.D. Pau), 1/J/897/5, Harriet to the government in Paris, 14 April 1777: 'Les habitans du pais de Labourt, privés de ses plus beaux privilèges, ... pensoient que M.M. les fermiers ne fauroient plus aucune attention à une province qu'ils avoient presque détruite: mais ils se trompaient: leur ambition ... ne s'arretra que quand il n'y a plus rien.' Translations are my own unless otherwise stated. Capitalisations, italicised words and underlined phrases in the translated quotations reflect the original.
16 A.D. Pau, 1/J/897/4, Harriet to the government in Paris, October 1773.
17 A.D. Pau, 1/J/897/4, Captain de l'Hôpital to the marshal and M. de Bertin, 14 September 1771: 'Les habitants du Pays de Labourt ne connaissent et n'admettent rien que par la voye de M. l'Intendant ou de leur syndic ou d'un Bilsar. C'est la seule forme qui leur soit familiere, tout ce qui vient d'ailleurs est suspect aux habitants et les echauffe aisement.'
18 A.D. Pau, 1/J/897/4, The *contrôleur général* to Marshal Derochelieu, 26 October 1773: 'fermentation ... le peuple trop grossier ... un moyen aussi inouï qu'extraordinaire, c'est ce que les fermiers ont fait, sans preuvoir les consequences dangereuses que pouvoient en resulter dans un pais prenevu de ses usages et de la liberté.'
19 Michael Kwass, *Contraband: Louis Mandrin and the Making of a Global Underground* (Cambridge, MA, 2014), 43–4.
20 Bell, *The Cult of the Nation in France*, 57.
21 Manex Goyhenetche, *Histoire générale du Pays basque. Évolution politique et institutionnelle du XVIe au XVIIIe siècle*, Volume 2 (San Sebastián and Bayonne, 2000), 115 and 169–70.
22 Jean-Baptiste Sanadon, *Essai sur la noblesse des basques: pour servir d'introduction à l'histoire générale de ces peuples* (Pau, 1785), 249.
23 Michael Kwass, *Privilege and the Politics of Taxation in Eighteenth-Century France: Liberté, Égalité, Fiscalité* (Cambridge, 2000), 33 and 95.
24 Frédéric Le Play, *L'Organisation de la famille selon le vrai modèle signalé par l'histoire de toutes les races et de tous les temps* (Tours, 1884), 63.
25 Étienne de Polverel, *Tableau de la constitution du royaume de Navarre, et de ses rapports avec la France* (Paris, 1789), 164.
26 A.D. Pau, C/1540, Response of the Estates of Navarre to the letter of convocation to the Estates-General of France, March 1789: 'La Navarre n'est point Province du Royaume de France; c'est un Royaume a part soumis au Roi de France, mais distinct et independant du Royaume de France. ... Telle est la constitution du Royaume de Navarre que ses Roys ne peuvent faire aucune Loy sans le conseil, consentement et volonté des gens des trois Etats: constitution plus ancienne que la monarchie

de la Navarre, car les Navarrois établirent cette constitution avant de se donner un Roy; constitution reconnüe, jurée et respectée par le Roy de Navarre pendant plus de neuf cent ans, depuis la fondation de la monarchie jusqu'en 1620; constitution que Louis XIII lui-même et tous ses successeurs ont juré de garder et maintenir inviolablement; constitution qui n'auroit pû être aneantie, ni par des infractions multipliées pendant une longue suite de siecles, ni par le silence des Navarrois, ni par aucun acte de l'autorité absolüe; non seulement parce que les droits des nations sont imprescriptibles, mais encore parce qu'il est dit dans les fors de la Navarre que les Rois ne pourront jamais les empirer.'

27 A.D. Pau, C/1601, Polverel to the president of the National Assembly, 12 October 1789; A.D. Pau, C/1601, Polverel's speech at the National Assembly on the proposal of abolishing the title of 'King of Navarre', 12 October 1789.
28 McPhee, *Liberty or Death*, 89.
29 Annie Jourdan, *Nouvelle Histoire de la Révolution* (Paris, 2018), 25.
30 Goyhenetche, *Histoire générale du Pays basque*, Volume 2, 205.
31 Vincent Wright, 'The Basses-Pyrénées from 1848 to 1870: A Study of Departmental Politics' (PhD thesis, University of London, 1965), 10–12.
32 For a reflection on the achievements and failures of the Revolution's reforms concerning the poor, see Alan Forrest, *The French Revolution and the Poor* (Oxford, 1981), 170–6.
33 Manex Goyhenetche, *Histoire générale du Pays basque. La Révolution de 1789*, Volume 4 (San Sebastián and Bayonne, 2002), 186.
34 Archives départementales des Pyrénées-Atlantiques in Bayonne (hereafter A.D.), E dépôt/Ustaritz/BB8, *Cahier de doléances* of Ustaritz, 1789.
35 Sharif Gemie, *Brittany, 1750–1950: The Invisible Nation* (Cardiff, 2007), 68.
36 Forrest, 'Reimagining Space and Power', 94.
37 Marie-Vic Ozouf-Marignier, *La Formation des départements. La représentation du territoire français à la fin du dix-huitième siècle* (Paris, 1989), 90–5.
38 Forrest, 'Reimagining Space and Power', 94.
39 Ozouf-Marignier, *La Formation des départements*, 82–4.
40 Forrest, 'Reimagining Space and Power', 94. Other historians disagree, though. See, for example, Michel Biard, *Les Lilliputiens de la centralisation. Des intendants aux préfets, les hésitations d'un 'modèle français'* (Seyssel, 2007).
41 A.D. Pau, C/1621, The *syndic* of Labourd to the Bilçar, 10 November 1789: 'Il nous semble qu'il seroit d'un très grand intérêt pour le Labourt de rester toujours seul, isolé, indépendant des autres contrées.'

42 Yturbide (ed.), 'Cahiers de doléances de Bayonne et du Pays du Labourt aux États Généraux de 1789', *Bulletin de la Société des sciences, lettres et arts de Bayonne* (1909), 29: 'Notre situation topographique, notre caractere particulier, nos usages, si l'on veut nos préjugés, les dispositions de notre coutume, notre idiome, nos allures'.
43 A.D., E dépôt/Bayonne/BB64, The town of Bayonne to the National Assembly, 1790.
44 Michel Etcheverry, 'Les Basques et l'unité nationale sous la Révolution', *Bulletin de la Société des sciences, lettres et arts de Bayonne*, 11 (January–June, 1933), 76: 'Leurs langue, leurs mœurs, les coutumes qui régissent leurs biens, leurs manières de concourir aux impositions, très souvent leurs intérêts de commerce, tout est différent. Ces différences ont fait naitre entre les Bayonnais et les Basques des sentiments de jalousie qui deviennent facilement de l'inimitié.'
45 McPhee, *Liberty or Death*, 89.
46 A.D. Pau, C/1621, The *syndic* of Labourd to the Bilçar, 10 November 1789: 'il seroit plus avantageux pour le Labourt, d'être par préférence uni à la Basse Navarre et à la Soule plutôt qu'à d'autre canton.'
47 Archives nationales de France (hereafter A.N.), D/IVbis/71, The municipal officials of Saint-Palais to the National Assembly, 1790: 'Les Basques de la Navarre, de Labourt et de la Soule, ont tous une origine commune, même langage, mêmes mœurs, même gout, mêmes usages. La nature les avait destinés tant par leurs rapports et le caractère National que par leur situation locale, à ne former qu'un seul peuple régné par les principes d'une administration commune et réglé par des lois uniformes.'
48 Ozouf-Marignier, *La Formation des départements*, 141.
49 A.N., D/IVbis/52, Table of citizens and voters of the *département* of the Basses-Pyrénées, 23 July 1791.
50 Goyhenetche, *Histoire générale du Pays basque*, Volume 4, 205–6: 'la grande minorité des Basques dans leurs assemblées politiques avec les Béarnais amèneroient nécessairement la nullité de leurs représentations.'
51 A.N., D/IVbis/71, The municipal officials of Saint-Palais to the National Assembly, 1790.
52 P.-J.-B. Buchez and P.-C. Roux (eds), *Histoire parlementaire de la Révolution française, ou Journal des Assemblées Nationales depuis 1789 jusqu'en 1815*, Volume 4 (Paris, 1834), 268: 'Réunissez des hommes dont les uns parlent une langue, les autres une autre; que voulez-vous qu'ils se disent? Ils finiront par se séparer comme les hommes de la tour de Babel.'
53 Bell, *The Cult of the Nation in France*, 171.
54 Yturbide (ed.), 'Cahiers de doléances de Bayonne et du Pays du Labourt aux États Généraux de 1789', 78.

55 A.D. Pau, C/1540, Response of the Estates of Navarre to the letter of convocation to the Estates-General of France, March 1789.
56 Anderson, *Imagined Communities*, 42 and 84.
57 Buchez and Roux (eds), *Histoire parlementaire de la Révolution française*, 268: 'un obstacle insurmontable. L'assemblage qu'on vous propose est physiquement et moralement impossible.'
58 Ibid., 269: 'L'italien, l'allemand et l'anglais ont leur source commune dans le latin et dans les langues du Nord. Le basque est la véritable langue antique.'
59 Ibid., 269: 'A peine trouvera-t-on dans cette contrée des familles assez aisées pour fournir des éligibles à l'assemblée nationale.'
60 Bell, *The Cult of the Nation in France*, 178–9.
61 Alyssa Goldstein Sepinwall, *The Abbé Grégoire and the French Revolution* (Berkeley, 2005), 96–7.
62 Buchez and Roux (eds), *Histoire parlementaire de la Révolution française*, 267: 'Le comité n'a pas cru que la différence du langage fût un motif suffisant pour oublier les convenances et s'écarter de l'exécution de vos décrets.'
63 Woloch, *The New Regime*, 51, 114 and 128.
64 Goyhenetche, *Histoire générale du Pays basque*, Volume 4, 209–10.
65 See, for example, Georges Lefebvre, *Les Paysans du Nord pendant la Révolution française* (Paris, 1972), 5–9.
66 Patrice Gueniffey, *Histoires de la Révolution et de l'Empire* (Paris, 2011), 70.
67 Woloch, *The New Regime*, 128; Malcom Crook, *Napoleon Comes to Power: Democracy and Dictatorship in Revolutionary France, 1795–1804* (Cardiff, 1998), 81.
68 D'Andurain de Maytie, 'Les Élections législatives de 1824 dans l'arrondissement de Mauléon', *Bulletin de la Société des sciences, lettres et arts de Bayonne*, 137–8 (1981–82), 355 and 361.
69 Karila-Cohen, *L'État des esprits,* 13. This argument counters Mona Ozouf's claim that the Napoleonic regime's obsession with order put an end to the *esprit public*. See Mona Ozouf, 'Esprit public', in François Furet and Mona Ozouf (eds), *Dictionnaire critique de la Révolution française* (Paris, 1988), 719.
70 Alain Corbin, *Le Monde retrouvé de Louis-François Pinagot. Sur les traces d'un inconnu, 1798–1876* (Paris, 1998), 248–9: 'science politique balbutiante'.
71 Marie-Vic Ozouf-Marignier, 'De l'Universalisme aux intérêts locaux: le débat sur la formation des départements en France (1789–1790)', *Annales: Économies, Sociétés, Civilisations*, 41:6 (1986), 1194.

72 Georges Lefebvre, *The French Revolution from its Origins to 1793*, Elizabeth Moss Evanson trans. (London, 1962), 154; Mona Ozouf, *De Révolution en République. Les chemins de la France* (Paris, 2015), 1112.
73 For a similar argument, see Ozouf, *De Révolution en République*, 1113.
74 Guillet, *Naissance de la Normandie*, 92.

2

Basque soldiers in a French nation

At the turn of the nineteenth century, war turned the *ancien-régime* myth of the warriorlike Basque man into an archetype of Basque identity. The Basques' natural disposition for war was a central feature of the historical narrative of Basque Cantabrianism, the myth that alleged that throughout history the Basques had fended off Carthaginian, Roman, barbarian and Moorish invasions and had hence never been conquered by foreign powers. The claim, like similar ones across Europe at the time, found legitimacy both in Roman texts and in early modern epics. The most famous one was the sixteenth-century Spanish Basque poem *Crónica de Vizcaya*, which recounted the wars between the Cantabrians and the Romans and the latter's failure to conquer Cantabria.[1] Due to the popularity of the Basque Cantabrian myth, at the end of the *ancien régime* local elites frequently associated the Basques with such features as physical agility, boldness in battle, valour, pride and passionate defence of liberty.[2] The *cahier de doléances* of the clergy of Labourd in 1789, for example, claimed that the Basques were valuable to the king because of their warriorlike nature, which made them the ideal guardians of the Pyrenean border. 'In times of need the Basques are all soldiers,' they wrote, 'and they will courageously sacrifice their lives and their possessions for the defence of their *patrie* and for the service of their King.'[3] In the following two decades, during the Revolutionary and the Napoleonic Wars, administrative and military officials recognised these characteristics as essential for the success of France's military enterprises and employed them as a defence of Basque exceptionalism within the French army.

In 1792, at the outset of the Revolutionary Wars, the National Assembly decided to create a Basque battalion, the *chasseurs basques*, that was to be deployed along the western Pyrenean border in case of Spanish attack. It was the first time that Basque soldiers from the three dismantled *pays* of Labourd, Basse-Navarre and Soule were joined together on the basis of their ethnic specificity. The *chasseurs basques* fought valiantly against Spain in the War of the Pyrenees (1793–5) and as a result, in the aftermath of the conflict, officials mythologised the archetype of the valiant Basque soldier for several military purposes: as an excuse for draft evasion, as an explanation for refusing to send the Basques to fight abroad and as a defence of Basque exceptionalism against the *chasseurs'* full integration into the French army. The Basque battalion was eliminated by Napoleon Bonaparte in 1800 but, in the final acts of the Peninsular War in 1813–14, the emperor decided to reinstate it in order to encourage both local and national patriotism in a last, desperate attempt to defend the Pyrenean frontier from Anglo-Portuguese and Spanish invasion. While the *chasseurs basques* were eventually dismantled for good after the One Hundred Days, their legacy lived on. In the nineteenth century, the battalion's valour became a symbol of the Basque country's allegiance to France, as well as proof of the survival of the ancient Cantabrians' qualities of bravery, fearlessness and invincibility. It was a myth that suited all regimes in power and that the Basques used repeatedly as evidence of both their jealous attachment to the *petite patrie* and their loyalty to the *grande patrie*.

As historians have recently pointed out, the *chasseurs basques*, like other ethnic, linguistic and religious minorities within the Revolutionary and Napoleonic armies, exposed the complexities, contradictions and limitations of the Revolution's ideal of a nation-state based solely on its citizens' civic will.[4] Since ethnic and cultural diversity persisted and produced alternative loyalties within France, the state was forced to negotiate its patriotic discourse of the nation-in-arms and adapt it to different local circumstances.[5] In this respect, French authorities did not struggle to enforce their 'civilising mission' only on those ethnic groups outside the boundaries of France, as the classic historiography has contended, but also within old France.[6] The Revolutionary and Napoleonic states were aware of their internal diversity, and the demands of war made them more pragmatic in their pursuit of ethnic and linguistic homogeneity than their professed ideology. In this respect, the constitution of the Basque battalion in 1792, as well as its reintroduction in 1813, was a pragmatic response to the needs of war and reflected the state's cultivation of local interests alongside the promotion of national uniformity.[7] While the battalion, which mirrored the system of local militias that the Revolution had abolished, underscored the persistence of a degree of *ancien-régime* localism in Revolutionary and Napoleonic France, it did not represent the mere survival of a pre-Revolutionary mode of thinking. Rather, military elites reinforced local loyalties as a means towards national integration, stressing the importance of the *chasseurs basques* for the success of the French army.

Becoming Basque soldiers during the French Revolution

The Revolutionary army was the first to unite the Basques together on the basis of their ethnic specificity. Before the Revolution, each Basque *pays* had its own individual militias that bore no sense of Basque cultural togetherness. In 1743, for example, Labourd had four companies, Soule five and Basse-Navarre eight. Even though, when major conflicts broke out, these militias could be employed on a national scale, their primary role was to patrol and protect the Pyrenean border from potential Spanish threats.[8] Local militias were made permanent in 1726 and did not involve large portions of the population, but they were resented across France because they often drew men from the unprivileged strata of local communities. They became the object of one of the most passionate complaints of the peasants' *cahiers de doléances* in 1789,[9] although, in the Basque *cahiers*, local notables also made reference to the militias as an example of both Basque utility for the king and independence vis-à-vis the kingdom of France. The clergy of Labourd, for instance, argued that they were satisfied with the special administration of the *pays* and that, as a result, they were showing their faithfulness to the king by protecting the border.[10]

The *chasseurs basques* were born out of the Legislative Assembly's decision, on the eve of the Revolutionary Wars in April 1792, to create an Armée du Midi, an army of volunteers that protected the southern border with Spain and the Italian states. A few months later, the *armée* was split into two: the Armée des Alpes and the Armée des Pyrénées. Forming part of the latter were four Basque volunteer companies stationed around Saint-Jean-Pied-de-Port, which rose to ten in September 1793. The 1,800 men forming the ten Basque companies became known as the *chasseurs basques*.[11] At the end of the year, the *représentants en mission* Monestier and Pinet, who were responsible for the army in the Basses-Pyrénées, reinforced the ethnic connotation of the *chasseurs*. They joined the Basque battalions together to form a Basque demi-brigade and appointed a Basque, the distinguished general Jean Isidore Harispe, as commander of the second battalion. His soldiers appreciated the Basque distinctiveness of their company. Harispe 'belongs to the *pays*', they wrote to General Mauco. 'The Basque is naturally distrustful and is rarely trustworthy; yet we trust him, we trust him entirely.'[12] As the French army joined Basque soldiers together for the first time, it favoured the emergence of both a self-aware sense of Basque identity, shared by members of all three Basque *pays*, and an ethnic definition of Basque community.

The 1,800 *chasseurs basques* fought valiantly in the War of the Pyrenees. In the summer of 1793, they crossed the border and occupied Zugarramurdi in Navarra. Spanish troops occupied the French Aldudes the following year, but the *chasseurs* pushed them back and launched a successful attack in the Bidassoa valley, occupying Irún, Hondarribia, San Sebastián, Bilbao and Vitoria. When the peace treaty was signed on 22 July 1795, they were about to threaten Pamplona. In the aftermath of the war, local and national propaganda hailed the *chasseurs basques* as heroes. With time, such narratives came to transcend Basque soldiers and to identify the behaviour of the Basques as a whole during the war. A military report in 1794, for example, explained that 'the Basques of this district rose *en masse* multiple times last year to push back the Spaniards'.[13] Another from a few years later noted that: 'From the moment that war was declared between France and Spain, when rumours began to spread of our first defeats, the entire Basque country took up arms, organised itself in battalions, in *compagnies franches*, to fight their ancient and eternal enemies.'[14] The War of the Pyrenees, in other words, turned the Basques into national heroes.

These heroic accounts were much exaggerated. The *chasseurs basques* represented only a minimal portion of the Basque population, and the latter frequently reacted differently from Basque soldiers to war and invasion. At the beginning of the war, some peasants, especially those from the villages along the border, continued to exercise their trading relations with the Spaniards, in spite of the interdiction.[15] The majority of the French Basque communities invaded by the Spaniards in 1794, moreover, offered little resistance to the enemy; some of them, alienated by both the war and the anti-religious policies of the *représentants en mission*, even decided to follow the Spaniards back across the Pyrenees once their troops retreated.[16] Similar behaviours were noted in other Pyrenean areas, such as the Cerdanya.[17] Finally, not all recruited soldiers behaved as well as the celebrated *chasseurs*. In February 1794, for example, forty-seven Basques from Itxassou deserted their regiment, prompting the administration to deport the population of entire villages along the border in retaliation. While the *chasseurs basques* were celebrated as heroes, then, the *représentants en mission* simultaneously accused deserters and their fellow villagers of fanaticism, treason and of selling the nation to the enemy. On 7 *ventôse* II (25 February 1794), for example, the deputies wrote to the Comité de salut public: 'This *pays* offers the rare and odious spectacle of simple farmers and shepherds who detest liberty and equality, who wish the success of the Spanish armies, to whom they clandestinely give their animals, and for whom they work as spies against us.'[18] As a result, as Chapter 6 will show, although the Basque notability itself repeatedly employed the myth of the *chasseurs basques* as proof of the Basques' allegiance to the French nation, memory of the Revolutionary experience remained a divisive one across the nineteenth century, and the violence of the Terror was revived by Basque militants at times of tension between the Basque country and the French Republic.

The trope of the Basque soldier as valiant yet prone to desertion and the *mal du pays* became increasingly popular in the aftermath of the War of the Pyrenees. Military personnel relied on Basque stereotypes to justify the intensification of Basque desertion at the end of the war and after the promulgation of the Loi Jourdan, which made conscription compulsory for a selected number of Frenchmen in 1798. The heroism of Basque soldiers and their propensity for desertion were not at odds, the letters alleged. 'The Basque', explained a note from year VIII (1799), 'unfortunately has an inconstant character', which made him prone to desertion.[19] Another added: 'We wish to assure you that the principal virtue of the Basques is their docility and love of glory. The inconstancy that is reproached to them derives from their inactivity, rather than from the danger that they may face; from the deprivations they endure, rather than from their unwillingness to defend the Republic.'[20] Desertion, in other words, was a result of circumstances, nothing to do with the inner valour and patriotism of the Basques.

Military authorities, nevertheless, were aware of the vacuousness of their claims. General Moncey, for example, who had led the Basque demi-brigade during the war and was a defender of Basque military exceptionalism, warned local administrators of the need to enforce order and respect of the law among Basque soldiers. Good behaviour, he reminded them in year V (1797), was essential for the preservation of a privileged treatment within the army. 'I spared as much as I could these dear Basques, your spoilt children,' he wrote to Fargues, a Basque member of the Council of Five Hundred, asking for confirmation that his requests would be implemented.[21] 'The Basques, whom the government treated with such predilection,' he added in a letter to the Basque cantons, 'forget every day what they owe it by leaving their posts; and they equally forget ... what they owe to their general [Moncey himself] ... who deeply compromised himself responding of their fidelity and of ... their valour.'[22] Thus, Moncey implied, Basque soldiers had to behave according to their idealisation for the myth to be credible.

Moncey defended Basque exceptionalism on the basis of the population's different cultural identity in January 1796, when the minister of war, Aubert du Bayet, ordered that the ninth, tenth and eleventh military divisions, to which the Basques belonged, joined the Armée d'Italie under the command of General Schérer.[23] Moncey opposed the Basques' departure, using an abundance of stereotypes to substantiate his claim. He wrote:

> I am not going to hide from you, citizen minister, that it would go against the general interest of the Republic and the particular interest of this *pays* to ask the Basques to leave ... The Basque, fierce, independent, has mores, a character and habits different from the people around him. His language, which has no relation with theirs, seems to prevent all foreign communication and to force him to live by himself; ... the love of his *pays* is his fanaticism; the moment that he loses sight of the valleys he inhabits [and] the mountains that surround them, he languishes, he loses his energy, or rather, he uses it all ... to return home.[24]

Moncey's appeal persuaded Aubert du Bayet to allow the Basques to continue to station in Bordeaux and to be deployed along the Basque border. The government's patience with Basque exceptionalism, however, was coming to an end. In 1800, First Consul Bonaparte decided to eliminate the Basque battalion because he did not want a 'corps privilégié' in the army.[25] Basque military personnel adopted once again Moncey's localist discourse, drawing on regional distinctiveness as an explanation for the Basques' privileged position. The soldiers of the second Basque battalion, for example, explained to General Dufour that Basque mores and language made 'amalgamation' impractical, and that they wished their chief to be a Basque, as he would know their idiom and habits.[26] The commander of the first Basque battalion, Colonel Harriet, moreover, listed the Basques' peculiarities to Bonaparte, concluding that, because of them, 'such men would be prone to boredom, disgust, discouragement; homesickness would prevail and … they would abandon their new colours'.[27] Paradoxically, military personnel claimed that, because of their different customs, the Basques were better French soldiers when they operated separately from the rest of the French army.

The petitions convinced Bonaparte to preserve the Basque battalion temporarily. That same year, however, he denied the *chasseurs* their geographical exceptionalism and deployed them to Switzerland and later to Italy to fight in the War of the Second Coalition. At the end of the campaign, the Basque battalion was eventually dissolved: the homogenising goal of the army had prevailed over the particularist approach of the *ancien régime*. It was not the end of the *chasseurs basques*, though. The pragmatic needs of the Napoleonic Wars called them back one more time during the most dramatic phase of the Peninsular War thirteen years later.

The *chasseurs basques* under Napoleon

The government decided to reinstate the *chasseurs basques* in the winter of 1813, when the Anglo-Portuguese and Spanish armies, fighting the French in Spain, approached the Franco-Spanish border and threatened to invade France through the French Basque country. The reason was practical: due to the high level of desertion of Basque soldiers, local authorities argued that it was preferable to have them contribute to the protection of the *patrie* along the Pyrenean border – where, it appeared, they were less likely to desert their companies – than not at all. Indeed, despite the popularisation of stories of courageous Basque enterprises during the Revolutionary Wars, the Basque population had resisted conscription from the very first *levée en masse* of 1793 and, when the Loi Jourdan made the draft compulsory five years later, the Basque country became one of the areas of France with the highest rates of draft evasion. Between year VII and year XIII (1798–1804), for instance, 39 per cent of men selected for military service in the Basses-Pyrénées deserted the army either by not joining it at all or by leaving *en route*, against the national average of 24 per cent.[28] As Alan Forrest has observed, in the Pyrenees avoiding the draft was a 'collective choice', which included the conscript's family, his neighbours, friends, fellow villagers, the mayor and local authorities.[29] In several instances during the Napoleonic decade, for example, the authorities complained that villagers openly protected deserters. They helped them flee to Spain, offered them accommodation, altered communal registers or even made the latter disappear altogether. Some inhabitants, moreover, reported prefect Castellane in 1806, welcomed not only deserters, 'but also their furniture, in order to avoid paying the garrison fee required for their disobedience'.[30] Along the border, desertion often merged with banditry, which made roads unsafe and eroded the power of the state. Napoleon was particularly sensitive to it, as, upon coming to power in 1799, he had presented himself as the restorer of law and order in France after the Revolution. War on crime, aimed to make French society safe for its respectable citizens, became a prerequisite of Napoleon's policy of *ralliement* and *amalgame* of the propertied classes to him.[31]

As a way of countering desertion, in April 1808, only a couple of weeks before France's invasion of Spain, Joachim Murat temporarily reinstated the *chasseurs basques*.[32] In August, the *chasseurs* became a part of the new thirty-four companies of *miquelets* that had been created, in *ancien régime* fashion, in order to patrol the external border of the Pyrenean *départements*. The problem with the *chasseurs*, as with the *miquelets* more generally, however, was that they patrolled only their portion of the border: they were reluctant to pursue the Spaniards onto the southern slope of the Pyrenees and failed to operate effectively if they were transferred to other war zones.³³ In the spring of 1809, indeed, Napoleon decided to send the *chasseurs basques* to Naples but, as had occurred a decade earlier, a Basque military report discouraged him from doing so because 'the disposition of the men who form this company is not favourable to this project at all'.³⁴ As a result, one year after their recreation, Bonaparte dissolved the *chasseurs*, incorporating them into the first battalion of the *chasseurs de montagne* of the Basses-Pyrénées.³⁵ Until 1813, many Basque soldiers were still granted the privilege of being deployed locally but without any official position of cultural or ethnic distinctiveness.

Discussions about the reintroduction of the *chasseurs basques* started again in the autumn of 1813 because, on 7 October, after years of fighting Napoleon's 'Spanish ulcer', a joint army of Anglo-Portuguese and Spanish troops led by Arthur Wellesley, the future duke of Wellington, forced Marshal Soult's Armée d'Espagne to retreat into France and invaded the French Basque country.³⁶ The invasion came at an enormous cost to the Basque people, causing further disaffection towards the Napoleonic regime. That winter, they had to produce 4,000–5,000 food rations per day to feed the soldiers, in addition to which soldiers and officers could come and go at their discretion from villages, requisitioning what they pleased and devastating households along the way.³⁷ As the mayor of Anglet put it to the sub-prefect of Bayonne, villagers 'are forever ruined, because a worker cannot recover from such disasters'.³⁸ The local population were also required to host soldiers, both French and later British and Portuguese, and to take care of the wounded when hospitals were full. Local physicians worked incessantly to treat soldiers' wounds, and villagers helped with what they could, an action branded as patriotic by the authorities but likely a humane reaction to the horrors of war.³⁹ Finally, the local population had to accommodate refugees, especially women, children and officials who were fleeing Spain and, like the soldiers, pillaged villages along the way.⁴⁰ War demands brought the Basques to the brink of starvation but, by 1813, the army, rather than the population, was the main concern of the French state. When the mayor of Halsou complained to General Darricau that the corn he was requisitioning was essential for the population's survival, the general replied that the corn was better off with the French than with the Spaniards, and that he would feed it to the horses if necessary.⁴¹ In such a chaotic situation, in which discontent with the regime was growing and the tide of war was turning against the French, the government submitted ideology to pragmatism, resorting once again to the *chasseurs basques* in order to foster a sense of patriotic duty among the Basque population. Although the wellbeing of the population was not the main concern of the French government during the Napoleonic Wars, people's compliance was essential for the state to pursue its war effort, and the question of conscription was pivotal.[42] Thus, in the winter of 1813, after the Anglo-Portuguese invasion of France, the state reintroduced the *chasseurs basques*, enrolling the Basque recruits of that year. Authorities viewed the *chasseurs* as a means of both decreasing Basque desertion and of cultivating local pride, drawing parallels with the heroic *chasseurs basques* of the Revolutionary Wars. The reintroduction of the Basque battalion, the minister of the interior, Montalivet, explained to prefect Vanssay, 'will have the double merit of rewarding the inhabitants of this *département* for their good conduct in these difficult circumstances, and of having excellent troops, united by the desire to push back the enemy far from their homes'.[43] The employment of the *chasseurs basques*, Vanssay added in a subsequent explanatory letter to the *directoire* of the Basses-Pyrénées, would also restore the memory of those glorious Basque battalions that greatly contributed to the Armée des Pyrénées Occidentales in 1793–5, raising spirits and improving the sense of national unity. He explained with regard to the restoration of the *chasseurs basques*:

> This measure, which will be well received by public opinion and which will contribute a lot to calm the alarm that has been exciting spirits since such a numerous *levée* of men who believed themselves to be free from conscription, will have significant advantages in the interest of national defence and of the good functioning of military service. The denominations that we propose to give to the corps will revive memories precious to the inhabitants of this *département*; it is important not to underestimate the effect that these recollections can have on men prone to enthusiasm and strong emotions. Twenty years ago, the Basque Battalions provided the most remarkable services to the armée des Pyrénées occidentales. The inhabitants of this county, and the Basques in particular, who have a passionate affection for their *pays*, struggle to get accustomed to the profession of arms when we take them away and amalgamate them; on the contrary, if they

are united together and are led by officers they trust, they are capable of doing wonders. In 1793 and 1794, they were the terror of the Spaniards; they will soon become the terror of the English and the Portuguese, as they will find the means to chase them tirelessly on our mountains.[44]

State officials, in other words, regarded local pride as a means of cultivating national patriotism. In order to further the memory of the War of the Pyrenees, authorities also decided to appoint General Harispe, commander of the second Basque battalion in 1793–95, as the new chief of the national guard in the Basque country. His appointment, Vanssay argued, would contribute to raising the morale of the population and resist the enemy.[45]

The Napoleonic state's pragmatism towards the Basques was revealing of authorities' understanding that military success in such a culturally different *pays* as the Basque country depended as much on locals' ability to assimilate the new system into their lifestyles as, crucially, on the state's willingness to compromise with local customs and demands. As prefect Vanssay pointed out in November 1813, the reintroduction of the *chasseurs basques* was an exception to military rules, but it was a risk worth taking as it was well justified by the Basques' good conduct and by the expected positive impact on their military performance.[46] In this respect, the Basque case bore similarities with Corsica, which also benefited from a degree of flexibility. Since the island, which had been annexed to France in 1769, was plagued by uprisings, in 1801 prefect Miot suspended the constitution and, among other things, awarded it a separate fiscal system, with much lower indirect taxation than the rest of the country.[47]

It remains unclear whether the reintroduction of the *chasseurs basques* improved the military allegiance of the Basques. The desertion rate decreased in 1813 in the Basque country as, according to some accounts, in the rest of France. While such statistics have prompted Isser Woloch to argue that, by ritualising the draft, the Napoleonic regime managed to convince people that conscription was part of their lives,[48] though, in the Basque country it seems more likely that the population was simply more inclined to accept the draft when danger was imminent. As Vanssay noted in January 1814, after the Anglo-Portuguese invasion, 'it seems ... that seeing danger increase, the opinion [of the *département*] has risen again'.[49] Thus, similarly to 1793–95, defensive war close to home, rather than offensive war elsewhere on the European continent, was an incentive for Basque men to accept the draft and fight in a French uniform. The valour of the Basques, however, was short-lived. When Wellesley offered the population the option of either joining the French army and fighting against the enemy or staying quietly at home under British protection, most inhabitants consented to his terms.[50] French authorities criticised the conduct of the British as treacherous and the compliant population as treasonous.[51] Yet Wellesley found a compromise that worked both for the British troops and for the French population. By behaving well, the troops found a quiet and safe environment in which to sojourn. By keeping calm and not indulging in guerrilla warfare, the local population managed to cohabit with British troops without severe damage to their property and local economy. The reopening of Basque ports during British occupation also benefited the maritime economy of Bayonne at the end of the Napoleonic era.

French troops, on the contrary, upon retreating into France, continued to pillage and cause disorder in villages, as they had done for five years in Spain. Local authorities were indignant and worried that such behaviour would lower the good *esprit public* of the *département*, demoralise the local population and contribute to turn people to the British.[52] As the mayor of Sare wrote: 'The tired inhabitant, burdened either with war or with heavy and unnecessary taxes, after making all kinds of sacrifices to save their own lives, expected to find in the French soldier a friend for his own protection, instead of a subtle persecutor, who deprives him of both his food and his home.' He concluded: 'Due to his indiscipline, the French soldier has become the enemy of the population.'[53] Although the reintroduction of the *chasseurs basques* allowed Basque draftees to fight close to home and protect their homes, at times contributing to their allegiance to the French military cause, then, for much of the Basque population it was concern about survival that defined their daily choices in the most critical moments of the war.

The majority of the Basque population's hostility to war and conscription, nevertheless, did not dissuade the authorities from boasting about Basque military exceptionalism after the end of the Peninsular War. Between May and June 1815, as France braced for another conflict during Napoleon's One Hundred Days, local and national authorities exchanged lengthy letters about the preparedness of the Basques to support the emperor militarily one more time. In May, the mayor of Saint-Jean-de-Luz, Labrouche, explained to Marshal Soult that the Basques were ready to fight another war with Spain but that, as before, they would have to be deployed close to home. He wrote:

> [I]n general the inhabitants of the French Basque country do not sympathise with those of the neighbouring villages in Spain and, if war were to take place between the two nations, we shall still find the French Basques ready to be armed to defend only their *foyers* under the command of officers chosen among their own; because if sent away and led by those who do not speak their language, they will always be bad soldiers.[54]

The following month, the minister of the interior, Carnot, wrote to the new prefect of the Basses-Pyrénées, Combe-Sieyès, soliciting him to fuel the Basque population's enthusiasm for the imminent war by reminding them of their glorious deeds during the Revolutionary and Napoleonic Wars. 'I was saddened to see that the population of your *département* risked falling into a dangerous apathy: are some perfidious insinuations suffocating the voice of honour, the love of the *patrie* in the Basques' heart?' he wrote. 'Remind this warriorlike people that the Emperor entrusts them with the defence of the Pyrenees ... I count on your zeal, Monsieur le préfet, to infuse your *département* with the enthusiasm that inflames our frontier provinces of the Alps and of the Rhine, as well as those of the Interior of France: the Basques have not degenerated.'[55] Thus, the authorities hoped that a mythologised version of recent Basque military history would inspire the population and make it rise above the brutal reality of war.

Eventually, the Franco-Spanish frontier did not see any military action during the One Hundred Days, but while the Napoleonic regime was over by July 1815, on 27 August, 19,000 Spanish troops crossed the Bidassoa river into France and were stationed around the towns of Urrugne, Saint-Jean-de-Luz and Saint-Jean-Pied-de-Port, aiming to capture Bayonne. The newly appointed prefect of the Basses-Pyrénées, d'Argout, lacking enough time to levy the national guard, restored the *chasseurs basques* one last time and appointed General Harispe at their head once again. 'Monsieur de Chauvigny had invited me to rouse the population and in order to rouse them, I had to employ people who had an influence on them. It is for this reason that I invited general Harispe to encourage the Basques to rebel,'[56] he explained to Marshal de Vioménil, adding in a letter to the minister of the interior Carnot-Feulin that: 'General Harispe, on his part, conducted himself perfectly; he employed with zeal the influence he has on the Basques in the service of the king.'[57] The Basque troops, together with a legion of national guards, defended their territory and pushed the Spaniards back across the border in early September.[58] The authorities celebrated the Basques for their prowess, but the inhabitants of Bayonne complained that the Basques had only risen to protect their *foyers* and not to defend their capital. 'Today the Bayonnais are proud of their excellent conduct,' prefect d'Argout wrote to Carnot-Feulin later that September. 'Their ancient enmity toward the Béarnais was replaced by gratitude, though at the same time they displayed a lot of anger toward the Basques who abandoned them to protect their own *foyers*.'[59] While local authorities celebrated the Basques as a homogeneous people, the population continued to be driven by internal animosities that defined the relations between *pays* and towns under the *ancien régime*.

Although old local hostilities still persisted in the early nineteenth century, the myth of Basque valour during the Revolutionary and Napoleonic Wars became increasingly popular among local officials and intellectuals in the following decades. In 1825, the *abbé* Bidassouet, in his *Histoire des cantabres*, for example, recalled the 1815 expedition and explained that the Bayonnais 'swore, like good Cantabrians, not to survive the capture of their town. *We can be destroyed*, they proclaimed, *but never defeated*.'[60] As Chapter 1 showed, the association of the Bayonnais with the Cantabrians, and hence with the Basques, was a result of the administrative reforms of 1789–90: before the Revolution Bayonne did not consider itself a Basque town, nor did the Basques consider it to be one. The myth of the *chasseurs basques* also emerged in local publications and correspondence in the following decades. In the 1830s, in the midst of the First Carlist War in Spain, the French Basque intellectual Augustin Chaho, a Carlist supporter, compared the heroic behaviour of General Harispe and the Basque battalion during the 1793 campaign to that of the Spanish Basque Carlist military leader Tomás de Zumalacárregui. 'It was during the war of 93 that Harispe first gave evidence of the reckless valour and rare cold blood that distinguished this general of the emperor,' he wrote. 'Ten thousand *chasseurs cantabres*, such as we were,' he added, greatly exaggerating the number of the *chasseurs basques*, 'will be more formidable to Zumala-Carreguy [sic] than fifty line regiments.'[61] Basque notables further revived the myth of the *chasseurs basques* in the aftermath of the proclamation of the Second Republic in 1848, in order to create a link between the Basques' support for the First Republic and the new republican government. The notability of Saint-Étienne-de-Baïgorry, for instance, wrote to Paris that: 'The heroism displayed by our fathers in 1793 for the defence of the republican soil against Spanish invasion awarded our village the glorious name of warriors of the Thermopylae. We have not degenerated since the time of our fathers, we are standing ready against all internal and external enemies.'[62] In the aftermath of the Napoleonic Wars, then, the myth of the *chasseurs basques* became part of French popular culture. The mythologisation of Basque soldiers, as the next chapter will show, continued during the First Carlist War.

Conclusion

The Revolutionary and Napoleonic Wars contributed to the characterisation of the Basque man as a brave soldier yet one who was resentful of the constraints of authority. In 1792, the Revolutionaries decided to create the *chasseurs basques*, a Basque battalion that was meant to protect the western Pyrenean border from Spanish invasion. Although the *chasseurs* were one of several companies of Pyrenean *miquelets* garrisoned along the Franco-Spanish frontier, the Basque battalion was peculiar insofar as it was ethnic-specific. Paradoxically, at a time when the army became the symbol of Revolutionary patriotic zeal and national unity, Basque soldiers were joined together militarily for the first time and began to develop a clearer and more structured understanding of the ethnic and cultural component of their identity. The Revolutionaries' creation of the Basque battalion was revealing of the extent to which local particularism still factored in military choices in the 1790s, as well as of the degree of pragmatism inherent in the new notion of the citizen-soldier.

Authorities' insistence on the preservation of the Basque battalion in the aftermath of the War of the Pyrenees continued to reflect such dualism. On the one hand, the defence of the *chasseurs'* exceptionalism against full incorporation into the French army was a perpetuation of the *ancien régime*'s notion of each province's utility for the king, which in the Basque *pays* took the form of border patrols. On the other, the celebration of Basque achievements was a way of fostering the population's sense of local pride, which, authorities hoped, would further its allegiance to the new French nation. Compromise between ideology and local concerns underscored the tension between the Revolutionary ideal of a civic nation and France's cultural, religious and ethnic diversity,[63] and also became key to military decision-making during the First Empire's final years of war, when Napoleon accepted prefect Vanssay's proposal of reintroducing the *chasseurs basques* as a means of curbing desertion. In this respect, war did not make the regime more rigid, as some historians have claimed.[64] Instead, it increased its flexibility, prompting the state to adapt its demands to regional cultural peculiarities.

Although the majority of the Basque population resented war and conscription during the Revolutionary and Napoleonic decades, the bravery and success of the *chasseurs basques* during the War of the Pyrenees transcended the battlefield and came to represent the Basque population as a whole. In the nineteenth century, this contributed to the reinforcement of the stereotype of the Basque man as valiant yet rebellious, as well as, importantly, to strengthening the bond between the Basque country and the French nation-state. According to the authorities, similarly to the Alsatians' display of valour along the Rhine,[65] the fact that the Basques had distinguished themselves during the Revolutionary Wars by defending France's southern border proved their desire to be French and their sense of national patriotism, despite their different language and mores. In this regard, the Basques, like the Alsatians, were true representatives of the ideal of a French civic nation.

Notes

1 Juaristi, *El linaje de Aitor*, 53.
2 Sanadon, *Essai sur la noblesse des basques*, 45–6.

3 Yturbide (ed.), 'Cahiers de doléances de Bayonne et du Pays du Labourt aux États Généraux de 1789', 30: 'Les Basques sont tous soldats au besoin, et ils sacrifieront courageusement leurs vies et leurs biens à la défense de leur patrie et au service de leur Souverain.'
4 Christopher J. Tozzi, *Nationalizing France's Army: Foreign, Black, and Jewish Troops in the French Military, 1715–1831* (Charlottesville and London, 2016), 2–5; Stewart McCain, *The Language Question under Napoleon* (Basingstoke, 2018), 152.
5 On the Revolutionary idea of the nation-in-arms, see Alan Forrest, *The Legacy of the French Revolutionary Wars: The Nation-in-Arms in French Republican Memory* (Cambridge, 2009).
6 Stuart Woolf, 'French Civilization and Ethnicity in the Napoleonic Empire', *Past and Present*, 124 (1989), 61. On the systematic attempt to apply policies of cultural imperialism to all old and new territories of the *Grand Empire*, see Michael Broers, *The Napoleonic Empire in Italy, 1796–1814: Cultural Imperialism in a European Context?* (London, 2004). Alexander Grab, though, disagrees with Broers, painting a more malleable version of the First Empire in Italy. See Alexander Grab, 'Army, State, and Society: Conscription and Desertion in Napoleonic Italy (1802–1814)', *Journal of Modern History*, 67:1 (1995), 25–54.
7 Christopher Tozzi, 'Soldiers of the *Pays*: Localism and Nationalism in the Revolutionary Era Army', in Philip Whalen and Patrick Young (eds), *Place and Locality in Modern France* (London and New York, 2014), 162.
8 Labouche, 'Le Chef de brigade Harispe et les chasseurs basques', *Bulletin de la Société des sciences, lettres et arts de Pau*, 22 (1892–93), 60.
9 Alan Forrest, *Conscripts and Deserters: The Army and French Society During the Revolution and Empire* (Oxford, 1989), 11–13.
10 Yturbide (ed.), 'Cahiers de doléances de Bayonne et du Pays du Labourt aux États Généraux de 1789', 30.
11 Labouche, 'Le Chef de brigade Harispe', 63–4 and 67.
12 Ibid., 100: 'est du pays. Le basque naturellement méfiant donne difficilement sa confiance; il a la nôtre, il l'a toute entière.'
13 A.N., F/7/3822, Report of the fourth division, 3 *thermidor* II (21 July 1794): 'les Basques de ce district se levèrent plusieurs fois en masse l'année dernière pour repousser les espagnols.'
14 Labouche, 'Le Chef de brigade Harispe', 148: 'Dès la déclaration de la guerre entre la France et l'Espagne, au bruit des premiers échecs que nous essuyâmes, le pays basque tout entier courut aux armes, se forma en bataillons, en compagnies franches pour combattre leurs anciens et éternels ennemis.'

Basque soldiers in a French nation   57

15 A.D., E dépôt/Bayonne/2D9, [The administration of the Basses-Pyrénées] to the general of the second division on the prohibition to export cattle to Spain, 29 March 1793.
16 F.-A. Aulard (ed.), *Recueil des actes du Comité de Salut Public avec la correspondance officielle des représentants en mission et le registre du conseil exécutif provisoire. 10 août 1794–20 septembre 1794*, Volume 6 (Paris, 1904), 475–7.
17 Sahlins, *Boundaries*, 176.
18 F.-A. Aulard (ed.), *Recueil des actes du Comité de Salut Public avec la correspondance officielle des représentants en mission et le registre du conseil exécutif provisoire. 9 février 1794–15 mars 1794*, Volume 11 (Paris, 1897), 398–9: 'Ce pays offre le spectacle, rare partout ailleurs et bien odieux, de simples agriculteurs et pasteurs détestant la liberté et l'égalité, faisant des vœux pour le succès des armes de l'Espagnol, auquel ils font passer clandestinement leurs bestiaux, et auquel ils servent d'espion contre nous.'
19 Service Historique de la Défense (hereafter S.H.D.), KX/11, Note on the composition of the second battalion of *chasseurs basques*, [year VIII (1799)]: 'Le Basque malheureusement est d'un caractère inconstant'.
20 S.H.D., KX/11, The officers of the second battalion of *chasseurs basques* to General Dufour, [year VIII–IX (1799–1800)]: 'Nous osons assurer que la principale vertu des basques est la docilité et l'amour de la gloire, que l'inconstance qu'on semble leur reprocher vient plutôt du peu de danger qu'il a à courir, de son inactivité, des privations qu'il éprouve, plutôt que l'envie de se soustraire à la défense de la république.'
21 S.H.D., B/4/112, General Moncey to the representative of the people Fargues, 29 *prairial* V (17 June 1797): 'j'ai épargné autant que j'ai pu ces chers basques, vos enfants gâtés.'
22 S.H.D., B/4/112, General Moncey to the municipal administrations of the Basque cantons, 2 *ventôse* V (20 February 1797): 'Les basques traités avec tant de prédilection par le gouvernement oublient chaque jour en abandonnant leur poste, ce qu'ils lui doivent, ils oublient aussi ... ce qu'ils doivent peut-être à leur général ... qui s'est bien gravement compromis en répondant pour ainsi dire de leur fidélité et ... leur valeur.'
23 Labouche, 'Le Chef de brigade Harispe', 148.
24 Ibid., 148: 'Je ne dois pas vous dissimuler, citoyen ministre, qu'il serait contraire à l'intérêt général de la République et à l'intérêt particulier de ce pays de faire partir les basques ... Le basque, fier, indépendant, a des mœurs, un caractère et une façon de vivre tout à fait différents des peuples qui l'avoisinent. Son idiome qui n'a aucun rapport avec le leur semble s'opposer à toute communication étrangère et l'obliger de ne vivre qu'avec lui; ... l'amour de son pays est chez lui son fanatisme;

dès qu'il a perdu de vue les vallées qu'il habite, les montagnes qui les couronnent, il languit, perd son énergie, ou bien l'emploie toute entière ... à revoler sur son foyer.'

25 Ibid., 158.
26 S.H.D., KX/11, The officers of the second battalion of *chasseurs basques* to General Dufour, [year IX (1800)].
27 S.H.D., KX/11, The chief of the first battalion of *chasseurs basques* to the first consul, 24 *messidor* VIII (12 July 1800): 'de tels hommes seroient en proye à l'ennui, au dégout, au découragement, la nostalgie s'en empareroit et ... ils finiroient par abandonner les nouveaux drapeaux.'
28 A.-A. Hargenvilliers, *Compte général de la conscription*, Gustave Vallée ed. (Paris, 1937), 74–5.
29 Alan Forrest, 'Conscription and Crime in Rural France during the Directory and the Consulate', in Gwynne Lewis and Colin Lucas (eds), *Beyond the Terror: Essays in French Regional and Social History* (Cambridge, 1983), 93.
30 A.N., F/9/236, The prefect to the minister of the interior, 3 November 1806: 'mais encore leur mobilier afin de les soustraire au paiement des frais de la garnison que leur désobéissance a nécessité'.
31 Michael Broers, *Napoleon's Other War: Bandits, Rebels and their Pursuers in the Age of Revolutions* (Witney, 2010), 85.
32 S.H.D., KX/11, The minister secretary of state to the minister of war, 25 February 1809.
33 Forrest, *Conscripts and Deserters*, 215–17.
34 S.H.D., KX/11, Report to the emperor, 17 May 1809: 'les dispositions des hommes qui composent cette compagnie ne sont nullement favorable à ce projet'.
35 S.H.D., KX/11, The commander of the eleventh military division to the minister of war, 11 July 1809.
36 On the Peninsular War, see David Gates, *The Spanish Ulcer: A History of the Peninsular War* (London, 1986).
37 A.N., F/1cIII/Basses-Pyrénées/10, The prefect to the minister of the interior, 22 December 1813.
38 A.N., F/1cIII/Basses-Pyrénées/10, The mayor of Anglet to the sub-prefect of Bayonne, 17 November 1813: 'sont ruinés pour jamais, car le laboureur ne peut se relever de semblables désastres'.
39 A.N., F/1cIII/Basses-Pyrénées/10, The prefect to the minister of the interior, 8 July 1813; A.N., F/1cIII/Basses-Pyrénées/10, The mayor of Sauveterre to the prefect, 1813.
40 Dominique Halty, *Épisodes des guerres napoléoniennes au Pays basque* (Pau, 1998), 60. On the demands of an invading army, see Jacques Godechot, 'Les Variations de la politique française à l'égard des pays

occupés, 1792–1815', in *Occupants-occupés, 1792–1815. Actes du colloque qui s'est tenu à Bruxelles, les 29 et 30 janvier 1968* (Brussels, 1969), 15–33.
41 A.N., F/1cIII/Basses-Pyrénées/10, The mayor of Halsou to the sub-prefect of Bayonne, 24 November 1813.
42 Margaret Levi, 'The Institution of Conscription', *Social Science History*, 20:1 (1996), 135.
43 A.N., F/1cIII/Basses-Pyrénées/10, The minister of the interior to the prefect, 5 December 1813: 'réussirait le double mérite de récompenser la bonne conduite que les habitants de ce Département ont tenu dans ces circonstances difficiles et d'avoir d'excellentes troupes unies par le désir de repousser l'ennemi loin de ses foyers'.
44 A.N., F/1cIII/Basses-Pyrénées/10, The prefect to the *directoire* of the Basses-Pyrénées, 26 November 1813: 'Cette mesure, qui serait très agréable à l'opinion publique et qui contribuerait beaucoup à calmer l'inquiétude que ne peut manquer d'exciter dans les esprits une levée aussi nombreuse d'hommes qui étaient fondés à se croire libérés sous le rapport de la conscription, aurait certainement aussi des grands avantages dans l'intérêt de la défense du pays et pour le bien du service. Les dénominations que je propose de donner aux corps à former rappelleraient aux habitants de ce Dép.t des souvenirs qui lui sont précieux; il importe de ne point négliger l'influence que ces souvenirs peuvent exercer sur des hommes très disposés à l'enthousiasme et à l'élan. Les Battaillons Basques rendirent, il y a vingt ans, les plus grands services à l'armée des Pyrénées occidentales. Les habitants de cette contrée et surtout les Basques, qui ont une affection passionnée pour leur pays, s'accoutument difficilement au métier des armes, lorsqu'on les éloigne et qu'on les amalgame; tandis que réunis et commandés par des officiers qui ont leur confiance, ils sont capables de faire des prodiges. En 1793 et 1794, ils étaient la terreur des Espagnols; ils le deviendraient bientôt aussi des Anglais et des Portugais qu'ils trouveraient moyen de harceler sans cesse sur nos montagnes.'
45 A.N., F/1cIII/Basses-Pyrénées/10, The prefect to the minister of the interior, 21 November 1813; A.N., F/1cIII/Basses-Pyrénées/11, The prefect to the minister of the interior, 23 January 1814.
46 A.N., F/1cIII/Basses-Pyrénées/10, The prefect to the *directoire* of the Basses-Pyrénées, 26 November 1813.
47 Nathalie Goedert, 'La Corse et l'exception administrative: les premiers pas de l'administration préfectorale', *La Revue administrative*, 54:320 (2001), 229–52.
48 Isser Woloch, 'Napoleonic Conscription: State Power and Civil Society', *Past and Present*, 111 (1986), 122–8. Woloch's thesis has been disputed

by other historians, who have argued that desertion, and in some *départements* even resistance, was on the rise towards the end of the Empire, as the impositions of the Napoleonic state increased sharply after the defeat at Leipzig in October 1813. See Thierry Lentz, *Nouvelle Histoire du Premier Empire. L'effondrement du système napoléonien, 1810–1814*, Volume 2 (Paris, 2004), 361–3; Munro Price, *Napoleon: The End of Glory* (Oxford, 2014), 171–5.

49 A.N., F/1cIII/Basses-Pyrénées/11, The prefect to the minister of the interior, 6 January 1814: 'il semble ... que voyant le peril s'augmenter, l'opinion [du département] se soit relevée.'

50 Arthur Wellesley, Duke of Wellington, *The Dispatches of Field Marshal the Duke of Wellington during his Various Campaigns in India, Denmark, Portugal, Spain, the Low Countries, and France*, Volume 7, Colonel Gurwood, C.B., K.C.T.S. ed. (London, 1845), 289–90.

51 A.N., F/1cIII/Basses-Pyrénées/11, The prefect to the minister of the interior, 19 February 1814; See also, A.N., F/1cIII/Basses-Pyrénées/11, The duc de Dalmatie to the army, 8 March 1814; A.N., F/1cIII/Basses-Pyrénées/10, The prefect to the emperor, 21 November 1813; A.N., F/1cIII/Basses-Pyrénées/10, The prefect to the minister of the interior, 30 November 1813.

52 A.N., F/1cIII/Basses-Pyrénées/11, The prefect to the minister of the interior, 6 January 1814; A.N., F/1cIII/Basses-Pyrénées/11, The sub-prefect of Orthez to the prefect, 20 February 1814.

53 A.N., F/1cIII/Basses-Pyrénées/10, The mayor of Sare to the sub-prefect of Bayonne, 11 October 1813: 'L'habitant fatigué, ou sous les armes ou sous des pesantes corvées gratuites, ayant fait toute espèce de sacrifices pour sauver sa propre existence, s'attendoit à trouver dans le soldat français, pour sa protection, un ami, au lieu d'une subtile persécuteur qui tantôt le dépouille du nécessaire à sa nourriture, et tantôt à sa couverture... Par son indiscipline le soldat français est devenu l'ennemi de la population.'

54 A.N., F/7/9689, The mayor of Saint-Jean-de-Luz to the duc de Dalmatie, 11 May 1815: 'en général les habitants des Pays basques français ne sympathisent pas avec ceux des communes limitrophes d'Espagne, et que si la guerre avoit lieu entre les deux nations, on trouveroit encore les Basques français disposés à s'armer pour défendre seulement leurs foyers sous le commandement des officiers, prix chez eux; car partout ailleurs, et commandés par ceux qui ne parlent pas leur langage, on n'en fera jamais que des mauvais soldats.'

55 A.N., F/7/9689, The minister of the interior to the prefect, 3 June 1815: 'J'ai vu avec peine que vos administrés se levaient à une dangereuse apathie: des insinuations perfides étoufferaient-elles donc dans le cœur

des Basques la voix de l'honneur, l'amour de la patrie? Rappelez à ce peuple guerrier que l'Empereur lui confie la défense des Pyrénées; il saura, je l'espère, les fers que l'étranger nous prépare: nous combattons encore une fois pour l'indépendance et la gloire de la France. ... Je compte sur votre zèle, M. le préfet, pour inspirer à votre département l'enthousiasme qui enflamme nos provinces frontières des Alpes et du Rhin et celles de l'Intérieur de la France: les Basques n'ont pas dégénéré.'

56 A.N., F/7/9689, The prefect to Marshal de Vioménil, 4 September 1815: 'M. de Chauvigny m'avoit invité à électriser la population, et pour l'électriser j'ai dû me servir des personnes qui avoient de l'influence sur elle. C'est par ce motif que j'ai invité le général Harispe à insurger les basques.' Monsieur de Chauvigny was Comte de Chauvigny de Blot, commander-in-chief in Bayonne.

57 A.N., F/7/9689, The prefect to the minister of the interior, 5 September 1815: 'Le général Harispe s'est parfaitement conduit de son côté, il a employé avec zèle, pour le service du roi, l'influence qu'il possède sur les Basques.'

58 A.N., F/7/9689, Second session of the provisional council of defence, 30 August 1815; A.N., F/7/9689, The prefect to the minister of the interior, 5 September 1815; A.N., F/7/9689, The prefect to the commander of the eleventh military division, 4 September 1815.

59 A.N., F/1cIII/Basses-Pyrénées/11, The prefect to the minister of the interior, 11 September 1815: 'Aujourd'hui les Bayonnais sont fiers de leur excellente conduite ... Leur ancienne inimitié contre les Béarnais a fait place à la reconnaissance, d'un autre côté ils témoignent beaucoup d'humeur aux basques qui les ont abandonnés pour défendre leurs propres foyers.'

60 Pierre d'Iharce de Bidassouet, *Histoire des cantabres ou des premiers colons de toute l'Europe avec celle des basques, leurs descendants directs* (Paris, 1825), 178: 'jurèrent en braves Cantabres de ne point survivre à la prise de leur ville. *Nous pouvons être détruits*, disoient-ils, *mais jamais vaincus.*'

61 Augustin Chaho, *Voyage en Navarre pendant l'insurrection des Basques (1830–1835)* (Bayonne, 1865), 80: 'C'était pendant la guerre de 93, où Harispe donna les premières preuves de la valeur téméraire et du rare sang-froid qui distinguent ce général de l'empereur. Dix mille chasseurs cantabres, tels que nous étions, seraient plus formidables à Zumala-Carreguy que cinquante régimens de ligne.'

62 A.D. Pau, 1/M/52, The commune of Saint-Étienne-de-Baïgorry to the government, 1848: 'L'héroïsme déployé par nos pères en 1793 pour la défense du sol républicain contre l'invasion espagnole mérita à notre commune le glorieux surnom des Thermopiles. Nous n'avons point

dégénéré de nos pères, nous sommes debout et prêts contre tout ennemi intérieur et extérieur.'
63 Tozzi, *Nationalizing France's Army*, 2.
64 Charles J. Esdaile, *The Wars of Napoleon* (London and New York, 2019), 109.
65 Vlossak, *Marianne or Germania?*, 5 and 15.

3

Liberty, liberties and legitimism in the First Carlist War

The Basque phase of the First Carlist War (1833–40) popularised a representation of the Basque country as the cradle of such conservative values as collective liberty, religion and tradition. The conflict, which was largely fought on Spanish Basque soil, was part of the European transition from an *ancien-régime* order to a liberal society, and French ultraroyalists supported Carlism and the Basque cause in order to challenge liberalism and recover the alleged pre-Revolutionary values of traditional, rural and pious France. The main champions of the Carlist cause in France were the legitimists, who had been ousted from power in 1830 and regarded the Spanish Basques' support for Don Carlos as their new hope for the restoration of absolutism in western Europe. At a local level, paradoxically, the main theorist of Spanish Basque demands in the Carlist War was a French Basque, the intellectual and politician Augustin Chaho, from the *ancien-régime pays* of Soule. Although Chaho was a republican whose main interest lay in the preservation of the Basque *fueros*, rather than in the restoration of a legitimate Bourbon to the French throne, his and legitimists' portrayal of Basque Carlists produced a similar characterisation of the Basque country as a land of liberty, faith and tradition. They both associated the Basque country with the *fueros* and, hence, with a collective understanding of liberty that was superior and antecedent to the individualist notion of liberty that stemmed from the Enlightenment and the French Revolution. Additionally, they idealised Basque traditional values and identified them with a model of rural society that liberalism allegedly wished to destroy. Finally, they characterised the French and Spanish Basques as one people, which contributed to the development of a shared sense of cultural identity between Basque communities on the two sides of the Pyrenees. Thus, the Basque phase of the First Carlist War contributed to the forging of a transnational conservative identity that came to define the Basque country in the late nineteenth century.

The Spanish Basque provinces rose in support of Carlism in 1833 when King Fernando VII, on his deathbed, rejected Salic Law, which would have made his brother Carlos king of Spain, and named as his successor his toddler daughter Isabel, under the regency of his wife María Cristina. The overruling of the traditional male order of succession enraged Don Carlos, who refused to recognise Isabel as the legitimate monarch of Spain and took up arms to defend his right to kingship. Two factions fought each other fiercely until the *cristinos*' victory in 1840: the conservative supporters of Don Carlos, who preached for a return to an *ancien-régime* style of monarchy and a decentralised approach to government, against the liberal supporters of María Cristina and Isabel, who championed a constitutional monarchy and administrative centralisation. One of the real and perceived goals of the liberals' administrative reconfiguration of Spain was the suppression of the Basque *fueros*, as the French Revolution had done in the French Basque country in 1789. As a result, Carlism's defence of tradition and provincial liberties found fertile ground in the Spanish Basque country, where the Basques endorsed Don Carlos's cause in the name of legitimism and the *fueros*.[1]

Since the French government of Louis-Philippe declined to engage militarily in the conflict, historians have neglected the influence of the First Carlist War on French politics and French political thought. Additionally, since legitimists had little involvement in French politics from 1830 to 1870, the role that Carlism played in the development of their political ideas has been overlooked.[2] As a result, except for Laëtitia Blanchard Rubio,[3] scholars have studied the war as a quintessentially Spanish conflict and have overlooked the impact of Carlism on French counterrevolutionary and antiliberal thought.[4] Yet France became involved in the war ideologically at both the national and the local level in the French Basque country. Legitimists' identification of the Basque uprising as a religious crusade in defence of *ancien-régime* principles and Chaho's depiction of the conflict as a liberal war of extermination against the Basques contributed to the theorisation of a traditionalist and conservative vision of French society against the perceived universalist and industrial 'modernity' of the liberal order.

The Basques, a legitimist people

French legitimists regarded the Carlist War as their new hope for the restoration of an *ancien-régime* style of absolute monarchy in France and Europe. As royalists who defended the dynastic succession to the French crown of the eldest branch of the Bourbon royal household, in 1830 they refused to recognise Louis-Philippe, of the Orléans cadet branch of the Bourbon dynasty, as the legitimate monarch of France, and had been waiting for a new propitious moment to counterattack since the duchesse de Berry's failed insurrection in the Vendée in 1832.[5] Legitimists recognised in the Carlist War many of the same element of their own crusade. Don Carlos, or Carlos V to his supporters, presented himself as the legitimate monarch of Spain against the usurper María Cristina, exactly as Charles X was, for them, the legitimate French monarch, who had been ousted by the usurper Louis-Philippe. Don Carlos's cause, moreover, stood for tradition, absolute monarchy and decentralisation against María Cristina's liberalism, constitutional monarchy and centralisation, similarly to the way in which Charles X considered himself an *ancien-régime* ruler, committed to traditional values and pre-Revolutionary decentralisation, against the liberal reforms of the July Monarchy.[6] Don Carlos's victory in Spain was desirable for legitimists as it would weaken the legitimacy of Louis-Philippe in France too. When the Spanish Basques rose in revolt in support of Carlism, legitimists portrayed both the French and Spanish Basque provinces as legitimist strongholds, devoted to monarchy, religion and provincial liberties.

The Basque Carlists' motto of 'legitimism and the *fueros*' embodied legitimists' counterrevolutionary political thought, which rejected the liberal principles of individualism and equality in the eyes of the law, as stated in *The Declaration of the Rights of Man and of the Citizen* of 1789, and espoused a collective vision of society whereby the individual, as a social being, could be free only as part of a natural and hierarchical civic community which operated according to a divine plan.[7] Legitimists regarded Carlism as the embodiment of the real principle of liberty, which they equated with man living in society and, consequently, with law and order. They contrasted it to María Cristina's liberalism, which deprived man of his natural collective and concrete state of being and threatened to lead Spain into usurpation and anarchy.[8] The protection of liberty, they argued, depended on the application of two concepts: the preservation of Salic Law and the principle of nationality. Legitimists believed that the maintenance of the male line to the throne through the application of Salic Law safeguarded both the legitimacy of kingship, as it prevented a foreign prince from becoming king through marriage, and the preservation of national identity itself, since they regarded the king as the embodiment of the people.[9] In turn, legitimists associated Isabel's sex with illegitimacy and weakness, claiming that María Cristina's overthrow of Salic Law threatened the survival of the Spanish nation.[10] The queen regent's substitution of political 'civilisation' with 'barbarism' was a representation of the inherent degeneracy of the whole liberal project.[11] Legitimism was also synonymous with the principle of nationality, as the king was seen as the embodiment of his people. Ultraroyalists presented the two pretenders to the throne, Don Carlos in Spain and the duc d'Angoulême in France, as the true representatives of the people in contrast to the liberal usurpers María Cristina's and Louis-Philippe's alleged support for the capitalist bourgeoisie. Additionally, they portrayed legitimate kings as exercising paternal authority in conformity with divine law, but respecting the concrete liberties of their subjects' respective communities.[12] Hence, they rejected the claim that legitimism stood for the principle of power while more progressive forces, such as liberalism and republicanism, represented the cause of the people. Rather, the opposite was true. Supporting the cause of the people, they argued, did not mean awarding power to the masses; it meant enforcing respect for the law, which was the foundation of the social order. Only within the pre-established social order could people be really free.[13] Thus, only a legitimate, monarchical government represented the people and, consequently, could guarantee people's liberty.

When the Basque provinces followed Bilbao into a pro-Carlist rebellion in the autumn of 1833, French legitimists were quick to identify the Basques as a legitimist people and their defence of local liberties as a part of their legitimist project. On the one hand, the Basques' defence of the *fueros* supported the counterrevolutionary understanding of man as a social creature whose liberty depended on life in civil society. On the other, the Basques' protection of the *fueros* became a symbol of the defence of the provincial liberties of the *ancien régime* and of an idealisation of rural life, based on respect for royal authority and divine law.

Legitimists adopted the historical narrative of Basque Cantabrianism to provide a historical foundation to the Basques' unique attachment to their liberty. They dated it back to ancient history, when the Cantabrians allegedly resisted multiple attempts at foreign invasion and subjugation. The legitimist newspaper *L'Europe*, for instance, explained that throughout the centuries Spain was ravaged by the Carthaginians, the Romans, the Saracens, the Moors, the Arabs and the Goths. None of them managed to subjugate the Cantabrians. Later, Charlemagne led his armies to northern Spain, but 'the conquest lasted only an instant'. Finally, Napoleon invaded Spain in 1808 but 'the people of Vizcaya, known in antiquity as the belligerent Cantabrians, believing that Napoleon would travel through their province, erected a triumphal arch on which they wrote these words: *Cantabrians never defeated*. Napoleon was informed of it and modified his route.'[14] The history of the invincible Basques explained their attachment to their liberty, which in the early modern period took the collective and concrete form of the *fueros*. The 'cries of glory and of liberty' that the Basques issued in defence of Don Carlos and their privileges in 1833 was, according to legitimists, a continuation of such distinguished tradition.[15]

The historical liberty of the Basques, legitimists argued, made them morally superior to other European peoples. They regarded the Basques as the preservers of the uncorrupted moral order, political authority and social hierarchy of an idealised European countryside, which the capitalist liberalism of towns was destroying. Through their support of the Basque *fueros*, then, legitimists positioned themselves politically as protectors of the people against the new forms of material and moral misery engendered by the capitalist and, especially, financial world.[16] Spain, explained Vocaltha, a French legitimist who volunteered in the war, was the only country to have been shielded from the 'démoralisation sociale' that affected the rest of Europe in the nineteenth century. He attributed such moral preservation to the Cantabrians first and later to the Basques, who were 'more friends of liberty than of their existence'. He relied on history to draw parallels between the past glory of the Cantabrians and the projected future glory of the Basques at the head of Don Carlos's army. It was in Vizcaya, he explained, that Pelagius of Asturias, an eighth-century king who was widely considered the initiator of the *Reconquista*, 'swore to die for God, liberty and religion: *Fueros y la religion* [sic]'.[17] As Vizcaya represented the province where Pelagius began the reconquest of Spain from the Moors, he implied, the four Basque provinces similarly represented the place where, eleven centuries later, Don Carlos would start his reconquest of Spain from the new infidel: liberalism.

Legitimists' accounts of the Basque phase of the Carlist War were permeated with religious metaphors. Religion was crucial to their mission, as it presented the monarchy as the restorer of divine sovereignty after Revolutionary dechristianisation.[18] Religious metaphors focused on two main themes: parallels between the contemporary Spanish Basque Carlist rebellion and the French counterrevolutionary uprising in the Vendée in the 1790s, and a comparison between the Spanish Basque military leader Tomás de Zumalacárregui and Christian heroes in Spanish and European history.

The comparison between the Spanish Basque country and the Vendée symbolised the continuity of European legitimists' counterrevolutionary mission between the 1790s and the 1830s.[19] As the Vendée was the sanctuary region of counterrevolution, whose Catholic and royalist army had resisted the Revolutionary troops in the name of 'God and the king', the Spanish Basque country was entrusted with the divine mission of halting the liberal and progressive forces of the nineteenth century.[20] In this respect, legitimists portrayed the *cristinos* as the heirs of the French Revolutionary tradition, and Carlism as a continuation of European ultraroyalists' counterrevolutionary mission. Vocaltha, for example, predicted: 'The reunion of these four [Spanish Basque] provinces [will] form the big Spanish Vendée, against which the efforts of all other provinces will be dashed.'[21] Similarly, a poem that the legitimist writer and historian Alcide de Beauchesne wrote as an obituary for Zumalacárregui in 1835, published in *La Mode* and *La Gazette de France* – both legitimist publications – described the Basque leader as rallying a new Vendean rebellion. The poem imagined Zumalacárregui shout:

> 'To arms! – Because tonight we have to crush
> Under our feet the regicidal hydra!
> We need world peace! We need God to decide
> Between the good and the wicked!' –
> He says, and the Lord heard his words:
> A unanimous tocsin shook the bell towers,
> And from the depths of the ravines, the woods and the rocks,
> Emerged seething the Spanish Vendée![22]

The new 'Spanish Vendée' represented both the continuity of legitimists' historical battle against the forces of progress and liberalism and a revival of hope for the legitimist cause in Europe. Such sense of continuity across the first few decades of the century was key to French legitimists, who were attempting to recover their momentum and restore their pride after the most recent Vendean defeat of 1832.[23]

As the leader of the 'Spanish Vendée', legitimists recognised Zumalacárregui as a both military and spiritual commander who was reviving Don Carlos's legitimist cause. He was the embodiment of the Carlist principles of the throne and the altar, and his symbolic role as a Christian soldier was fundamental to the cause after the Carlists were deprived of the support of the pope and of most Spanish bishops.[24] Zumalacárregui and his Basque army were associated with religious figures of the past. Some legitimist publications portrayed the Spanish Basque uprising as a new Maccabean Revolt, the rebellion that a group of Jewish warriors had initiated against the Seleucid Empire in the second century BCE. The outcome of the revolt was the Jews' recovery of control over Judea and the reconsecration of the temple of Jerusalem. Legitimists compared Zumalacárregui to the leader of the Maccabees, whom the First Book of Maccabees identified as the Kohen Mattathias ben Johanan. As Mattathias had led the rebellion against the Seleucid king Antiochus IV, who had forbidden Jewish religious practice and imposed Greek polytheism, legitimists saw Zumalacárregui as the leader of the uprising against María Cristina's illegitimate rule and imposition of liberal values. The struggle between 'Judaism' and 'Hellenism', as the Second Book of Maccabees interpreted the Maccabean Revolt, was now a conflict between legitimism and liberalism. 'It is beautiful to unite the thoughts of strength and of religion in one sentiment of independence,' Vocaltha wrote. '[I]t is beautiful to be at the same time a Christian and a soldier, it is beautiful to become the Maccabee of an entire people that you set free thanks to victory and sovereign reason; it is beautiful to be called Zumalacarreguy [sic]!!!'[25] As the Maccabees, after the cleansing of the Temple and the re-establishment of Jewish worship, had eventually installed Jonathan Maccabee as high priest, legitimists identified the Basques as the ones who would ultimately consecrate Don Carlos to the throne of Spain and, consequently, help to re-establish legitimist rule.

Other accounts compared Zumalacárregui to El Cid, a medieval Castilian knight turned Spanish and Christian hero. While the real Rodrigo Díaz de Vivar, known as El Cid, had served both Moorish and Christian armies in the eleventh century, the medieval epic poem *Cantar de mio Cid* had turned him into a Catholic hero who had contributed to the *Reconquista* and the Christian unification of Spain, fighting the Moors on behalf of the king of Castile, Alfonso VI. Legitimists adopted the Christian interpretation of El Cid and claimed that Zumalacárregui was El Cid of Navarra, who was fighting against the latest threat to Christian Spain, the liberal army of María Cristina, on behalf of Don Carlos. *La Mode*, for example, wrote in 1835 that Zumalacárregui, 'this Spanish hero, who deserved the name of El Cid of Navarra, ... already provided more services to his king than the valiant soldier of Burgos did to Alfonso VI'.[26] A few months later, after Zumalacárregui's tragic death during the siege of Bilbao, the magazine insisted that the Basque leader should be celebrated as a national hero and his statue erected next to that of El Cid in the monastery of El Escorial near Madrid, the symbol of the Spanish Catholic monarchy. 'Say, all of you, that Zumalacarreguy [sic], who fell under the walls of Bilbao, should receive funeral honours only in the cathedral of Madrid,' it wrote, 'and that the statue of El Cid of Castile awaits at El Escorial the statue of El Cid of Navarra.'[27] Such religious metaphors, then, aimed at the creation of a symbolic, providential, historical narrative for the contemporary Carlist cause, as well as a sense of continuity in the European counterrevolutionary mission since 1789.

In the first years of the war, legitimists regarded Zumalacárregui's Basque army and the Carlist cause almost as synonyms. Indeed, between the first weeks of the uprising in October 1833 and his death in June 1835, Zumalacárregui temporarily turned the course of the war in favour of the Carlists thanks to his gifted guerrilla leadership skills.[28] Importantly, it was because of his initial victories that Don Carlos decided to travel back to Spain from his exile in England, arriving in Urdax, in Navarra, in July 1834. The popularity of the two men fed off each other. Don Carlos's cause took momentum as a result of the victories of the Basque general and his arrival in the Basque country provided Carlism with its natural leader.[29] Zumalacárregui, with his charisma, military abilities, royal support and premature death, became a legendary hero. As Don Carlos established his headquarters in Navarra, legitimists saw the triumph of his cause as inextricably tied to that of the Basque provinces and the Basque uprising as representative of the Carlist cause as a whole. As the Spanish Basque country came to embody legitimism, the local *juntas*, which defended the *fueros*, became the defenders of all Spanish liberties. 'The real liberty is in Navarra with Charles V and these *juntas* truthfully popular and national, which defend the sacred rights and laws of the country,' *La Gazette de France* wrote in 1836. '[I]n Madrid, there are only arbitrary decisions, injustice, confiscation; everywhere else, violence, massacres, riots, insurrections.'[30] Legitimists contrasted such bleak portrayals of Madrilene life, determined by a view of the urban world as morally corrupted by industrialisation, speculation and 'modernity', with the Basques' preservation of moral purity and traditional values. As a result, the historical rights and alleged moral principles of the Basque country became the concrete representation of the legitimist cause.

Crucially, legitimists did not consider the Basques' political and economic independence within Spain to be at odds with the principles of monarchical authority and national unity that they preached. On the contrary, they took it as an opportunity to reinforce the counter-revolutionary myth that the *ancien régime* had been the golden age of provincial liberties that the French Revolution had violated.[31] The problem, they claimed, lay with the egalitarian principles of the Enlightenment and of 1789, which prioritised an abstract, universalistic, individualistic definition of liberty over the notion of liberty in a concrete, collective, anti-individualistic sense that they associated with the provincial privileges of the old order.[32] Provincial *franchises*, the newspaper *Le Légitimiste* pointed out, represented 'the guarantees of the last citizen', which legitimism protected insofar as 'they are rights whose principle is sacred'.[33] The paper *Le Rénovateur* reminded its readers that the Revolutionary events themselves were proof that the monarchy was the defender of provincial liberties, as it was the French Revolution that had abolished privileges, not the legitimate government of Louis XVI. It wrote:

> It was not the royalists who overturned the estates of Provence, of Languedoc, of the Dauphiné, of Bourgogne, of Bretagne, of Artois and of Béarn; it was the Revolution. Neither our fathers nor we have ever abandoned the cause of the provincial *franchises*. Our fathers protested against the decrees of the constituent assembly that destroyed the internal organisation of the kingdom; we still demand decentralisation every day. One should not be surprised by our sympathy for the four insurgent provinces, since they write on their banners: LEGITIMACY AND LIBERTY.[34]

French legitimists, then, took their support of the Basque *fueros* as an opportunity to position themselves in favour of regional decentralisation in France. It was not a coincidence that it was between 1836 and 1837 that the lawyer Ferdinand Béchard, a deputy of the Right during the July Monarchy, theorised the legitimist notion of administrative decentralisation in his *Essai sur la centralisation administrative*. Protection of provincial liberties became an inherent aspect of legitimist ideology.[35]

While liberal publications accused the Basques of self-interest and of fighting only to protect their local privileges, legitimists rejected the claim, arguing that the defence of legitimism and of the *fueros* went naturally hand in hand. The paper *La Quotidienne*, for example, explained that it was a 'grave mistake' to think that the Basques were fighting only for the preservation of their privileges, for two main reasons. First, in the moral hierarchy of the rationale for war, legitimism took precedence over provincial concerns. '[T]he Basque country and Navarra are fighting for legitimacy and civilisation against usurpation and revolutionary barbarism,' it wrote. '[T]he material interests of these provinces are only secondary.'[36] Second, the protection of Basque liberties was an intrinsic part of legitimist ideology. 'While usurpation admits that it can hold up only by means of servitude, legitimacy signals its accession by solemnly recognising Spanish liberties,' the paper insisted. 'Charles V swears that he will preserve the *fueros*, and he will keep his promise, because the liberties of a country are also legitimate rights.'³⁷ Ultimately, legitimists portrayed the preservation of the Basque *fueros* as a legitimist prerogative aimed at the restoration of a naturally collective and hierarchical civil society, which they contrasted with the isolation of the 'modern' man and his subjugation to the state, inherent consequences of the abstract notions of individualism and equality preached by the liberal and revolutionary ideologies.³⁸

The French Basques, also a legitimist people

Although legitimists' primary interest was Spain, the characterisation of the Basques as a pure, moral, religious and traditional – hence legitimist – people transcended national boundaries and included French and Spanish Basques alike. In 1835, for example, the legitimist paper *La Gazette du Languedoc* educated its readership on the identity of the Basques and explained that the French and the Spanish Basques were one and the same people. Speaking of the Spanish Basques, it wrote that:

> The people who live in these counties have the greatest relations of habit and, without any doubt, of origin with those who, on the northern slopes of the Pyrenees, inhabit part of the *arrondissements* of Bayonne and of Mauléon in France. In general, we call them *Basques*, in France and in Spain, and from it derives the name of *Basque* Provinces [*Provinces Vascongades*]; but they, both on this and on the other side of the Pyrenees, call themselves *Escualdunac*, and their language, so remarkable for its forms, they call it *Escuara* [sic]. Travelling through the [Spanish] Basque Provinces, the inhabitant of Mauléon or of Bayonne finds his brothers, as well as the dialects of the language that he learnt to mumble in the cradle.³⁹

French and Spanish Basques, *La Gazette du Languedoc* added, were different from their French and Spanish neighbours not only because of their distinctive mores and language, but also because of their special attachment to an understanding of liberty that was characteristic of the legitimist cause.⁴⁰

The inclusion of the French Basques in the legitimist narrative of the Carlist War was arguably not only a question of cultural boundaries. It also aimed to further French readers' sense of identification with the Carlist and legitimist causes by emphasising that the war and the values the Carlists were fighting for were not only Spanish, and hence foreign – they were French and concerned France too.[41] The legitimist volunteer Robert de Custine, for instance, explained that the French Basques were the preservers of the legitimist tradition within liberal France. Writing in 1838, he alleged that a local nobleman told him about the Basques: 'It is nice ... to find in the middle of France, so selfish and corrupted, a corner of land where faith, simple mores and the rigid integrity of our fathers have been preserved.'[42] The legitimist cause, he claimed, was not lost in France. There was still a region that preserved legitimist principles.

The French Basques, moreover, contributed to the war more actively than through ideology alone. While military action did not extend to France, the French Basques featured in the war effort through a huge contraband network that extended across Europe and reached even the American continent. Legitimists hailed such an activity as heroic, which was an unusual and self-serving stance. After 1815, the restored Bourbon regime had committed to curbing smuggling on France's borders, including in the Basque country, as it associated public order with political stability and, consequently, with a legitimist identity for France.[43] The liberal press, instead, had romanticised the figure of the contrabander, presenting him as a symbol of liberty and deriding customs guards.[44] During the Carlist War, the two positions were reversed. Legitimists encouraged Basque smuggling, as a way both of supporting the legitimist war on the international stage and of undermining Louis-Philippe's support of María Cristina and the legitimacy of his regime at home. Liberals, on the contrary, attempted to prevent contraband as it compromised Louis-Philippe's international relations with Spain and eroded the solidity of his government in Paris. In 1834, for example, the crown prosecutor of Bayonne complained that the Basques' illicit trade contributed to 'fuel the insurrection [in Spain] against the government of Isabel II, which is recognised and somehow guaranteed by France'.[45] The Carlist War, then, was as much a military conflict as a war of ideas.

Legitimists employed the prototype of the Basque contrabander in order to forge an ideal version of the legitimist man. He was strong, brave, warriorlike, yet equally just, pious and loyal, attached to his land, his traditions and his country. He was the idealisation of a chivalric medieval knight, which Romanticism popularised at the beginning of the nineteenth century.[46] Additionally, the Basque smuggler was necessarily a staunch legitimist, whose illegal commerce represented an act of resistance against the illegitimate government of Louis-Philippe. Legitimists popularised their version of the myth of the Basque contrabander especially in 1838, when French Basque smugglers helped Don Carlos's fiancée, the Portuguese María Teresa de Braganza, known as the princess of Beira, across the border into Spain on the eve of their wedding. Custine, who had accompanied the princess on her journey across France and witnessed her crossing, alleged that they were hosted by a local legitimist nobleman, the marquis Henri de Belzunce, who reassured Custine that he should not doubt the loyalty of the Basque *montagnards* to the legitimist and Carlist causes. 'You can enter all the huts with the certainty of finding an inviolable asylum against the chasing of governmental agents,' Belzunce allegedly explained. 'All the men you will meet will serve as guides; you can entrust them with your person and your belongings without fear; they will risk their lives to defend one and the other, especially if you tell them that you support the cause of Charles V, to which they are all devoted.'[47] Such a dogmatic portrayal of the Basque people was misleading. While it was true that the French Basques engaged in a gigantic contraband network extending across two continents and involving the smuggling of both merchandise and people across the Pyrenees, ideology was hardly the principal factor behind smuggling. For much of the Basque population, contraband was a source of material gain. Many in Bayonne saw it as an opportunity to restore the prosperity of the port, while the merchants and manufacturers in towns such as Saint-Jean-Pied-de-Port, whose local factory produced shoes for the Carlist insurgents, perceived it as a chance to improve their industrial profits.[48] At the same time, as Chapters 7 and 8 will reveal, the popularisation of the myth of the Basque contrabander as a Romantic hero, which originated in the Peninsular War and legitimists perpetuated,[49] was influential and determined both the literary depiction of the Basque man and the Basques' self-portrayal vis-à-vis the emerging tourist industry in the later part of the nineteenth century.

The most famous archetype of the Basque contrabander was Ganix de Macaye, the smuggler who had escorted the princess of

Beira across the Pyrenean border.[50] Custine was the first to mention the 'famous chief of contrabanders', though omitting his name, but Ganix transcended political loyalties and came to represent a stereotypical example of the Romantic Basque smuggler. The liberal *La Sentinelle des Pyrénées*, for example, reported that the princess of Beira had crossed the Nive river 'on the back of a famous contrabander',[51] while the Orleanist *Le Phare de Bayonne* revealed that the princess had been helped by the smuggler G., who lived in Macaye.[52] Further, the story of Ganix was later publicised during the Second Empire by a Basque writer and member of the *conseil général* of the Basses-Pyrénées, Jean-Baptiste Dasconaguerre, in his most famous book, *Les Échos du Pas de Roland*. At the time, Ganix was living in poverty and Dasconaguerre hoped that reminding his fellow Basques of his heroism during the Carlist War would trigger local aid. In the book, the story of Ganix transcended his personal experience and came to represent the qualities of the Basques as a whole. Dasconaguerre imagined the princess of Beira asking the marquis of Belzunce, who was hosting her before the border crossing, whether Ganix was to be trusted. He had Belzunce reply, mirroring Custine's text: 'I shall respond to it, Madam, on my honour. Ganich [*sic*] is a brave and loyal Basque ... We still find here [in the Basque country] the faith and integrity of our fathers; the smallest cottage is an inviolable asylum for foreigners. Entrust your person and your possessions to a Basque, and he will risk his life to save one and the other.'[53] Thus, legitimists' representation of the Basque smuggler bypassed the legitimist cause itself and became a model of traditional, conservative values in the nineteenth century.

Augustin Chaho and the 'war of extermination' against the Basques

Support for the Basque phase of the First Carlist War as a defence of 'the doctrine of historical rights'[54] was also embraced by the Soule-born and Paris-educated intellectual and politician Augustin Chaho. Like the legitimists, Chaho portrayed the Basques as the embodiment of the Carlist cause, but his political position was different, insofar as he was neither a legitimist nor a liberal. He was a republican who supported Carlism on the basis of the alleged superiority of the Basque race. He presented the Basques as superior to all other European peoples in two main respects. On the one hand, he argued for the historical primacy of Basque liberty and independence, which were guaranteed by the *fueros*. On the other, he reinvented the myth that the Basques had never been polytheist, arguing that the Basques were a chosen people who would soon achieve a new golden age through territorial unification. As a democrat and a republican, Chaho was critical of both legitimists and liberals. He accused legitimists of self-interest and of appropriating the Basque cause as 'the instrument of their political goals'.[55] At the same time, he accused the liberal *cristinos* of being the oppressors, as he believed that the Basques' original liberty was superior to contemporary liberalism and interpreted María Cristina's attempt to impose liberal reforms on the Basque provinces as a form of enslavement. 'Be aware, liberal sophists from Madrid,' he warned the *cristinos* in *Paroles d'un Bizkaïen* in 1834, 'that the Basques will always reject your illegitimate liberalism with disdain, your ignoble oppression with horror.'[56] Having rejected both legitimism and liberalism, Chaho proclaimed that the only way of supporting the Basque cause 'without betraying my democratic principles' was to support Carlism.[57]

In *Voyage en Navarre pendant l'insurrection des Basques*, an account of his largely fictional participation in the Carlist War as a volunteer, Chaho portrayed the conflict as a liberal war of extermination against the Basque people. In similar fashion to legitimists, he depicted liberals as despots driven by a centralising mission whose aim was the deliberate annihilation of the original liberty and independence of the Basques. Chaho pushed the argument further, though, claiming that the *cristinos* were engaging in a war aimed at the elimination of the Basques as an ethnic nation. The Castilians, he had a Carlist chief say, 'would like to annihilate the glorious titles of our independence and of our nationality, aroused by despotic views and by the deep-rooted jealousy that they harbour against the Basques'.[58] In turn, he added in another fictional conversation with a Labourdin peasant, the Basques were in arms 'to defend their noble independence and the individuality of our primitive and solar race, under the command of a freely elected chief, Zumala-Carreguy [*sic*], and under the nominal flag of a Lord and King, D. Carlos'.[59] It was because they were under threat of national extinction, Chaho explained, that the Spanish Basques were rising in support of Don Carlos.

Chaho theorised his support of Carlism and parallel antagonism to liberalism by adopting the myth of Basque Cantabrianism and narrating a heroic history of Basque resistance to oppression. Throughout the centuries, he argued, the Basques had resisted all invasion and even when the barbarians had substituted 'primitive liberty with slavery', they had managed to preserve their ancient liberties.[60] As a result, Chaho believed that progressive ideas deriving from the Revolutionary tradition of 1789 were regressive when applied to the Basques, because the latter already possessed the original and highest form of liberty and equality, and any attempt to reproduce them was but an imitation. 'The Basques are all equal, all free, in theory and in practice,' he explained to María Cristina in *Paroles d'un Bizkaïen*. 'You wish to make Castile French; our neighbouring Spaniards can gain from this change; we, the Basques, can but lose. Your progressive institutions would be reactionary for us. The Basques are a model-people; they just wish to imitate the Republic of their ancestors.'[61] Chaho, then, did not denounce Revolutionary principles themselves, as legitimists did, but he rejected them when they threatened the political and economic particularism of the Spanish Basque provinces. As a result, he distinguished between the original and pure liberty of the Basques and the liberal and corrupted notion of liberty originating in the French Revolution.

Similarly to legitimists, Chaho adopted the myth of Basque Cantabrianism to demonstrate the continuity between the wars of independence that the Cantabrians, the ancestors of the Basques, had allegedly fought throughout history and the present Carlist War.[62] He adapted the traditional version of Basque Cantabrianism to a philosophy of history of his own invention, founded upon the belief that history was cyclical and repeated itself every 60,000 years. The history of the past 60,000 years was divided into four ages. First, there was the age of the Children of the Sun, between 6,000 and 3,000 BCE, a Basque golden age, during which the Cantabrians occupied Europe, Asia and Africa. The second age corresponded to the invasions of the Children of the Night, that is, other Indo-European peoples, from 3,000 BCE to year zero. At this time, Paradise disappeared and Basque territory was reduced to the seven Pyrenean provinces. The third age corresponded to Chaho's current one. It began after year zero and was a time of constant warfare between the Basques and the Celts, the Phoenicians, the Carthaginians, the Romans, the Goths and the Moors. This phase formed the core of the traditional Basque Cantabrian narrative. Around 1830, at the time when Chaho was writing, signs suggested that a fourth age was approaching, when the People of the South, the Basques, would regain their hegemonic role. Such early indicators, for Chaho, included the Carlist War, which he saw as the beginning of a new Basque age of freedom and of a new golden age, headed by Zumalacárregui as the chosen leader.[63] Given that the Basques were the new elected people, Chaho concluded that it was only natural that it was they, and not the *cristinos*, who should lead the process of regeneration in Spain.[64]

Chaho's definition of the Basques as an elected people and the prediction of an incoming Basque golden age were imbued with messianic undertones, which were widespread in Europe at the time. In France, for instance, Edgar Quinet had predicted that the bearer of a new gnostic religion would soon appear in a people of the Pyrenees, while in the Polish lands, Andrzej Towiański, who later influenced the Polish nationalist poet Adam Mickiewicz, had argued that the Poles were the new elected people.[65] While legitimists and Carlists, however, associated the Basques with the Christian version of the myth of primitive monotheism, Chaho rejected Christianity. Influenced by his studies of Sanskrit, a language that had also fascinated such Romantic contemporaries as Claude Fauriel and Johann Gottfried Herder, Chaho argued that the only true faith was the primitive religion of the sun, professed in ancient times by Indians and Iranians. Basque religion, he claimed, derived from India and Euskara descended from Sanskrit. Descending from India, the Basques had not been corrupted by barbarian influences and in ancient times had worshipped Iao, the god of the seers and bearer of the primogenital trinity: life, incarnated god and spirit.[66] Iao was a pre-Christian divinity, which proved, according to Chaho, that, unlike other European civilisations such as the Greeks and polytheist Romans, the Basques had never been idolatrous.[67] While legitimists and, later, the supporters of the *fueros*, or *fueristas*, disagreed with Chaho on the identity of the Basque divinity, they were influenced by two ideas on which Chaho's theory was founded. First, the Basques were a new suffering Israel, whose ancient liberties, independence and language had to be preserved or recovered. Second, the Carlist War was a Basque religious crusade aimed at protecting the guardians of Basque liberty, the *fueros*, from liberalism's centralising mission.

The definition of the Basques as the elected people who would lead the world towards a new golden age prompted Chaho to claim that the Basques could fully achieve their process of regeneration only if they were united among themselves and independent of foreign powers. 'Our race, for too long plunged into a lethargic sleep, woke up at my call,' Chaho had a fictional Zumalacárregui proclaim in the final pages of *Voyage en Navarre*. 'Our blood, spread in battle, will give birth in our mountains to a generation of heroes; witnesses of the tears of the *patrie* and of our wounds, our children, cradled with warlike songs, will nourish in their hearts the inextinguishable hatred of oppression; they will press themselves as brothers around the oak of liberty, they will wave the flag of liberation.'[68] For Chaho, then, the Carlist War did not represent only the latest in a long series of conflicts for the protection of Basque liberty; it was also the beginning of a new era of Basque political independence.

In case of French military intervention against the Spanish Carlists, Chaho incited the French Basques to disregard their duty towards France and join the Spanish Basques for the greater cause of Basque independence. '[I]f the French government, intervening against Zumalacárregui, were to declare a war of extermination against the independence of our race,' he imagined telling a peasant from Labourd in *Voyage en Navarre*, 'I have reason to believe that instead of marching against their Spanish brothers, the Basques of France will not recoil from a daring resolution, dictated by the interests of their glory and their liberty.'[69] Eventually, Chaho predicted, the Basques from the two sides of the border would reunite to form one independent nation. He wrote:

> 'The Pyrenees start at the [river] Ebre and end at the [river] Adour,' the Romans used to say of the ancient Basques. The *Euskariens* believed they were an integral part of it; they did not conceive that, disregarding their perfect identity of origin, language, mores and laws, the circumstance of living on the northern or southern slope of a mountain would be enough to politically separate peoples that touch and confuse themselves at the intersection of valleys. Founded upon this principle and upon historical right, perhaps one day the Basques will attempt to recover the national unity that they once enjoyed.[70]

Scholars of Basque nationalism have identified Chaho as a protonationalist whose ideas had a direct impact on the *fuerista* movement that developed after the abolition of the Spanish Basque *fueros* in 1876 and on Sabino Arana's invention of Basque separatist nationalism in the final decade of the nineteenth century.[71] Although the influence of his ideas on both movements, as Chapter 5 will show, is undeniable, Chaho was not a separatist. He was a French intellectual and politician who militated in favour of French republicanism, not of Basque nationalism. On the one hand, he seemed more interested in creating a stereotypical cultural identity for the Basque country than a political one. Emblematically, it is likely that his expedition to Navarra as a volunteer in the Carlist War, which he recounted in *Voyage en Navarre*, never happened. When it came to politics, his commitment was to French republicanism. When the Second Republic was proclaimed in 1848, he campaigned in his native Soule, becoming commander of the national guard of Bayonne, a member of the *conseil général* of the Basses-Pyrénées and, as a Democratic-Socialist candidate, narrowly failing to be elected to the Constituent Assembly in 1849.[72] On the other hand, despite his arguments for Basque independence in *Voyage en Navarre*, his vision for the future of the Basque country was not consistent. In a reflection on the political situation of France under the July Monarchy, published during the Carlist War in 1838, he even seemed to suggest that the ideal future for the four Spanish Basque provinces was not to be independent, but to be united to France.[73] Chaho, in other words, appeared to consider the French, and perhaps even Spanish, Basque country as a cultural region of France, rather than an independent nation with political and territorial claims. As a result, Chaho's ideas concerning the Basque country rarely left the realm of theory, making him an influential thinker but not a Basque militant.

Conclusion

Although legitimists and the republican Chaho became partisans of both Carlism and the Basque *fueros* for different reasons – legitimists to restore reactionary monarchism and Chaho to defend Basque particularism – their claims converged and developed a quintessentially traditional and conservative identity for the Basque country. For one thing, they associated the Basque country with a conservative notion of social and collective liberty, embodied by the *fueros*, which they contrasted with the individualistic and universalistic definition of liberty that derived from the Enlightenment and the French Revolution and that was embraced by nineteenth-century liberalism. As a result, they employed the notion of foral liberty to espouse the 'doctrine of historical rights', which favoured *ancien-régime* decentralisation against progressive, liberal centralisation. Additionally, legitimists theorised the existence of the *fueros* on the basis of historicism and the idealisation of rural society, which were key values of the right, and to which Chaho also committed in his protection of Basque tradition.[74] Although the *fors* were eliminated in France in 1789, legitimists shared with Chaho an understanding of the seven Basque provinces as united by common linguistic and cultural traits that distinguished them from France and Spain and protected them from centralisation, liberalism and 'modernity'. Finally, both Chaho and the legitimists portrayed the Basques as a chosen people selected to restore true faith in Europe, although Catholics were suspicious of Chaho because of his anti-clericalism. As the next chapters will show, Chaho's and the legitimists' representation of the Basques as defenders of tradition, morality and religion had long-term consequences for the relationship between the Basques and the French government. In particular, it perpetuated the association between Basque identity and political conservatism that had originated in the French Revolution. At the turn of the twentieth century, it became a dominant trait of French Basque conservatives' resistance to the secularising and centralising reforms of the Third Republic.

Notes

1 Mark Lawrence, *Spain's First Carlist War, 1833–1840* (London, 2014), 3–5 and 14–15; John F. Coverdale, *The Basque Phase of Spain's First Carlist War* (Princeton, 1984), 265–6.
2 There are some works on legitimism in the period 1830–70, but no text focuses specifically on the First Carlist War. See Bernard Rulof, *Popular Legitimism and the Monarchy in France: Mass Politics Without Parties, 1830–1880* (New York, 2020); Jean Charbonnel, *Les Légitimistes. De Chateaubriand à de Gaulle* (Paris, 2006); Jean-Philippe Luis, 'France

and Spain: A Common Territory of Anti-Revolution (End of the 18th Century–1800)', in Matthijs Lok, Friedemann Pestel and Juliette Reboul (eds), *Cosmopolitan Conservatisms: Countering Revolution in Transnational Networks, Ideas and Movements (c. 1770–1930)* (Leiden, 2021), 261–82; Steven D. Kale, *Legitimism and the Reconstruction of French Society, 1852–1883* (Baton Rouge, 1992).

3 Laëtitia Blanchard Rubio, 'Les Provinces basques et la Navarre en guerre vue par les français, 1833–1839' (PhD thesis, Université Paris 3, 1999); Laëtitia Blanchard Rubio, 'La Première guerre carliste ou la guerre de la dernière chance: la communauté légitimiste face à son destin', *Amnis*, 10 (2011); Laëtitia Blanchard Rubio, 'La Mémoire du conflit carliste et ses enjeux: entre usage politique et mise en ordre du passé', *Amnis*, 18 (2019).

4 On the First Carlist War, see Coverdale, *The Basque Phase of Spain's First Carlist War*; Jordi Canal, *El Carlismo. Dos siglos de contrarrevolución en España* (Madrid, 2000); Lawrence, *Spain's First Carlist War*. On French counterrevolutionary thought, see Gerard Gengembre, *La Contre-révolution ou l'histoire désespérante* (Paris, 1989); Tort, *La Droite française*.

5 On the failed legitimist insurrection of 1832, see Eric Martone, 'The Last Vendée: The Duchesse de Berry, Legitimist Propaganda, and Alexandre Dumas', in Eric Martone (ed.), *Royalists, Radicals and les Misérables: France in 1832* (Newcastle upon Tyne, 2013), 13–73.

6 María Cristina was in fact an absolutist. She was forced to seek liberals' help in response to the Carlist uprising.

7 Pierre Lévêque, *Histoire des forces politiques en France, 1789–1880*, Volume 1 (Paris, 1992), 168; Gengembre, *La Contre-révolution*, 157.

8 Gengembre, *La Contre-révolution*, 149 and 157.

9 *Le Légitimiste*, 5 July 1835.

10 Lawrence, *Spain's First Carlist War*, 64.

11 *Le Légitimiste*, 5 July 1834.

12 Lévêque, *Histoire des forces politiques en France*, 166; Tort, *La Droite française*, 284.

13 *Le Légitimiste*, 12 July 1835.

14 *L'Europe*, 10 May 1837: 'conquête n'a duré qu'un instant'; 'les peuples de la Biscaye, que l'antiquité appelait les belliqueux Cantabres, croyant que Napoléon passerait par leur pays, érigèrent un arc de triomphe sur lequel ils inscrivirent ces mots: *Les Cantabres jamais vaincus*. Napoléon en fut instruit et dirigea sa route d'un autre côté.'

15 Vocaltha, *Zumalacarreguy et l'Espagne, ou Précis des évènemens militaires qui se sont passés dans les provinces basques depuis 1831* (Nancy, 1835), 5: 'cris de gloire et de liberté'.

16 Tort, *La Droite française*, 284; Lévêque, *Histoire des forces politiques en France*, 162 and 169.
17 Vocaltha, *Zumalacarreguy et l'Espagne*, 13: 'jurait de mourir pour Dieu, la liberté et la religion: *Fueros y la religion*'.
18 Lévêque, *Histoire des forces politiques en France*, 162; Gildea, *The Past in French History*, 227.
19 Laëtitia Blanchard, 'Violence politique et légitimisme pendant la première guerre carliste: une occasion manquée', *Amnis*, 17 (2018).
20 Michel Winock, 'L'Héritage contre-révolutionnaire', in Michel Winock (ed.), *Histoire de l'extrême droite en France* (Paris, 1993), 21.
21 Vocaltha, *Zumalacarreguy et l'Espagne*, 15: 'La réunion de ces quatre provinces, forme la grande Vendée espagnole, contre laquelle viendront se briser les efforts de toutes les autres provinces.'
22 *La Mode*, 5 July 1835 and *La Gazette de France*, 15 September 1835: '"Aux armes! – Car il faut ce soir sous nos talons / Écraser l'hydre régicide! / Il faut la paix au monde! il faut que Dieu décide / Entre le brave et les félons!" – / Il dit, et le Seigneur entendit sa parole. / Un tocsin unanime ébranla les clochers, / Et du fond des ravins, des bois et des rochers / Sortit en bouillonnant la Vendée espagnole!'
23 Lawrence, *Spain's First Carlist War*, 69.
24 Ibid., 52 and 65.
25 Vocaltha, *Zumalacarreguy et l'Espagne*, 59–60: 'Il est beau d'allier ainsi les pensées de force et de religion dans un même sentiment d'indépendance; il est beau d'être à la fois chrétien et soldat, il est beau de devenir le Machabée de tout un peuple que vous faites libre par la victoire et la souveraine raison; il est beau de se nommer Zumalacarreguy!!!' On the comparison between Zumalacárregui and the leader of the Maccabean revolt, see also *La Mode*, 5 April 1835.
26 *La Mode*, 5 April 1835: 'ce héros espagnol, qui a mérité le nom de Cid de la Navarre, ... a déjà rendu plus de services à son roi, que le vaillant de Burgos n'en rendit à Alphonse VI'.
27 *La Mode*, 5 April 1835: 'Dites-vous tous que Zumalacarreguy, tombé sous les murs de Bilbao, ne doit recevoir les honneurs funèbres que dans la cathédrale de Madrid, et que la statue du Cid de la Castille attend à l'Escorial la statue du Cid de la Navarre.'
28 Lawrence, *Spain's First Carlist War*, 13.
29 Ibid., 63.
30 *La Gazette de France*, 7 March 1836: 'La veritable liberté est en Navarre auprès de Charles V et de ces juntes véritablement populaires et nationales qui défendent les droits et les lois sacrées du pays; à Madrid, il n'y a qu'arbitraire, injustice, confiscation, partout ailleurs, violence, massacres, émeute, insurrection.'
31 Gildea, *The Past in French History*, 166.

32 Gengembre, *La Contre-révolution*, 149; Charbonnel, *Les Légitimistes*, 99–101.
33 *Le Légitimiste*, 12 July 1835: 'les garanties du dernier citoyen ... elles sont des droits tout aussi sacrés quant à leur principe.'
34 *Le Rénovateur*, 20 September 1834: 'Ce ne sont pas les royalistes qui ont renversé les états de la Provence, du Languedoc, du Dauphiné, de la Bourgogne, de la Bretagne, de l'Artois et du Béarn; c'est bien la révolution. Ni nos pères, ni nous, nous n'avons jamais abandonné la cause des franchises provinciales. Nos pères protestaient contre les décrets de l'assemblée constituante, qui détruisaient l'organisation intérieure du royaume; nous réclamons tous les jours encore la décentralisation. Il ne faut donc pas s'étonner de nos sympathies pour les quatre provinces insurgées, puisqu'elles ont inscrit sur leurs bannières: LÉGITIMITÉ ET LIBERTÉ.'
35 Lévêque, *Histoire des forces politiques en France*, 166.
36 *La Quotidienne*, 5 August 1834: 'le pays Basque et la Navarre combattent pour la légitimité et la civilisation contre l'usurpation et la barbarie révolutionnaire; les intérêts matériels de ces provinces les occupent secondairement.'
37 *La Quotidienne*, 13 September 1835: 'Tandis que l'usurpation avoue qu'elle ne peut se soutenir que par la servitude, la légitimité signale son avènement en reconnaissant solennellement les libertés espagnoles. Charles V jure le maintien des *fueros*, et ce serment il le tiendra, car les libertés d'un pays sont aussi des légitimités.'
38 Lévêque, *Histoire des forces politiques en France*, 168.
39 *La Gazette du Languedoc*, 10 December 1835: 'Le peuple qui habite ces contrées a les plus grands rapports d'habitudes et sans doute d'origine avec celui qui, sur les revers septentrionaux des Pyrénées, possède en France une partie des arrondissemens de Bayonne et de Mauléon. En général, on les nomme *Basques*, en France et en Espagne, et de là vient le nom des Provinces *Vascongades*; mais eux, tant en deca qu'au-delà des Pyrénées, prennent le nom national d'*Escualdunac*, et leur langue, si remarquable par ses formes, est nommée par eux la langue *Escuara*. En parcourant les Provinces Vascongades, l'habitant de Mauléon ou de Bayonne retrouve des frères, et les dialectes du langage qu'il a appris à bégayer au berceau.'
40 *La Gazette du Languedoc*, 10 December 1835.
41 On the notion of an *Internationale Blanche*, see Luis, 'France and Spain', 269–77.
42 Robert de Custine, *Les Bourbons de Goritz et les Bourbons d'Espagne* (Paris, 1839), 184: 'Il est bien heureux ... de retrouver au milieu de cette France, si égoïste et si corrompue, un coin de terre où se sont perpétuées la foi, les mœurs si simples et la rigide probité de nos pères.'

43 Aurélien Lignereux, *La France rébellionnaire. Les résistances à la gendarmerie (1800–1859)* (Rennes, 2008), 106.
44 David Todd, *L'Identité économique de la France. Libre-échange et protectionnisme, 1814–1851* (Paris, 2008), 163.
45 A.D., E dépôt/Came/2D5, The crown prosecutor of the *arrondissement* of Bayonne to the mayor of Came, 12 August 1834: 'alimenter l'insurrection contre le gouvernement d'Isabelle II, reconnu et en quelque sorte garanti par la France'.
46 Chris Jones, 'Middle Ages', in Christopher John Murray (ed.), *Encyclopedia of the Romantic Era, 1760–1850*, Volume 2 (New York and London, 2004), 743–4.
47 Custine, *Les Bourbons de Goritz*, 184–5: 'Vous pouvez entrer dans toutes les cabanes avec la certitude d'y trouver un asile inviolable contre la poursuite des agents du gouvernement. Tous les hommes que vous rencontrerez vous serviront de guides; vous pourrez leur confier votre personne et votre bourse sans crainte; ils exposeront leur vie pour défendre l'une et l'autre, surtout si vous leur dites que vous allez pour servir la cause de Charles V, à laquelle ils sont tous dévoués.'
48 Marie-France Chauvirey, *La Vie quotidienne au Pays basque sous le Second Empire* (Paris, 1975), 154–6; Théophile Gautier, *Voyage en Espagne* (Paris, 1859), 16.
49 Laëtitia Blanchard Rubio, 'Impressions de guerre: images et imaginaires de la première guerre carliste (1833–1840)', *Cahiers de la Méditerranée*, 83 (2011), 147–62.
50 Ibid., 147–62.
51 *La Sentinelle des Pyrénées*, 23 October 1838: 'sur le dos d'un contrebandier célèbre'.
52 Blanchard Rubio, 'Impressions de guerre'; Alain Pauquet, '*Le Phare de Bayonne* et *La Sentinelle des Pyrénées*: regards croisés de deux journaux français sur l'actualité espagnole de 1838', *Cahiers de civilisation espagnole contemporaine*, 29 (2022).
53 J.-B. Dasconaguerre, *Les Échos du Pas de Roland* (Paris, 1867), 51: 'J'en réponds, Madame, sur ma tête. Ganich est un Basque brave et loyal … On trouve encore ici la foi et la probité de nos pères; la moindre chaumière est un asile inviolable pour l'étranger. Confiez votre personne et votre cassette à un Basque, et il exposera volontiers sa vie pour sauver l'une et l'autre.'
54 Jacques Godechot, *La Contre-révolution: doctrine et action, 1789–1804* (Paris, 1961), 7: 'la doctrine des droits historiques'.
55 Chaho, *Voyage en Navarre*, iii: 'l'instrument de leur politique'.
56 Augustin Chaho, *Paroles d'un Bizkaïen aux libéraux de la reine Christine* (Paris, 1834), 17: 'Sachez, libéraux-sophistes de Madrid, que les Basques

repousseront toujours, avec dédain votre libéralisme bâtard, avec horreur votre ignoble joug.'

57 Chaho, *Voyage en Navarre*, iii: 'sans être infidèle à mes principes démocratiques'.

58 Ibid., 371: 'voudraient anéantir les titres glorieux de notre indépendance et de notre nationalité, excités par des vues despotiques et par la jalousie invétérée qu'ils nourrissent contre les Basques'.

59 Ibid., 91: 'pour défendre ... leur noble indépendance et l'individualité de notre race primitive et solaire, sous le commandement d'un chef librement élu, Zumala-Carreguy, et sous le drapeau nominal d'un Seigneur et Roi, D. Carlos'.

60 Chaho, *Paroles d'un Bizkaïen*, 9–11; Augustin Chaho, *Histoire primitive des Euskariens-Basques* (Madrid and Bayonne, 1847), l: 'l'esclavage à la liberté primitive'.

61 Ibid., 17–18: 'Les Basques sont tous égaux, tous libres, de droit et de fait ... Vous voulez franciser la Castille; les Espagnols nos voisins peuvent gagner à ce changement; nous Basques, nous ne pouvons qu'y perdre. Vos institutions progressives seraient pour nous rétrogrades. Les Basques sont un peuple-modèle; ils ne veulent imiter que la République de leurs aïeux.'

62 Chaho, *Voyage en Navarre*, 393.

63 Xabier Zabaltza, *Augustin Chaho, precursor incomprendido-un précurseur incompris, 1811–1858* (Vitoria-Gasteiz, 2011), 23–5.

64 Chaho, *Paroles d'un Bizkaïen*, ii.

65 Zabaltza, *Augustin Chaho*, 26.

66 Juaristi, *El linaje de Aitor*, 81.

67 Chaho, *Histoire primitive*, 242.

68 Chaho, *Voyage en Navarre*, 443 and 444: 'Notre race, trop longtemps ensevelie dans un sommeil léthargique, s'est réveillée à mon appel ... Notre sang, répandu dans les combats, fera naître dans les montagnes une génération de héros; témoins des larmes de la patrie et de nos blessures, nos enfants, bercés avec des chants guerriers, nourriront dans leurs cœurs la haine inextinguible de l'oppression; ils se presseront en frères autour du chêne de la liberté, ils arboreront le drapeau de la délivrance.'

69 Ibid., 80: 'si le gouvernement français, en intervenant contre Zumala-Carreguy, déclarait une guerre d'extermination à l'indépendance de notre race, j'ai lieu de croire qu'au lieu de marcher contre leurs frères espagnols, les Basques de France ne reculeraient point devant une résolution hardie, dictée par les intérêts de leur gloire et de leur liberté.'

70 Ibid., 213: '"Les Pyrénées commencent à l'Ebre et se terminent à l'Adour," disaient aux Romains les anciens Basques. ... les Euskariens

croyaient en faire partie intégrante; ils ne concevaient point que, sans égard pour l'identité parfaite d'origine, de langage de mœurs et de lois, la circonstance d'habiter le nord ou le midi d'une montagne fût suffisante pour scinder politiquement des peuplades qui se touchent et se confondent à l'intersection des vallées. Fondés sur ce principe et sur le droit historique, peut-être, quelque jour, les Basques tenteront de recouvrer l'unité nationale dont ils jouissaient autrefois.'

71 Juaristi, *El linaje de Aitor*, 76–106.
72 Eugène Goyheneche, 'Un Ancêtre du nationalisme basque. Augustin Chaho et la guerre carliste', *Euskal Herria (1789–1850). Actes du colloque international d'Études Basques* (Bayonne, 1978), 231; Zabaltza, *Augustin Chaho*, 20.
73 Augustin Chaho, *De l'agonie du parti révolutionnaire en France. Lettre à Monsieur Jacques Laffitte* (Paris, 1838), 42.
74 Juaristi, *El linaje de Aitor*, 40.

4

Euskara or the spirit of the Basque nation

In the nineteenth century, philology perpetuated the myth of the ancient and divine origin of the Basques. The Basques possessed two interrelated myths of ethnic descent: the myth of Basque Iberianism, the theory according to which the Basques were the first and only population of Spain, and the myth of primitive monotheism, according to which they had never been polytheist and were the first monotheistic people in the history of the world. These two myths, like most European theories of ethnogenesis, were founded upon two traditions, one classical and one biblical. The two primary old authorities on which such mythology was based were Strabo's *Geography* and Pliny's *Natural History*. Although neither of the two Roman authors had affirmed that Euskara was the language of the entire Iberian Peninsula, disputed interpretations attributed such meaning to their writings. Strabo, in particular, had described the Celtiberians' night dances in honour of a local divinity, which suggested that pre-Christian Basques worshipped one god, which in turn proved their primitive monotheism. The biblical tradition, as in much of Europe at the time, relied on the Genesis. It was a common Christian belief that ethnic groups, with their respective languages, derived from the three sons of Noah – Shem, Ham and Japheth – who had spread across the earth after the Flood (Genesis 10:1–32) and the fall of the Tower of Babel (Genesis 11:1–9). The Basques believed that one of Japheth's sons, Tubal, was the ancestor of the Basques, who had travelled to Spain and gifted the ancient Basques with their language and their monotheistic religion. In the nineteenth century, philologists attempted to prove 'scientifically' the veracity of these myths of ethnic descent through the study of Euskara, which they believed revealed the superiority of the Basque race.

The use of language to prove theories of ethnogenesis was by no means a Basque-specific endeavour. Comparative philology became a fashionable discipline across Europe in the nineteenth century, as it claimed that languages possessed unique information about the history of races and, consequently, that different tongues reflected the innate character of a people.[1] In such stateless nations as Germany, philology enabled nationalists to advocate for national self-determination, as they associated the German language with cultural and ethnic traits that allegedly all German peoples shared.[2] The Basque case, though, was peculiar in two respects. On the one hand, the study of Euskara was as much a transnational and international effort as it was national and local. Since Basque scholars considered themselves to be both Basque and either French or Spanish, their texts often responded to specific French and Spanish political and cultural stimuli respectively, but they also cultivated a Basque identity that transcended the national boundaries of France and Spain. In the first half of the nineteenth century, the popularisation of the Basque language and the exhortation to protect it came from Basque and non-Basque scholars alike. While European philologists regarded Euskara primarily as an object of study, though, Basque scholars considered it a means to ensure the active preservation of Basque autonomy and tradition. As Chapters 5 and 6 will show, such endeavour acquired an increasingly militant character in the second half of the nineteenth century. On the other hand, the study of linguistics in the Basque country differed from its counterparts in central Europe, insofar as Basque scholars did not regard language as a tool for the creation of an independent nation-state. Instead, their goal was the preservation of a degree of autonomy vis-à-vis the increasingly centralising measures of the French and Spanish states.

As historians of the Spanish Basque country have recently argued, Basque philological works were not pre-nationalist texts. They were the foundation of a political and cultural regionalism that served as a reinforcement of the Basques' position within Spain.[3] The study of the Basque language, then, went hand in hand with the rise of the 'modern' state and its administrative centralisation, of the 'modern' nation and its urge for cultural uniformity, and with the consequent loss of autonomy of the Basque provinces. While in Spain such movement was centred around the protection of the *fueros*, though, in the French Basque country, where the *fors* were abolished in

1789, Basque linguists tried to reinvent the position of the French Basque country within the new ideas of France that the different French governments enforced upon their population in the nineteenth century. In this respect, Basque philology constructed a historical representation of the region's ancient past that was both quintessentially Basque and resonant with French national meaning.[4]

Euskara and the myth of Basque Iberianism

French Basque philologists were influenced by the Spanish Basque Iberian myth of ethnic descent, which, in the Spanish Basque country, aimed to validate 'scientifically' the existence of the *fueros* and defend them from state centralisation. While texts attempting to justify 'historically' the exceptionalism of the Basques had been circulating since Juan Martínez de Zaldibia's *Suma de las cosas cantábricas y guipuzcoanas* in 1564, from the eighteenth century, local men of letters, influenced by comparative philology's subdivision of peoples by language and its quest for the recovery of a prehistorical Indo-European original language,[5] employed Euskara in order to provide validity to the claims of the ancient and divine origin of the Basques vis-à-vis Spain. Both the myths of Basque Iberianism and of primitive monotheism found authentication in the assertion that Euskara was a primitive and underivative language that bore no similarities with neighbouring idioms and had remained largely unaffected by the passing of time.

One of the most influential and cited texts in the nineteenth century was the Jesuit priest Manuel de Larramendi's *Diccionario trilingue del castellano, bascuence y latin*, published in 1745, in which he defined Euskara as a 'lengua matriz': 'a matrix language'. The syntax of Basque, especially in its compound and derivative forms, he explained in the preface of the dictionary, made Euskara the most perfect language; its grammatical rules made it the most harmonious language; and the copiousness of its vocabulary made it the richest and most abundant language.[6] In this regard, Larramendi predated early Romantics' historicisation of languages, according to whom beauty and perfection lay only in ancient idioms.[7]

The definition of Basque as a 'matrix language' had three important and influential consequences. First, it supported the biblical tradition that such a perfect language as Euskara possessed divine origins and had reached Europe after the dispersion of languages that followed the fall of the Tower of Babel. 'It is evident that no matrix Language was born in Spain ... This invention is impossible because only God is the Author of matrix Languages,' Larramendi wrote, adding: 'This is confirmed by the most singular advantages of Basque and the perfection of its structure ... certainly, no man can be the Author of such admirable harmony.'[8] The philological study of Basque grammar, then, proved that Euskara was a divine language.

Second, the alleged perfection of the Basque tongue supported the Basque Iberian claim that Euskara was the original language of Spain and, consequently, that the ancestors of the Basques were the first population of the Iberian Peninsula. Larramendi's argument that Euskara was the original idiom of Spain because it could not be a derivative language was expanded in 1803 by the Spanish clergyman Pablo Pedro de Astarloa in another influential text, *Apología de la lengua bascongada*. The book was a treatise against Don Joaquín de Tragia's counterclaim to the antiquity of Euskara in the *Diccionario geográfico-histórico de España*, published the year before. In his book, Astarloa argued that languages could be created only in three different ways: by imitation, by imitation and invention, or by pure invention. Euskara, however, he argued, did not belong to any of these categories. It could not have been created by imitation or by imitation and invention, as it did not resemble any other known languages, including neighbouring ones, and was completely different from the tongues of the populations who had conquered Spain. Additionally, it could not have been the result of pure invention because, as Larramendi had pointed out, the Basques did not possess the means of inventing a language second to no other for 'culture, richness, energy and suavity'. Thus, Astarloa concluded, the origin of Euskara had to be antecedent to the Basques' arrival in Spain and, consequently, the ancestors of the Basques were the first population of Spain.[9] 'We are all the sons of the ancient Basques and the glorious descendants of the first inhabitants of Spain,' he wrote.[10] Three years later, the Basque Carlist statesman Juan Bautista de Erro y Azpiroz claimed, in another renowned yet much criticised volume, *Alfabeto de la lengua primitiva de España*, that he had studied the previously unknown characters engraved on ancient vases, stones and medals across the whole of the Iberian

Peninsula and could prove that the language of the engravings was Euskara. This, he argued, served as the ultimate proof that Euskara was the original language of Spain. Through a study of the Basque alphabet, its syllables and word endings, he alleged that the engravings were not of Greek and Phoenician origin, as had been believed, but that, on the contrary, it was the Basques who had taught to the Phoenicians, the Greeks and even the Romans their alphabet, the use of coinage and other useful inventions.[11] According to Erro y Azpiroz's interpretation of Basque Iberianism, Euskara was the first language not only of Spain but of the whole ancient Mediterranean world.

The most famous proponent of this thesis was the Prussian linguist Wilhelm von Humboldt, who was friends with Erro y Azpiroz and Astarloa and visited the Basque country at the turn of the nineteenth century to study its language. The comparative study of Iberian place nomenclature and of the Basque language, he wrote at the conclusion of his research, demonstrated that Euskara was the one and only language of the first Iberians. 'Two points seem to be perfectly established,' he wrote in *Prüfung der Untersuchungen über die Urbewohner Hispaniens vermittelst der vaskischen Sprache*, published in 1821. 'The ancient Iberians are the ancestors of the contemporary Basques; the Iberians were spread across the whole Peninsula, they spoke one and the same language and formed multiple peoples with different dialects. The Basque language, then, was that of the primitive inhabitants of Spain.'[12] Humboldt, like many Romantic scholars at the time, regarded language as the highest expression of the character of a people and considered the purity of Euskara as revealing of the superior essence of the Basque people.[13] His contribution to the study of Basque ethnography and philology cannot be understated, as he was one the first to provide Basque Iberianism with a 'scientific' formulation and, crucially, he was also the first to promote it in European academic circles. The popularity of the Basque country among European scholars was due to a large extent to Humboldt and his writings about Euskara and what he called the Basque nation.

The third important consequence of Basque being a 'matrix language' was that it validated the claim of the primitive monotheism of the Basques. That the Basques were never pagan, philologists believed, was a direct consequence of the fact that Tubal transmitted both Euskara and true religion to their ancestors. In this respect, Basque philologists claimed that Euskara was what the Germans called the *Ursprache*, the lost primordial Indo-European language that was supposed to be the idiom that mankind spoke in the Tower of Babel and hence the language of God. The claim of the divine origin of Euskara, as well as the ensuing myths that the Basques were the first population of Spain and the bearers of the first monotheistic religion, were adopted by French Basque philologists, who adapted them to the political and cultural circumstances of France and Europe, furthering both the national ties between France and its Basque *pays* and the transnational ones between the seven Basque provinces.

Dominique-Joseph Garat and the 'Nouvelle Phénicie' project

The most prominent thinker to adopt Larramendi's definition of Euskara as a 'matrix language' in the French Basque country was Dominique-Joseph Garat, who was one of Labourd's representatives at the Estates-General in 1789. In a report on the Basques to Napoleon entitled *Recherches sur le people primitif de l'Espagne*, completed in 1811, Garat argued that the only way for contemporary Basques to fulfil their military duty towards the First Empire was to recover the warriorlike prowess of their ancestors, which was possible only if they spoke Euskara. A lawyer, man of letters and *idéologue*, Garat spent the 1770s and 1780s in Paris, where he engaged with such philosophers as Diderot, Helvétius, d'Alembert and Condorcet, and wrote for *Mercure de France* and the *Encyclopédie méthodique*. During the French Revolution, he was both minister of the interior and minister of justice, and after Thermidor he was appointed professor of ideology and philosophy at the École Normale, as well as being member of the moral sciences of the Institut. In 1799, he welcomed Napoleon's coup, which won him a seat in the Senate and later the title of Count of the Empire and membership of the Académie française. Because of his official role in the First Empire, he was disgraced after its fall and spent the last twenty years of his life in the Basque country, where he died in 1833.[14]

In *Recherches,* Garat adopted the myth of Basque Iberianism to describe the Basques as the descendants of the Cantabrians, the first population of Spain, who had preserved their ancient character until the present day thanks to the use of Euskara. The glorious character of the Cantabrians was dormant, he acknowledged to Napoleon, but the contemporary Basque population could easily recover it if the seven Basque provinces were united together under the French Empire, if the Basques were employed in the imperial navy, rather than in the *armée de terre*, and, crucially, if they were allowed to speak their native language.[15] If the Basques were put in the same conditions as their ancestors, Garat elaborated, they would recover the same fierce attitude and enthusiasm of the Cantabrians. 'If you leave the Spanish and French Basques separated, as they currently are, they will always be but Basques,' he wrote. '[I]f you unite them, suddenly all together they will become the Cantabrians, they will regain their name, their attitude and they will cultivate the immense glorious heritage attached to this name with the enthusiasm that is so natural to them.'[16] Since Garat was writing in the midst of the Napoleonic Wars, the most pressing issue was to allow the Basques to enrol in the navy. The Cantabrians, he explained, used to distinguish themselves as excellent seamen, and to recover such heritage would mean putting the Basques' ability at sea at the service of the Empire. Here Garat was striking a sensitive chord, as Napoleon was aware of the inferiority of France's fleet compared to the British navy. While the Basques formed pretty poor soldiers, prone to desertion and to 'mal du pays', Garat opined, in a fully Basque ship they would speak Euskara and would not be homesick. The position of the Basques within the Empire, then, he concluded, was to be seafarers. 'Serving in the fleet', he explained, 'they can resuscitate their ancient glory and contribute to the prosperity of Napoleon's Empire.'[17] Garat could argue that the ancestors of the Basques, the Cantabrians, were good seafarers because he identified them, albeit with no historical evidence, with the Phoenicians.[18] A return to greatness, for him, corresponded to a union of the seven Basque provinces to form a new Phoenician region: the 'Nouvelle Phénicie'.[19]

Key to the successful implementation of the 'Nouvelle Phénicie' project was the preservation of the Basque language. The plan for the future of the Basque provinces, Garat argued, was founded upon the ancient character of the Basques, which had been preserved throughout the centuries because of the use of Euskara. '[I]t is this barrier of languages and not that of mountains, rivers and seas,' he alleged, 'that prevents people from merging, from mixing with each other and from disappearing, confusing the originality and original purity of their primitive character.'[20] Influenced by Larramendi's *Diccionario* and Astarloa's *Apología*, Garat argued that Euskara needed to be preserved because it was a primitive language, one of the oldest languages on earth and as old as the Basques' first ancestors, the Cantabrians or Phoenicians. This made of Basque a language of nature, a tongue that had 'remained as it was born'.[21] Garat distinguished between *patois* and pure languages, a distinction, he argued – likely remembering the French Revolution's repressive legislation against all minority idioms in France – that was constantly confused in modern Europe. While a *patois* derived from the mixing of languages and resulted from the corruption and decadence of a tongue, he explained, a pure language was the opposite: it was an idiom uncorrupted by external influences, which still preserved its original purity and perfection. 'The language of a Simple people who did not merge with any other people, who did not know greatness nor decadence, neither the refined delicacy nor the corruption of taste and of the arts, even after the long centuries,' he wrote, 'is like a nascent language.'[22] Euskara was a pure language, containing in itself the history and morality of the Basque people.

Garat, like fellow *idéologues*, believed that all intellectual faculties derived from man's organisation of the body. He consequently thought, as did Cabanis, that language also preceded distinct sensations and the first ideas and progressed slowly from primitive signs to abstract, philosophical thinking.[23] Populations who, like the Basques, spoke a very ancient language were the ones closest to pure ideas.[24] Comparing French and Euskara, Garat argued that Basque was a more 'living language' than French because it was a self-explanatory idiom: a language whose words defined themselves and could therefore be understood without the use of a dictionary. 'It is not enough for a language to be spoken by a people in order to be alive,' he explained. '[T]here has to be a lively and dazzling light that spreads from its most elementary words to its most compound words.'[25] Drawing on Larramendi's *Diccionario*, he argued that a language, to be considered pure, had to have clear connections between the original word and its derivative words. Additionally, it had to build on words and ideas and to have the ability to grow and perfect by itself.

Thus, in order to recover the ancient greatness of the Basques, Garat told Napoleon, Euskara needed to be protected and promoted. '[I]t is then essential that [the Basques] watch over the sacred fire of this language that warms them up and enlightens them,' he wrote. 'All of their thoughts must be expressed in and limited to this language if they want to play a great role on earth again.'[26] As a result, Garat argued, there were two main reasons why it was crucial that pupils spoke Euskara in Basque schools. First, the perpetuation of Euskara was essential for the preservation of the Basque character. '[I]f the character of these people has so jealously protected the repository of their language,' he wrote, 'their language, in turn, will preserve their character, on which more than one hope resides.'[27] Second, given that Euskara had nothing in common with French or Spanish, pupils wasted a lot of time in school learning those languages. By translating key notions into Basque instead, Garat believed, students would learn even the most difficult subjects easily, thanks to the nature of their mother tongue, 'so analogical, so clear, so transparent'.[28]

Garat's historical account of the Basques responded to two specificities of the Napoleonic Empire. One was the regime's pervasive policy of myth-making. Napoleon was an ambitious man who aimed not only at military victories but at eternal glory. During his years as general, consul and then emperor, he enshrined his military successes in an aura of legend by means of popular imagery and the press, and sought to restore an empire in the guise of such masters of the world as Alexander the Great, Julius Caesar, Augustus and Charlemagne. He was particularly charmed by Charlemagne as the restorer of the Roman Empire, a name that implied the idea of the universal and the eternal; the First Empire's propaganda machine frequently compared Napoleon, his empire and policies to Charlemagne's.[29] Garat's retelling of the myth of Basque Iberianism, then, was not only part of the European philological recovery of myths of ethnic descent, but also part of the myth-making agenda of the First Empire.

Second, Garat's emphasis on the Basque language was suggestive of his attempt, alongside other minorities within France, to take advantage of the greater pragmatism of the Napoleonic homogenising agenda, compared to the radical Revolution, by emphasising the value of a people's specificities for the Empire. Indeed, although

Michael Broers has suggested that mainland France was more prone to cultural amalgamation than the 'outer Empire',[30] the treatment that the Basques received, as Chapter 2 showed, revealed that there was linguistic pragmatism within old France too.[31] Garat's report, then, came at a time when notions of amalgamation allowed for a wider degree of diversity than during the radical phase of the Revolution, as well as when – again unlike the First Republic – the Empire took little interest in primary schooling. One similar example was that of the Grand Sanhedrin, an assembly of Jewish notables that Napoleon instituted in 1806 aiming to assimilate the Jews. The notables of the Sanhedrin, in similar fashion to Garat, reimagined Franco-Jewish relations according to the utility the Jews possessed for the Napoleonic Empire.[32] At the same time, Garat's search for a role for the Basques within the First Empire likely derived from his concerns about Napoleon's policy of cultural assimilation. During a visit to the Batavian Republic, soon to become annexed to France under the name of Holland, he was struck by the fact that its prosperity was jeopardised by France's occupation, which did not allow the maritime nation to thrive through its commerce.[33] In this respect, Garat's *Recherches* was arguably an implicit criticism of Napoleon's policies of amalgamation and homogenisation in other parts of France and Europe, and an attempt to spare the Basques the same fate.

It is unclear how serious Garat was about the 'Nouvelle Phénicie' project, or whether Napoleon read his report at all. He was committed, nevertheless, to its principles. In a letter to the emperor in which he informed him of the delivery of his report to the duc de Bassano, Garat reiterated the importance of the Basques for the subjugation of Spain and the humiliation of Britain, with which France was at war at the time. Additionally, he stressed again the importance of Euskara. Although his work was nothing more than a historical essay, he added, by translating imperial orders into Basque, Napoleon could ensure the loyalty of the Basques, which would perpetuate his success.[34]

Garat's theory of the Phoenician origin of Euskara never met the favour of comparative philology, but it was popularised across France at the beginning of the Restoration by the French writer Étienne de Jouy, who travelled across France to produce a popular ethnographic study of its peoples, published as *L'Hermite en province*. In the

Basque country, he was hosted by Garat, whom he referred to as 'mon docte compagnon'. Garat's influence was evident in Jouy's description of the Basque language. Euskara, he reported, was of Phoenician origin; French and Spanish Basques were the descendants of the Phoenicians and formed 'one and only race of men'; and Euskara was likely the original language of the whole Iberian Peninsula.[35] The philological and ethnographic study of the different peoples of France was a popular endeavour during the Restoration, as the Bourbons tried to recover the values of *ancien-régime* France, starting with those rural areas of France that they perceived to be less affected by the Revolution.

The *abbé* Bidassouet and the Basque origin of France

It was during the Restoration that the *abbé* Pierre d'Iharce de Bidassouet published his renowned reinterpretation of the myth of Basque Iberianism, which affirmed the centrality of the Basques to the ancient history of France and Europe. A staunch legitimist supporter, Bidassouet's work mirrored the Bourbons' attempt to recover the union of the throne and the altar, by producing a historical account of the Basques that emphasised their superior religiosity and loyalty to the French crown.[36] Born in Hasparren in 1765, Bidassouet was ordained as a priest in 1792. A member of the refractory clergy after the Revolution's promulgation of the Civil Constitution of the Clergy, he fled to Spain during the Terror and lived in Navarra and in Galicia before returning to the French Basque country. Back in France, he dedicated his time to the publication of works on the Basque language and on Basque history, which included claims that Euskara derived from Sanskrit and a mathematical theorem that allegedly proved that Basque was the language spoken by Adam and Eve in the Garden of Eden.[37] His most famous book, the *Histoire des cantabres*, was published in 1825 and became the most influential work of Basque linguistics in the French Basque country. Bidassouet hoped that the book, which was accompanied by his own Basque grammar and dictionary, would bridge the gap between the Basque country and France.

Like many philologists of the time, Bidassouet idealised the Basque past as a model of cultural renaissance within contemporary France.

He dedicated the *Histoire des cantabres* to King Charles X and, similarly to Garat, he argued that a study of the Basque language was crucial to understand the role that the Basques could play in nineteenth-century Bourbon France. The book presented two main goals. First, Bidassouet hoped that philology would not merely recover the history of the Basques but also reveal those Basque identarian traits that could be of service to the current monarch. 'I thought that the study of languages was not only important to study the monuments of antiquity,' he wrote, 'but also to compare the mores of ancient times that history passes on to us with those of the century in which we live, which can but improve in the reign of a Prince like you, SIRE.'[38] Second, by adding a Basque grammar and dictionary to his book, he wished to favour the integration of the Basque country into France, which would in turn promote commerce, industry, agriculture, the transport network and closer relations between the French and the Basques. As a result, he argued, the glory of the ancient Cantabrians would merge with the glory of contemporary France. '[T]he ashes of the Cantabrians, so proud of having defeated, one after the other, the Phoenicians, the Carthaginians, the Romans, the Goths, the Visigoths, the Ostrogoths, even the Franks and finally the Saracens,' he wrote, 'will seem to come to life again, in order to merge their ancient glory with that of the beautiful and thriving France, glorious and proud to be governed by Charles X.'[39] Thus, Bidassouet anticipated that his study of Euskara would strengthen the bond between the Basques and the Bourbon dynasty that governed and represented France.

Influenced by the works of comparative philology that were fashionable at the time, Bidassouet set out to determine the superiority of the Basque race through a study of its language. Languages, he argued mirroring Larramendi and Astarloa, were either primitive or imitated. Since Euskara was not the result of imitation, it was necessarily a *langue mère*. Primitive languages, he added, were antediluvian, included in their syntax the different ages of mankind and possessed a meaningful alphabet that reflected the world at its primordial stage. The language that incorporated all these characteristics, he concluded, was Euskara, which made it likely that Basque was the language with which Adam communicated with God in the Garden of Eden.[40] The antiquity of Basque origin and the purity of Euskara, he claimed, proved both the superiority and ambidexterity of the Basques, 'that is, the *righteousness*, the *finesse*, the *deep genius* of the *Escualdunac* to establish some elementary and fundamental laws that they were able to support with loyalty and to defend with bravery'.[41] Such characteristics, he added in a unique twist to the myth of Basque Iberianism, did not belong to the Basques alone but were shared by the French, because the Cantabrians were the common ancestors of both the Basques and the French. He relied on the traditional biblical version of the origin of the Basques, according to which the ancestors of the Basques were the descendants of Japheth, who moved westwards from Asia, arriving first in Turkey and then colonising the rest of Europe. While the traditional Basque Iberian myth argued that the ancestors of the Basques had settled directly in Spain after the fall of the Tower of Babel, however, Bidassouet claimed that the Basques were not only the first population of the Iberian Peninsula but of the entire European continent. Thanks to a study of toponymy inspired by Humboldt and Erro y Azpiroz, he concluded that 'the descendants of Japheth must necessarily be the Basques, the Escualdunac, because, as we have said, the provinces, the mountains, the rivers, the ponds of the counties where these colonies have passed through and where they sojourned, have meaningful topographic Basque names'.[42] As a result, Euskara, the language of the first inhabitants of Europe, was also necessarily the first language of the entire European continent.

Such a claim was significant, as it allowed Bidassouet to shift the centrality of Basque history from Spain to France. Through the study of toponymy, he alleged that the Cantabrians could be found in northern, western and central Europe.[43] He compared the claims of ancient French authors, who had argued that the 'Zaldibériens ou Cantabres' had arrived in Spain through the Rhine, the Pyrenees and the Alps, to those of Spanish authors, who had argued that a colony of Cantabrians had arrived directly in Spain from Armenia without stopping or conquering any piece of land in between, and he concluded that the former interpretation was more probable. The word 'Zaldibériens' itself, he claimed, derived from the Basque word 'Zelaïetes', which meant inhabitants of the plains. This further proved that, before arriving in Spain, the Cantabrians had conquered the central European and French plains.[44] Since the Cantabrians had moved to Spain through northern and eastern Europe, Bidassouet argued, it was only natural that they had peopled Gaul before reaching

Spain. As a result, 'the Spanish Cantabrians descend from the French Cantabrians, despite prejudice to the contrary'.[45] Given that the Gallic colonisers of Spain were Basques, he added, Gaul must have necessarily been Basque, and given that Gaul was Basque, all of Europe must have been Basque, as in the first pre-Babelic epoch of mankind there was only one nation and one language (Genesis 11:1). Bidassouet's argument satisfied both the French and the Basques. On the one hand, it supplied the Basques with a central position in the history of Europe and with a key place in the cultural origin of France. On the other, it provided a Basque twist to the myth of *nos ancêtres les Gaulois* and made of France the dominant nation in Europe since the beginning of time and of the French the chosen people. In this sense, Bidassouet replaced Basque Iberianism with a form of 'Basque Gaulishism' or even 'Basque Europeanism'.

The historicisation of Euskara allowed Bidassouet to argue that the ancient culture of the Basques was not lost. It was to be found in Labourd, which he defined as the most culturally important of the seven Basque cantons. This was an additional departure from Spanish Basque literature, which considered Vizcaya, Guipúzcoa and Álava to be the traditional cradles of Basque tradition. 'It is there that primitive traits were better preserved,' Bidassouet wrote of Labourd. 'The Labourdins are the real types of ancient Cantabrians, of this ancient race of men whose bravery made the greatest heroes of Europe tremble.'[46] The affirmation was not only a display of local patriotism. Bidassouet historicised Euskara in order to match the conservative values of religion, morality and tradition that the Bourbons were trying to recover after the French Revolution. History, in this regard, was not only a means of recovering the past but an attempt to use the past to build a better future. To the life in cities, filled with 'darkness, perfidy and gossip', Bidassouet added, writing in the first person, he preferred an isolated life in Labourd, among 'brave and simple peasants' and 'the marvels of nature'. There, he explained, he could see 'an *anticipated apparition of future beatitude*'.[47] In this respect, Bidassouet shared conservative monarchists' antipathy towards the emerging industrial bourgeoisie who were replacing the landed aristocracy as the dominant social group, and defended the environment as a criticism of the urban middle classes and the misery to which they subjected the working classes.[48] Thanks to the preservation of their language and their primitive character, then, Bidassouet suggested, the French Basque country was a cradle of monarchical conservative values.

Bidassouet's work was extremely influential among scholars of Euskara, who considered his *Histoire des cantabres* as one of most significant studies of Basque philology. His claim that Euskara was the language of Adam, in particular, became especially popular. The Basque clergyman Jean-Pierre Darrigol, for example, who published his *Dissertation critique et apologétique sur la langue basque* two years after Bidassouet's *Histoire des cantabres*, produced a study of Euskara that claimed to prove the closeness between the Basque language and the original creation, and argued that all Basque words ending in 'a' had much in common with the language of Abraham.[49] Bidassouet, moreover, was also a crucial influence on his most famous student, Augustin Chaho.

Augustin Chaho and Euskara as the divine language

Chaho, whom we encountered in the previous chapter in the guise of a staunch supporter of the First Carlist War as a war of Basque liberation, similarly elevated Euskara in an effort to protect the Basque country from the alleged threat of liberalism. His interpretation of Euskara owed much to his teacher. Like Bidassouet, he claimed that Euskara was the divine language of the Garden of Eden and that Basque had much in common with Sanskrit. While Bidassouet employed the history of Euskara to help the Basques fit into the present history of Bourbon France, however, Chaho, writing during the liberal July Monarchy, hoped that the revival of Euskara would protect the Basques and favour autonomy over administrative centralisation.

Chaho was a complicated thinker. His writings were often utopian and difficult to interpret and his political allegiances seemed contradictory for his time, as he was an antiliberal and culturally conservative republican. His work on language, nevertheless, appeared to have two main purposes. On the one hand, his elevation of Euskara to the universal language of God awarded the Basque country a prominent place in the genesis of the world. Such position, he believed, protected Basque culture from administrative centralisation, which threatened it with disappearance. On the other hand, his work on

Euskara underlined his wish to see the seven Basque provinces one day united to form an autonomous, if not independent, Basque country. As Chapter 3 showed, the extent to which Chaho was serious about such a proposition remains unclear, as much of his work never acquired a practical dimension. His claims, though, mirrored contemporary concerns that centralisation was destroying local cultures, as well as his understanding of local languages as a shield that protected provincial cultures and traditions from disappearing. In this respect, Chaho's political thought predated the more militant role that regionalist movements came to play in the late nineteenth century.

Chaho defended the alleged antiquity of Euskara by attacking the French archaeologist Alexandre du Mège, who, in the second volume of his *Statistique générale des départements pyrénéens*, published in 1829, had criticised the claim that Basque was an ancient language, arguing instead that Euskara was a medieval language, whose vocabulary derived to a large extent from Hebrew, Greek and especially Latin.[50] By means of his own study of toponymy, Chaho rejected the thesis that Euskara derived from the languages of such pagan peoples as the Greeks, the Phoenicians or the Celts. Instead, he claimed that linguistic similarity proved that Euskara had much in common with Sanskrit, a classical language of South Asia.[51] Sanskrit was spoken in antiquity by Iranians and Indians who, according to Chaho, were as pure a people as the Basques, as they preceded the age of barbaric invasion and hence had never experienced polytheism. While Bidassouet had also found similarities between the two languages, Chaho pushed the argument further and argued that in antiquity Sanskrit was a form of Euskara and hence Iranians and Indians shared with the Basques the same ancestors. Basque civilisation, he argued, extended from the Iberian Peninsula to Hindustan, and as in Europe it had preceded Illyrian and Celtic occupation, in Hindustan it had preceded Scythian invasion.

After consulting ancient Greek texts, he reached two conclusions. First, Basques, Iranians and Indians were part of the same 'race patriarcale'. Second, Iranians and Indians 'had for sole representatives in the subsequent centuries the *Euskariens cantabres et vascons*, the ancient Basques'.[52] As a result, he argued, the origin of Euskara could be traced back 'to the most remote centuries of the era rightly called primitive and patriarchal, higher and further back than polytheism and mythological fairy tales'.[53] Although Chaho never mentioned the studies that in the early nineteenth century scholars were conducting on the newly named Indo-European languages, which compared Latin and ancient Greek to Sanskrit, it seems likely that he was aware of them and that, to an extent, he was responding to them. In particular, his emphasis on Basque and Sanskrit as languages of the south appeared to challenge the German dominance of the philological field, as Chaho considered the Peoples of the North inferior to the Peoples of the South.[54]

The Peoples or 'Patriarchs of the South', Chaho argued, were the only peoples who descended directly from God. Euskara was proof of it because the simplicity of its 'improvised Language' revealed the 'divine truth' in its original, authentic and 'virginal' state. This was the case both for the name with which the ancestors of the Basques were allegedly known and for the name with which they referred to God. On the one hand, Chaho explained that, in the first age, the Peoples of the South were called 'Children of the Sun and of the Lamb', which was the same word in both Basque and Sanskrit. This was the word 'chourien', which referred to both the sun as light in the moral sense of 'civilisation and truth' and to the lamb as the 'celestial lamb', which once a year triumphantly crossed the belt of the zodiac. 'The astronomical language of the *Euskariens* reflects poetically the simple and rural mores of this shepherd people,' he wrote.[55] On the other hand, Chaho argued that the name that the ancient Basques employed to refer to God, Iao or Jao-on-Goika, equally revealed the spirit of the earliest time, when the Euskariens, ecstatic in face of the divine light, cried out the name of the divinity, Iao, whose syllables 'ia' and 'ô' summarised 'all the power of the word, all the harmony of the verb'. The name, he added, was the result of the 'grace', 'innocence' and 'beauty' that the Euskariens embodied in the first days of the genesis in the Garden of Eden where God had placed them. It was a spontaneous act, which differed from the religion of the barbarians, with its 'painful reflections' and 'degrading spectacle of idolatry'. Thus, Euskara, according to Chaho, was the language of God and the Basques the real predestined people.[56] The revival of Euskara, he believed, would determine the arrival of a new Messiah in the Pyrenees and of a new golden age for the Basque people. Like many of his contemporaries, Chaho's writings were permeated with anti-Semitic undertones. By claiming that

Euskara was the language of the Garden of Eden and that the Basques descended directly from God, Chaho perpetuated the myth of the primitive monotheism of the Basques, which stripped Judaism of the title of most ancient monotheistic religion and the Jews of the title of chosen people.

While philologists tended to meet Chaho's personality with a degree of scepticism, his and Bidassouet's association of Euskara with such Asian languages as Sanskrit became popular. The trend was part of a Europe-wide linguistic interest in the relationship between European languages on the one hand, and Iranian and Indian on the other. The 'craze for India' took off in 1808 when Friedrich Schlegel claimed, in his *Über die Sprache und Weisheit der Indier*, to have identified the location of the Garden of Eden in Indian territory and declared that Sanskrit was the closest idiom to the lost *Ursprache*, the divine language of revelation.[57] The French chemist Alexandre Baudrimont, for example, similarly to Bidassouet and Chaho, argued in 1854 that the Basque language had much in common with those of western Asia and Europe, and was the world's most ancient idiom.[58] In 1864, moreover, the Dutch linguist Willem van Eys claimed that the problem with Larramendi's grammar was that it looked for similarities between Euskara, Latin and Spanish, when in fact Basque was part of the family of the Turanian languages, which, he alleged, encompassed much of Asia and northern Europe.[59] Additionally, as the next chapter will further show, Chaho was one of the first Basque scholars to adopt a Romantic understanding of language and folklore as essences of a people. As an early advocate of the use of language and folk literature as shields against the disappearance of local tradition, he was a precursor of such later nineteenth-century regionalist concerns about the weakening effect of centralisation on minority languages and cultures. In this respect, Chaho was not a pre-nationalist but a regionalist militant ante litteram.

Élisée Reclus and the disappearance of Euskara

By the mid-nineteenth century, such authors as Bidassouet and Chaho were renowned and widely studied by French linguists, and Garat even had one of his works published posthumously in 1869. These studies, however, were accompanied by an increasing amount of criticism. The philologist Francisque Michel, for example, in his much-cited anthropological work *Le Pays basque*, published in 1857, called Bidassouet's arguments and the alleged relationship between Euskara and the Semitic languages of Asia 'rêveries', adding that the claim of the Babelic origin of the Basque language was ridiculous.[60] One decade later, Jean-François Bladé, in his *Études sur l'origine des basques*, reproached all his predecessors for using Euskara to prove the myth of Basque Iberianism. The ancient texts, he argued, proved only that a variety of dialects were spoken in the Iberian Peninsula, one of which was the Vascons', but there was no historical proof of the existence of Euskara before the twelfth century. Over time, he added, Basque had undergone so many changes that it was impossible to compare the contemporary idiom with its ancient version. Finally, Euskara, as Darrigol had already noted, had no specific alphabet and the phonetic phenomena that his predecessors claimed to be so special were in fact similar to those of the neighbouring romance languages.[61] Such mounting criticism was revealing of two new understandings of history that came to dominate the scholarly and political debate in Europe in the second half of the nineteenth century. First, this period witnessed the professionalisation of the humanities. Although professional scholars also invented national histories and local philologists continued to be popular, the former placed their authority in the service of nation-states and criticised amateur *savants*' perpetuation of myths of national origin.[62] Second, western Europeans began to view the history of the west as a tale of genealogical success from 'primitivism' to 'modernity'. The elites believed that those 'traditional' societies that still existed within Europe, such as the Basques, lacked the ability to change and the drive towards progress and 'civilisation', and as such they were destined to disappear.[63] In this regard, despite the preservation of its ancient language and tradition, the Basque country was not a 'modern' nation, but a remnant of a pre-modern society that had no place in the western world.

The text that best embodied French scholars' uneasiness about the coexistence of myth and history, tradition and 'modernity' in the French Basque country was an essay entitled 'Les Basques. Un peuple qui s'en va' that the French geographer Élisée Reclus published in the *Revue des Deux Mondes* in 1869. The piece was in part a response to Humboldt's above-mentioned *Prüfung der Untersuchungen über die Urbewohner Hispaniens vermittelst der vaskischen Sprache*, which had been translated into French three years earlier. An opponent of imperialism and a defender of minorities and their cultures, Reclus exalted the Basque traditions of liberty, equality and independence from oppression, which he identified with the peasant rural world and which, together with Euskara, represented the essence of Basque identity. At the same time, he claimed that Basque culture's slow disappearance as a result of administrative centralisation was a deplorable yet necessary part of the Basques' integration into the process of universal progress.[64]

Similarly to Bidassouet, Reclus identified the Basques of Labourd as the true bearers of Basque tradition. While all 'populations euskariennes' had been able to preserve their 'national integrity' throughout the centuries, he argued, it was the Basques of the coast who still incarnated the values of 'the ancient Iberian race' and especially those of Labourd, who still preserved 'the politeness and simple dignity of their ancestors'.[65] Although he admitted that the loss of the *fors* in 1789 had led the Basques towards assimilation, in their much-idealised rural world they still seemed to lead a happier life than people living in urban and industrial France. He wrote: 'We find ourselves driven to wonder, by a natural inclination of the spirit, if these joyful populations do not represent the remains of a luckier humanity that were free from our miseries and sadness.'[66] The emphasis on France over Spain allowed him to exalt traditional French country life and to show that a traditional peasant society still lived on in France in the Basque country.

For Reclus, it was language that distinguished the Basques from their neighbours. While philologists before him had attempted to draw connections between Euskara and the ethnogenesis of the Basques, however, Reclus limited himself to drawing conclusions about the language itself. The time when linguistics corroborated the divine origin of the Basques, he argued, was over. He praised the work of Humboldt, who had popularised Euskara in Europe and had prompted other linguists from Germany, France and the Basque country to take the Basque language seriously as a 'langue par excellence', distinct from all other western European languages for the structure of the word, the mechanism of the sentences and the multiple verb conjugations. Additionally, he commended those 'literary patriots' who 'declared their language superior to all others'[67] and the language of the divine, first spoken by Adam and Eve in the Garden of Eden. Chaho, in this sense, Reclus believed, was 'the last and valiant champion of Euskarian glories'. Times had changed, though. 'Henceforth', he wrote, 'science will not discuss any more the question of whether Basque is a divine language, superior in dignity to those of the people of the earth born far from the Pyrenees.'[68] As non-Basque scholars began to apply a more rigorous methodology to the study of Euskara, they began to view the Basque language exclusively as a valuable object of research, rather than the mother tongue of a European people.

Reclus predicted that Euskara was about to disappear as a result of progress and 'modernisation'. On the one hand, he conceded, the fading of the Basque language was a source of sadness, as it put an end to the Basque race, 'one of the most noble' among human races.[69] On the other, however, it was the price to pay for the Basques to partake in 'modern' civilisation. Like many liberal thinkers at the time, he believed that the rural world was a cradle of ignorance and superstition that led to both economic and intellectual poverty. What still protected Euskara against the interferences of French and Spanish, Reclus argued, 'is the ignorance in which the people still languish'.[70] The Basque population did not read newspapers nor books, he explained, the majority of children did not attend primary schools and the *instituteurs* were forced to mix the official language with 'un dialecte eskuara [sic]' in order to be understood. As a result, Basque parents bore sons who were 'lazy or without intelligence' and who were incapable of engaging in successful farming activities. Poverty of the mind, he claimed, resulted in poverty of the land. The new generation of Basques was unwilling to invest time and effort into agriculture, Reclus added, and preferred to emigrate to South America, where they hoped to make their fortune faster and more easily.[71] Here Reclus was pinpointing a mounting concern of Second Empire officials: the 50,000 Basques who left home to emigrate to South America in the mid-nineteenth century. Emigration to the American continent was unusual in France, where most people preferred internal migration from the countryside to towns. Reclus's depiction of emigration as the result of a state of mind was simplistic, as the latter was to a large extent the result of the endemic indigence of the interior of the French Basque country, which in turn derived from the innate deficiency of the soil.[72] Reclus's analysis, nevertheless, reflected that of Napoleon III's administrators, who associated the poverty of the Basques with their ignorance, paucity of education and of knowledge of French, and lack of sense of duty towards the French nation. The integration of the Basque country into the Second Empire's programme of economic 'modernisation', which included agricultural and industrial development, a stronger banking system and an improved transport network, they believed, would minimise such disadvantage and reduce emigration.[73]

In order to remove all obstacles to the arrival of the 'urban era' in the Basque country,[74] Reclus argued, Euskara and Basque culture had to be sacrificed altogether. Such a drastic claim echoed the view, deriving from the French Revolution, that linguistic diversity caused internal division within France and, consequently, that minority languages were to be eliminated in order to foster national unity.[75] 'In this century of prodigious activity ... the Basques will learn to walk at a faster pace too, but this will be at the cost of their nationality and their language itself,' he wrote. 'Of their magnificent idiom, from now on relegated among the things of the past, will remain some words, some grammar books, a few *pastorales*, some bad modern tragedies and some *chants* of contested antiquity.'[76] Despite the inevitable regret for the loss of such an ancient culture, Reclus was optimistic that the Basques would soon recognise the benefits of progress and 'modernity', as they would partake in a higher form of civilisation. '[T]he *Euskariens*, belonging now to the modern world, will work towards the common good and, thanks to it, they will enter a much superior civilisation to the one that was special to them,' he wrote.[77] Such greater civilisation, he argued, was seeking to pursue the same values of liberty and equality that were so dear to the Basques, but to a greater extent, which he hoped would one day encompass the whole of humanity. As a result, he explained in the universalistic idiom of the Revolution, the qualities of the Basque race would not disappear by means of the fusion of the Basques with their neighbours, but would be put to better use: they would be employed for the greatness of France and of humanity as a whole.[78]

Conclusion

The study of Euskara in the nineteenth century was a political endeavour. Philologists were interested not only in studying the

Basque language per se but in the characteristics it allegedly revealed about the Basque community of speakers. Such studies were founded upon a number of assumptions that were popular among intellectuals in nineteenth-century Europe. First was the idea that nations were innate and diachronic, and that language was what best expressed the national character of a people. Second was the Romantic notion that tongues were closest to perfection in the ancient past, after which an inevitable process of degeneration ensued. Linguistic degeneration automatically meant the degeneration of the people who spoke that language, too, but a people's golden age could be recovered if the speakers of a certain tongue were brought together and awarded the right conditions of national autonomy. Comparative philology, then, did not only idealise the past; it equally presented models for a nation's cultural rebirth.[79]

While in such stateless nations as Germany the political goal of philological works was national self-determination, in the Basque country scholars were committed to preserving the autonomy of the Basque provinces vis-à-vis the centralising efforts of the French and Spanish nation-states. French Basque scholars relied on myths of ethnic descent similar to their Spanish counterparts, but they responded to specific French concerns that reflected the country's frequent regime changes in the nineteenth century. Scholars of Euskara in the French Basque country had two primary goals in mind. First, such linguists as Garat and Bidassouet strove to find a position for the Basques within evolving ideas of what constituted the French nation-state in the first decades of the nineteenth century. Second, they sought to protect the Basque language from succumbing to the use of French. While to an extent they all worked towards this goal, Chaho was the most militant and idealistic thinker. He showed a commitment that prompted Reclus to call him 'le dernier des Basques', a title that Chaho himself had attributed to the Carlist general Zumalacárregui in his *Voyage en Navarre* of 1834.[80] As Reclus's essay revealed, however, in the second half of the nineteenth century the existence of the Basque language became increasingly at odds with French notions of progress and civilisational advance, which considered language uniformity to be an essential step towards national unity and social evolution. As the next two chapters will reveal, such hierarchy of languages prompted Basque men of letters to attribute an increasingly militant character to Euskara, which challenged the Third Republic's centralising and anti-clerical measures at the end of the nineteenth century.

Notes

1 Pietro Bortone, *Language and Nationality: Social Inferences, Cultural Differences, and Linguistic Misconceptions* (London, 2022), 209.
2 Benes, *In Babel's Shadow*, 4.
3 Molina Aparicio, 'La disputada cronología de la nacionalidad', 221–4.
4 On the attribution of national meaning to history, see Beth S. Wright, *Painting and History During the French Restoration: Abandoned by the Past* (Cambridge, 1997), 8 and 19.
5 Benes, *In Babel's Shadow*, 3.
6 Manuel de Larramendi, *Diccionario trilingüe del castellano, bascuence y latin* (San Sebastián, [1745] 1853), i–xi.
7 Jan Fellerer, 'Theories of Language', in Paul Hamilton (ed.), *The Oxford Handbook of European Romanticism* (Oxford, 2016), 793.
8 Larramendi, *Diccionario*, lxi and xii: 'Es evidente, que ninguna Lengua matriz nació en España ... esta invención es imposible, assi porque solo Dios es el Autor de las Lenguas matrizes'; 'Y esto se confirma por la singularisimas ventajas de el Bascuence, y las perfecciones de su extructura ... pues de cierto no puede ningún hombre ser Autor de tan admirable harmonia.'
9 Pablo Pedro de Astarloa, *Apología de la lengua bascongada, ó ensayo crítico filosófico de su perfeccion y antigüedad* (Madrid, 1803), 3 and 45–6: 'cultura, riqueza, energía y suavidad'.
10 Ibid., 28: 'Todos somos los hijos de los antiquísimos Bascos, y gloriosos descendientes de los primeros pobladores de España.'
11 Juan Bautista de Erro y Azpiroz, *Alphabet de la langue primitive de l'Espagne et explication de ses plus anciens monumens, en inscriptions et médailles; suivi de la critique de cet ouvrage*, Éloi Johanneau trans. (Paris, 1808), 12, 17, 35–6.
12 Wilhelm von Humboldt, *Recherches sur les habitants primitifs de l'Espagne, à l'aide de la langue basque*, M. A. Marrast trans. (Paris, [1821] 1866), 153: 'Deux points me paraissent parfaitement établis ... Les anciens Ibères sont la souche des Basques actuels; les Ibères étaient répandus dans toute la Péninsule, parlaient une seule et même langue, et formaient plusieurs peuplades avec des dialectes divers. La langue basque était donc celle des habitants primitifs de l'Espagne.'
13 Aranzadi, *Milenarismo vasco*, 428.

14 Claude Laharie, *La Révolution dans les Basses-Pyrénées* (Pau, 1989), 114; E. Maron, 'Preface', in Dominique-Joseph Garat, *Mémoires de Garat* (Paris, 1862), xiii.
15 Dominique-Joseph Garat, 'Recherches sur le peuple primitif de l'Espagne; sur les révolutions de cette péninsule; sur les Basques espagnols et françois. Rapport établi en 1811 pour Napoléon Ier', Jean Casenave ed., *Lapurdum*, 11 ([1811] 2006), 108.
16 Ibid., 108: 'Si vous laissez les basques Espagnols et François dans leur séparation actuelle, ils ne seront jamais que basques; si vous les réunissez, à l'instant tous ensemble seront les Cantabres, ils en reprendront le nom, l'attitude et ils cultiveront avec cet enthousiasme qui leur est si naturel l'immense héritage de gloire attaché à ce nom.'
17 Ibid., 109: 'Dans le service de mer ils peuvent faire renaître toute leur antique gloire et ajouter à toutes les prospérités de l'Empire de Napoléon.'
18 On the use of the myth of the Phoenicians, see Josephine Quinn, *In Search of the Phoenicians* (Princeton, 2017); Asher Kaufman, *Reviving Phoenicia: The Search for Identity in Lebanon* (London, 2014).
19 Garat, 'Recherches', 113.
20 Ibid., 114: '[C]'est cette barrière des langues et non pas celle des montagnes, des fleuves et des mers, qui empêche les peuples de se mêler, de se confondre et d'effacer en se confondant l'originalité et la pureté originelle de leur caractère primitif.'
21 Ibid., 115: 'restée comme elle est née'.
22 Ibid., 115: 'La langue d'un peuple Simple qui ne s'est mêlé à aucun autre peuple, qui n'a connu ni la grandeur ni la décadence, ni la délicatesse recherchée ni la corruption du gout et des arts, même après un long cours de siécles, est comme une langue naissante'.
23 Sergio Moravia, *Il pensiero degli Idéologues: scienza e filosofia in Francia (1780–1815)* (Florence, 1974), 295 and 298; Martin S. Staum, *Minerva's Message: Stabilizing the French Revolution* (Montreal, 1996), 102.
24 Dominique-Joseph Garat, 'Analyse de l'entendement', in *Séances des Écoles Normales, recueillies par des sténographes, et revues par les professeurs*, Volume 2 (Paris, 1795), 33.
25 Garat, 'Recherches', 117: 'Il ne suffit pas qu'une langue soit dans la bouche d'un peuple pour qu'elle soit vivante; il faut qu'une lumière vive et éclatante se répande de ses mots les plus élémentaires dans ses mots les plus composés.'
26 Ibid., 114: '[I]l faut donc qu'ils veillent plus que jamais sur le feu sacré de cette langue qui les échauffe et qui les éclaire … Il faut que toutes leurs pensées soient exprimées et renfermées dans cette langue s'ils veulent jouer encore un grand rôle sur la terre.'

27 Ibid., 115: 'si le caractère de ces peuples a si fidellement gardé le dépôt de leur langue, leur langue à son tour conservera leur caractère, ce caractère sur le quel on fonde plus qu'une espérance.'
28 Ibid., 115: 'si analogique, si claire, si transparente'.
29 Thierry Lentz, *Nouvelle Histoire du Premier Empire*. *Napoléon et la conquête de l'Europe, 1804–1810*, Volume 1 (Paris, 2002), 62–9; Jean Tulard, *Napoleon: The Myth of the Saviour*, Teresa Waugh trans. (London, 1984), 19 and 127–8; Georges Lefebvre, *Napoléon* (Paris, 1953), 67–8. For an example of the use of Charlemagne propaganda in Napoleonic Italy, see Michael Broers, 'Cultural Imperialism in a European Context? Political Culture and Cultural Politics in Napoleonic Italy', *Past and Present*, 170 (2001), 158.
30 Michael Broers, *Europe Under Napoleon, 1799–1815* (London, 1996), 99–100 and 180; Michael Broers, 'Napoleon, Charlemagne and Lotharingia: Acculturation and the Boundaries of Napoleonic Europe', *Historical Journal*, 44:1 (2001), 135–54.
31 On the linguistic pragmatism of the First Empire, see McCain, *The Language Question under Napoleon*.
32 Ronald Schechter, *Obstinate Hebrews: Representations of Jews in France, 1715–1815* (Oakland, 2003), 197 and 209.
33 Dominique-Joseph Garat, *Mémoire sur la Hollande* (Paris, 1805); Simon Schama, *Patriots and Liberators: Revolution in the Netherlands, 1780–1813* (London, 1992), 483, 553 and 655.
34 Garat, 'Lettre de D. J. Garat à Napoléon 1er', Jean Casenave ed., *Lapurdum*, 11 ([1811] 2006), 131–2.
35 Étienne de Jouy, *L'Hermite en province, ou observations sur les mœurs et les usages français au commencement du XIXe siècle*, Volume 1 (Paris, 1819), 100–2: 'une même et seule race d'hommes'.
36 Benes, *In Babel's Shadow*, 11.
37 Madariaga Orbea, *Anthology of Apologists and Detractors of the Basque Language*, 481–2.
38 Bidassouet, *Histoire des cantabres*, viii–ix: 'J'ai pensé que l'étude des langues ne servoit pas seulement à connoître les monuments de l'antiquité, mais encore à comparer les mœurs des temps reculés que l'histoire nous transmet avec celles du siècle où nous vivons, et qui ne peuvent manquer de s'améliorer sous le règne d'un Prince tel que vous, SIRE.'
39 Ibid., xvii: 'les cendres des Cantabres, si fiers d'avoir vaincu tour-à-tour les Phéniciens, les Carthaginois, les Romains, les Goths, les Visigoths, les Ostrogoths, les Francs mêmes, et enfin les Sarrasins, sembleront se ranimer pour venir mêler leur gloire antique à celle de la belle et florissante France, glorieuse et fière d'être gouvernée par Charles X.'

40 Ibid., 281–2.
41 Ibid., 6: 'c'est-à-dire la *droiture*, la *finesse*, le *génie profond* des *Escualdunac*, pour établir des lois élémentaires et fondamentales qu'ils surent soutenir avec fidélité, et défendre avec bravoure'.
42 Ibid., 12: 'les descendants de Japhet devoient être nécessairement Basques, Escualdunac, puisque, comme nous l'avons dit, les provinces, les montagnes, les rivières, les étangs des contrées, où ces colonies ont passé et où elles ont séjourné, ont leurs noms significatifs et topographiques basques, Escüarac.'
43 Ibid., 25.
44 Ibid., 26.
45 Ibid., 27: 'les Espagnols Cantabres descendent des Cantabres français, malgré le préjugé contraire.'
46 Ibid., 169: 'C'est là que se sont le mieux conservés tous les traits primitifs. Aussi les Labourtains sont les véritables types des anciens Cantabres, de cette ancienne race d'hommes dont la bravoure a fait trembler les plus grands héros de l'Europe.'
47 Ibid., 172–3: 'la noirceur, la perfidie, la médisance'; 'ces paysans simples et braves'; 'les merveilles de la nature'; 'une *apparition anticipée de la béatitude future*'.
48 Tort, *La Droite française*, 275–6.
49 Jean-Pierre Darrigol, *Dissertation critique et apologétique sur la langue basque par un ecclésiastique du diocèse de Bayonne* (Bayonne, 1827), 35–6 and 46.
50 Alexandre du Mège, *Statistique générale des départements pyrénéens, ou des provinces de Guienne et de Languedoc*, Volume 2 (Paris, 1829), 290.
51 Chaho, *Histoire primitive*, 137–60.
52 Ibid., 163: 'eurent pour uniques représentants dans la suite des siècles les Euskariens cantabres et vascons, les anciens Basques'.
53 Ibid., 139: 'aux siècles les plus reculés de l'ère appelée à juste titre primitive et patriarcale, plus haut et plus loin que le polythéisme et les fables mythologiques'.
54 Benes, *In Babel's Shadow*, 70–2.
55 Chaho, *Histoire primitive*, xxi: 'Verbe improvisé'; 'vérité divine'; 'civilisation et vérité'; 'Le langage astronomique des Euskariens reflète avec poésie les mœurs simples et agrestes de ce peuple pasteur.'
56 Ibid., 242: 'toutes les puissances de la parole, toutes les harmonies du verbe'; 'reflexions pénibles'; 'spectacle dégrandant de l'idolatrie'.
57 Benes, *In Babel's Shadow*, 73–4.
58 Alexandre Baudrimont, *Histoire des basques ou escualdunais primitifs* (Paris, 1854), 178–9.

59 Willem van Eys, *Essai de grammaire de la langue basque* (Amsterdam, 1867), v.
60 Francisque Michel, *Le Pays basque. Sa population, sa langue, ses mœurs, sa littérature et sa musique* (Paris, 1857), 11 and 14.
61 Jean-François Bladé, *Études sur l'origine des basques* (Paris, 1869), 240–1, 268–9 and 304–5.
62 Stefan Berger, 'National Histories and the Promotion of Nationalism in Historiography – the Pitfalls of "Methodological Nationalism"', in Stefan Berger and Eric Storm (eds), *Writing the History of Nationalism* (London, 2019), 24–5.
63 Wolf, *Europe and the People Without History*, 5 and 12.
64 Madariaga Orbea, *Anthology of Apologists and Detractors of the Basque Language*, 630–1.
65 Élisée Reclus, 'Les Basques. Un peuple qui s'en va', *Revue des Deux Mondes*, 68:2 (1867), 320: 'l'ancienne race ibérique … la politesse et la dignité simple de leurs ancêtres'.
66 Ibid., 318–19: 'on se trouve entraîné par une pente naturelle de l'esprit à se demander si ces populations joyeuses ne représentent pas les débris d'une humanité plus fortunée qui ne connaissait point nos misères et nos tristesses.'
67 Ibid., 323: 'déclaraient leur langue bien supérieure à toutes les autres'.
68 Ibid., 323: 'le dernier et vaillant champion des gloires euskariennes'; 'Désormais la science n'a plus à discuter la question de savoir si le basque est un langage divin, supérieur en dignité à ceux de tous les peuples de la terre nés loin des Pyrénées.'
69 Ibid., 334: 'une des plus nobles'.
70 Ibid., 330: 'c'est l'ignorance dans laquelle croupissent encore les populations'.
71 Ibid., 330–1: 'paresseux ou sans intelligence'.
72 A. de Saint-Léger and E. Delbet, 'Paysan du Labourd (Basses-Pyrénées, France)', in Frédéric Le Play (ed.), *Les Ouvriers des deux mondes*, Volume 1 (Paris, 1857), 212. On the Basque diaspora, see Gloria P. Totoricagüena, *Identity, Culture, and Politics in the Basque Diaspora* (Reno, 2015); Pierre Force, *Wealth and Disaster: Atlantic Migrations from a Pyrenean Town in the Eighteenth and Nineteenth Centuries* (Baltimore, 2016); Álvaro Aragón Ruano, 'French Basque and Béarnais Trade Diaspora from the Spanish Basque Country During the Eighteenth Century', *Atlantic Studies*, 16:4 (2019), 452–81.
73 A.N., F/1cVII/46, The sub-prefect of Mauléon to the *conseil d'arrondissement* of Mauléon, 1866. On Napoleon III's plan of economic growth, see Robert Tombs, *France 1814–1914* (London and New York, 1996), 399–402.

74 Quentin Deluermoz, *Le Crépuscule des révolutions, 1848–1871* (Paris, 2012), 142–3: 'ère urbaine'.
75 Douglas A. Kibbee, '"The People" and their Language in 19th-Century French Linguistic Thought', in Sheila Embleton, John E. Joseph and Hans-Josef Niederehe (eds), *The Emergence of the Modern Language Sciences: Studies on the Transition from Historical-Comparative to Structural Linguistics in Honour of E.F.K. Koerner. Volume 1: Historiographical Perspectives* (Amsterdam, 1999), 122–3.
76 Reclus, 'Les Basques', 330: 'Dans ce siècle de prodigieuse activité ... les Basques apprendront, eux aussi, à marcher d'un pas de plus en plus rapide, mais ce sera au prix de leur nationalité et de leur langue elle-même. De leur magnifique idiome, désormais rangé parmi les choses du passé, il ne restera plus que des lexiques, des grammaires, quelques pastorales, de mauvaises tragédies modernes et des chants d'une antiquité contestée.'
77 Ibid., 339: 'les Euskariens, appartenant désormais au monde moderne, se mettront, eux aussi, à l'œuvre commune pour le salut de tous, et par cela même ils entreront dans une civilisation bien supérieure à celle qui leur était spéciale.'
78 Ibid., 339.
79 Benes, *In Babel's Shadow*, 11.
80 Reclus, 'Les Basques', 336.

5

Inventing a Basque literary tradition

In 1897, at the Congress of Basque Tradition in Saint-Jean-de-Luz, the Béarnais federalist scholar Adrien Planté gave an address entitled 'Les Basques, ont-ils une histoire?' ('Do the Basques have a history?'). He reassured the Basque public that they did. It rested on popular literature, on the Basque language and on people's love of their homeland.[1] Planté's talk reflected a concern that had been troubling Basque scholars since the beginning of Romantic nationalism: whether the Basques, who possessed a weak literary tradition and no comprehensive written history, could claim to be a cultural nation. It was a serious apprehension because, for nineteenth-century western Europeans, being a historical nation was not only a matter of participating in progress and 'modernity'; it also involved the preservation and restoration of the national past. As Astrid Swenson has pointed out, western European states regarded the conservation of historical monuments as a sign of 'civilisation', insofar as their ability to recognise the value of their own past distinguished Europeans from the indigenous populations of the colonies, whom they regarded as 'peoples without history'.[2] Disregard for one's own past was a sign that a nation did not deserve the right to self-determination.

French Basque elites, like their Spanish counterparts, were aware of being considered a 'people without history' and worried that the Basque country's lack of a written tradition risked placing it among the ahistorical nations, whose neglect of their past denied them the right to exist. They were therefore wary of outsiders' scholarly interest in their language and culture, as they believed that such studies turned the Basque country into a heritage site whose value lay exclusively in its past. The *curé* of Tardets, Gratien Adéma, for example, wrote in 1887 that the Basques were 'a people with almost no history' and with few 'monuments of our past'. While European scholars were committed to protecting Basque culture from extinction, he warned, they were not interested in keeping the Basque country alive as a nation. Rather, 'they would like to preserve us as a prodigious historical and philological monument'.[3] Thus, French Basque scholars worked hand in hand with Spanish Basque ones to invent a Basque literary tradition that constituted a reaction to the hierarchy of cultures that Europe's obsession with the past initiated in the decades following the French Revolution.

Basque elites' efforts to equip the Basque country with a literary history produced paradoxical results. On the one hand, the construction of a Basque 'literary renaissance', as it was custom to call the revival of regionalist cultures in the late nineteenth century, was a transnational and international endeavour. It involved European scholars, as well as the concerted effort of French and Spanish Basque *savants* whose work strengthened the sense of a shared Basque cultural identity across the Pyrenees. Curiously, although the Spanish Basques possessed a more organised regionalist movement, the *fuerismo*, with a more proliferating literature than the French Basques, a surprising amount of artistic works and cultural activities that came to characterise Basque literary identity originated in the French Basque country. On the other hand, regionalist culture strengthened the relationship between the Basque country and France. Similar to what occurred in other regions such as Flanders, French intellectuals regarded Basque folklore as a means of enriching the cultural patrimony of the French nation.[4] Basque *savants*, in turn, viewed their transnational literary culture as a way of articulating and strengthening their position within the bigger nation. Local culture, they believed, instilled in people a sense of pride of and belonging to the *petite patrie*, which engendered love of and loyalty to the *grande patrie*.[5] While this was especially the case of France, it was also true of *fuerismo* in Spain, despite the emergence of Sabino Arana y Goiri's Basque separatist movement in the 1890s.[6] As a result, the Basque opus, although it referred to the Basque country as a nation, was not an attempt to break away from France and Spain. It was a way of providing the Basque country with a literary history that strengthened both the position of the region within the bigger nation and that of the nation within the new Europe of nation-states.

Inventing a written literary tradition

Basque intellectuals worried about the lack of a Basque written literary tradition. They were aware that the strength of 'modern' European nations was measured by their relationship with their past and, as a result, a nation without a literature was 'a nation without history' that had no place in the 'modern' world.[7] Some attempted to joke about it, deeming literature as overrated and irrelevant. Augustin Chaho, for example, claimed in 1855 that throughout the centuries the Basques had been too busy making history to write it down.[8] Additionally, Dr Albert Goyenèche, a local *savant* and conservative mayor of Saint-Jean-de-Luz in the 1890s, upon being asked why a complete history of the Basques did not exist, allegedly replied: 'The Basques are like honest women: they do not have a history.'[9] The jokes, nevertheless, failed to dissimulate intellectuals' malaise. The lack of a literary tradition implied, in Herderian terms, a low consciousness of one's past and a consequent weak sense of identity, which placed the Basques towards the bottom of the civilisational hierarchy of nations.[10] In the final decades of the nineteenth century, with the abolition of the *fueros* in Spain and the wave of anti-clericalism in France, scholars felt that Basque culture was especially fragile and that, without literature, it failed to legitimise its existence. The Spanish Basque *fuerista* Arturo Campión, for instance, wrote in 1880 that '[e]very time a literary work is produced in our noble and unfortunate *Patria Euskara*, some weak hope awakens in my heart'. The Basque literary renaissance, he explained, was revealing of the survival of Basque values vis-à-vis the abolition of the *fueros*, as literary works were 'keepers of traditions, avengers of justice, and the nerve and vital fluid of invincible revendications'.[11] Only a written literary tradition could save Basque culture from oblivion.

In the first half of the century, Basque intellectuals forged a pseudo-medieval literary tradition. As Stephen Bann has argued, the nineteenth century was a 'historical-minded' period of western European history, where scholars tried to narrow the gap between 'history as it happened' and 'history as it [was] written'. They regarded national history as the foundation of contemporary national greatness and a national literature as validation of such historical claims. In this sense, authenticity and forgery were 'two sides of the same coin'.[12] Inspired by the Romantic celebration of troubadour literature,

Basque intellectuals regarded medieval literature as the emblem of national heritage and the highest form of poetic achievement.[13] The Spanish Basque *fuerista* Hermilio de Olóriz, for instance, wrote in the *Revista Euskara* in 1878 that the romance was the most important form of poetry because 'it is the means through which people have cried their misfortunes and sung their glories and their myths ... In its pages lives the soul of a race, its pages describe its customs and its feelings.'[14] In this respect, forging a pseudo-medieval literary tradition meant affording greater historical value to the Basque Cantabrian myth of Basque invincibility and military glory.[15]

Although it was the *fueristas* who primarily popularised Basque literature to give historical foundation to their political demands to the Spanish state in the late nineteenth century, many of the most popular Basque epics were forged in France between the 1830s and the 1850s. They were only later adopted by the *fueristas* as representations of the strength and historicity of the Basque nation. In their reproduction of medieval songs, French Basque *savants* were influenced by two main texts. One was the old *Cantar de Beotibar*, which first appeared in the Spanish Basque scholar Esteban de Garibay's *Compendio Historial* in 1571 and was widely considered the first Basque medieval epic. It recounted the story of the battle of Beotibar of 1321 between the kingdom of Navarre and the province of Guipúzcoa for the annexation of the latter's territory to Navarre. Guipúzcoa's unexpected victory inspired the song.[16] The second poem was the more recent *Canto de los Cantabres* or *Canto de Lelo*, which narrated a five-year war that the Basques had fought against Augustus's Roman armies in the first century BCE. While it mourned the death of the Basque hero Lelo, it equally celebrated the Cantabrians' resistance to invasion, perpetuating the Basque Cantabrian myth of Basque independence.[17] The song was discovered in the Basque country by Wilhelm von Humboldt, who published it in 1817 in Johann Adelung's *Mithridates*, accompanied by a German translation. He claimed that the manuscript had originally been found in 1590 by Juan Ibáñez de Ibargüen while doing research in the archives of Simancas and Vizcaya, and had then been forgotten again until Humboldt stumbled upon it two centuries later.[18] The poem was likely written in the fifteenth century but many contemporaries, including Humboldt, believed that it dated back to the time of the war and reacted enthusiastically to its publication, as they regarded it as a remnant of the purest literary form of ancient European civilisation. The French historian Claude Fauriel, for example, wrote in his *Histoire de la Gaule méridionale* that the *Canto de Lelo* was 'a mountaineer's song, a real primitive song, where art still relies on the simplest inspirations of nature'.[19] Despite widespread doubts about the authenticity of the poem,[20] scholars were ready to accept its legitimacy, as they revered literature that, unlike historical fiction, claimed to be founded on history.[21]

In the following two decades, French Basque *savants* claimed to have discovered four ancient manuscripts, which allegedly proved the existence of a flourishing Basque romance tradition. The most famous epic was the *Chant d'Altabiscar* or *Altabizkarko Kantua*, which Michel, who recovered the manuscript of *La Chanson de Roland* in Oxford in 1837, popularised as a Basque *chanson de geste* in the early 1830s. The poem, which the *fueristas* later embraced as a national epic, was written in 1828 by a French Basque scholar, Eugène Garay de Monglave, who claimed, however, that it was based on a manuscript that was a contemporary of *La Chanson de Roland*. The manuscript, he explained, had been discovered by the grenadier and amateur philologist La Tour d'Auvergne in San Sebastián in 1794 and had eventually ended up in Dominique-Joseph Garat's house. The poem, formed of eight stanzas, described the battle of Roncesvalles and the death of Roland from the point of view of the Cantabrians, who were depicted as the winners. It began with the narrator counting from one to twenty to describe the impressive size of Charlemagne's army that the Cantabrians were preparing to face on Mont d'Altabiscar near Roncesvalles, and ended with a countdown from twenty to one to depict the Cantabrians' defeat of the Frankish soldiers one by one. In the end, the eighth stanza sang: 'One! Not even one is left alive. / It is over.'[22]

From the start, the authenticity of the *Chant d'Altabiscar* became the object of intense scrutiny and criticism. In 1866, in particular, the French scholar Jean-François Bladé wrote an entire dissertation that denounced both the *Canto de Lelo* and the *Chant d'Altabiscar* as apocryphal and mocked Garay de Monglave for his convoluted explanation of the origin of the manuscript.[23] The *Chant*, nevertheless, had staunch defenders among the *fueristas*. They saw it as an epic poem which awarded the Basques an epic genre whose quality equalled ancient Greek and medieval epic literature. In 1878, for example, Olóriz compared the *Chant* to the most famous European *chansons de geste* and criticised Bladé's scepticism, claiming that the poem was a 'cry of independence in which the indomitable spirit of the Basque race [*raza euskara*] is felt throbbing. [It is the] holy anthem of our mountains, simple and grandiose like the most sublime Homeric creations.'[24] The comparison between Homeric and medieval epics was widespread across Europe. In *A Critical Dissertation on the Poems of Ossian* of 1765, for example, the Scottish clergyman Hugh Blair compared another forgery, James McPherson's Ossian cycle, to ancient Greek epics. He believed that the highest form of poetry was produced in the infancy of society and compared Homeric and Celtic poems not on the basis of contemporaneity but on the basis of stages of social development.[25]

The *Chant d'Altabiscar* acquired further political meaning in 1877 when Campión published a ballad inspired by the *Chant*, which he called 'our national song', entitled *Orreaga*, the Basque word for Roncesvalles. The eight stanzas, which mirrored the structure of the *Chant*, described the Basques' defeat of the Franks from Charlemagne's point of view. On the night before the decisive battle, Campión wrote, Charlemagne was kept awake by an eerie sound. When he asked what it was, Turpin, the archbishop of Rheims, replied: 'This noise is the war song of the Basque country [Basconia], and today is the last day of our glory.'[26] After the abolition of the Spanish Basque *fueros* in 1876, the *fueristas* equalled the Cantabrians' struggle against the Romans to the contemporary Basques' fight against the 'foreign' demands of the Spanish state and used literature as a forewarning of the battle that the Basques were ready to engage in against the central government's intrusion into local affairs. The ending of Campión's ballad, which read that '[t]here are no longer foreigners in the Basque country', could be interpreted as a contemporary looming threat.[27]

Michel was also responsible for the publication of another allegedly medieval French Basque poem, *Abarcarer Cantua* (*Abarca's Song*), which he published in the English periodical *The Gentleman's Magazine* in 1858. The song, whose quality Michel compared to the *Chant d'Altabiscar*, narrated one of the two victories that King Sancho II of Navarre, supported by the fearless Basques, gained over the Moors in the tenth century. The poem, Michel explained, was discovered by the French Basque *abbé* Emmanuel Inchauspé, author of the *Verbe basque* (1858), who, together with the linguist Louis-Lucien Bonaparte, testified to its authenticity. Michel had his doubts, as the poem seemed likely to have been written to prove the antiquity of the Basse-Navarrese aristocratic family of the Belzunce, whose ancestor was celebrated in the poem as the 'lion of the battles' and a military counsellor to Sancho II.[28] Nevertheless, Michel argued that he could confirm that the song was old and that, as such, it vindicated 'the poetical genius of the Basques' against critics who called them a people without literature.[29] 'Listen to this shepherd's song', he exhorted his distinguished readership. '[P]erhaps you will agree with me that its notes … are not inferior to those which we are accustomed to admire.'[30] Interestingly, Basque *savants* relied on renowned French and European scholars in order to publish and popularise the texts that they discovered or forged, as internationally read publications provided Basque literature with the confirmation it required of its value and quality.

Augustin Chaho was the author of the two other texts that became an integral part of Basque metahistory:[31] the *Chant d'Annibal* and the *Légende d'Aïtor*. Unlike other *savants*, who relied on international publications, Chaho published the two texts himself in 1845 in his newspaper *Ariel*, where he was attempting to compile the first collection of Basque folkloric poetry.[32] The narrator of both stories was the Cantabrian bard Lara, who had first been mentioned by the Roman poet Silius Italicus in the sixteenth volume of his work *Punica*. The *Chant*, which Chaho attributed to 'an unknown Bard of Cantabria', sang the story of those Cantabrians who fought valiantly alongside Hannibal against the Romans in the Second Punic War. Upon their arrival in Italy, though, they decided to retreat before getting the chance of sacking Rome, as they preferred to return to their mountains and their loved ones.[33] To the theme of Basque valour, then, Chaho added in his *Chant* the Romantic motifs of love and nostalgia. The *Légende*, which read as a scholarly text rather than as a poem, took off where the *Chant* ended, occurring during the Cantabrians' celebrations of the end of the Second Punic War. The first night was dedicated to the commemoration of 'national history', and Lara was given the honour of recounting the legend of Aïtor. The latter, Lara explained, was 'the great ancestor, the patriarch, the father of the Indo-Atlantic race and the first born of the Euskarians'.³⁴ The story of Aïtor was invented by Chaho to replace the Christian Tubal as the mythical founder of the Basques. According to Jon Juaristi, Chaho replaced Tubal with Aïtor for two reasons. First, he wished to provide the Basques with a separate myth of origin to that of the rest of Spain. Second, driven by anti-Semitism, he wanted to remove any Semitic origin from Basque genealogy. As a result, Aïtor was an 'Aryan' patriarch, as were the founding fathers of the Indian and the Iranian races.³⁵

Although the *fueristas* initially met the legend of Aïtor with scepticism because of its lack of Christian roots and of Chaho's rejection of Catholicism, it acquired a timeless place in Basque mythology when, in 1877, the Navarrese writer Francisco Navarro Villoslada made it the central tenet of his renowned book *Amaya o los vascos en el siglo VIII*, a Romantic historical novel inspired by Sir Walter Scott's *Ivanhoe* (1819). The influence of Chaho's metahistory on Villoslada was not accidental. The two authors met in Vitoria during Chaho's brief sojourn there in the mid-nineteenth century, and Villoslada became deeply influenced by his French Basque counterpart's ideas.³⁶ The story of *Amaya* took place during the Moorish invasion of Visigothic Spain in the eighth century when, according to Villoslada, the Basques were still divided between Christians and pagans. The protagonist was Amaya, a princess who was the daughter of the Visigoth Ranimiro and of a Basque woman, as well as the niece of the pagan leader Amagoya and the heiress to the secrets of Aïtor. At the end of the novel, Amagoya eventually revealed to Amaya the secret of the Basque patriarch: Christianity as true religion. '[O]ur father Aïtor wishes that all his children recognise the law of Christ,' Villoslada had Amaya say. Pagan Basques converted to Christianity, Amaya married the Basque resistance leader García and the couple became the first monarchs of Navarra.³⁷ Additionally, on top of canonising the legend of Aïtor, *Amaya* contributed to the validation of the *Chant d'Annibal* as an ancient Basque song. In the novel, Amagoya accepted Amaya as the heiress of Aïtor only when the latter, in agonising spiritual pain, sang to the pagan leader an enriched version of the final stanza of the *Chant d'Annibal*, which the book cited in full, implying that the *Chant* was an ancient and renowned Basque song. The final stanza read:

> Bird, sweet singer,
> continue to sing to me.
> No one in the world was born
> more unfortunate than me.
> I lost my mother, I lost
> my home, my native valley...
> Never, never will
> my eyes stop crying!³⁸

Villoslada, then, turned Chaho's invented traditions into an essential part of the Basque literary canon.

Villoslada's novel was important for the codification of Basque identity in both France and Spain for a number of reasons. First, the book, like Villoslada's other historical novels, contributed to the Romantic celebration of the Basques' medieval heritage, which was part of their quest for a mythology of ethnic descent.³⁹ Villoslada was indeed known as 'the Walter Scott of Basque traditions'.⁴⁰ *Amaya*, moreover, popularised Chaho's literary texts, which became a part of the canon of Basque literature. The year after the publication of the novel, Campión also published a translation of *La Légende d'Aïtor* in the *Revista Euskara*, as part of a series of classic Basque works.⁴¹ Finally, *Amaya* codified two key themes that defined Basque identity in the early twentieth century: the purity of the Basque race and Catholic integralism. Except for a small group of separatists emerging in Vizcaya at the end of the nineteenth century, though, Basque intellectuals on both sides of the Pyrenees regarded these tenets as universal virtues that protected not only the Basque country but the true identity of Spain and France.⁴² As Campión put it in his review of *Amaya* in 1880, when Spain seemed to be on the brink of death, there came the Basques, 'the eternal defenders of the [whole of the] national soil'.⁴³

Recovering an oral literary tradition

While scholars admitted that the Basque country did not possess a rich written literary tradition, they claimed that it had one of the strongest oral literary traditions in Europe. They shared European intellectuals' belief that the *poésie populaire* was the most significant form of literature because it preserved the original essence of a people, and they regarded the cultivation of Basque folklore as both a local and a pan-European effort. G. Olivier, for example, wrote in the *Dictionnaire de la conversation et de la lecture* in 1834 that 'the folk song is the devoted child of the *patrie*, which embodies its mores, protects its customs and is the arch-depository of its most precious memories'.[44] The Alsatian historian Louis Spach, moreover, claimed in the *Encyclopédie des gens du monde* in 1835 that '[t]o sing is to live',[45] and Michel argued in 1857: 'Unlike poetry that is born of literature, [popular poetry] is inspired by reality. Its productions have a historical and psychological interest; they reveal the private adventures of a people, the details of its character, the attitudes of its spirit: they are memories, or rather confessions, in which a people opens its heart without reserve.'[46] Thus, recovering a Basque oral tradition meant recovering the quintessence of the Basque nation.

Additionally, French scholars felt that the collection of a Basque folk tradition was significant for France too, as they believed that the latter did not possess as rich a repertoire of folk tales as Britain, Germany or Spain.[47] Spach, for example, argued that if scholars made an effort to collect the *chants primitifs* from all French provinces, 'the harvest would look richer than we imagine'. In particular, he added, folklorists should look at the 'melancholic songs' that the Basques had preserved in the Pyrenees, as 'mountains are the trustworthy repositories of old traditions'.[48] As Natalie Morel-Borotra has pointed out, in the first half of the nineteenth century Basque folk songs were 'invented' by foreign, French and Basque men of letters, in part with the purpose of enriching French literature and recovering the purity of France's social infancy.[49] Basque folklore served the nationalist goals of the French nation as much as the regionalist goals of the French Basques.

The production of a Basque oral tradition took, to an extent, the form of those learned societies, publications and folkloric collections that were popular across Europe at the time. While many of these groups were ostensibly apolitical, such as the Société des sciences, lettres et arts de Bayonne, founded in 1873, others, such as the weekly paper *Eskualduna*, crossed the line between culture and politics, as their celebration of Basque culture and language was a form of resistance to the pressure of state centralisation and uniformity. The same was true of other scholarly groups across France, such as the Association bretonne, founded in 1843, the Comité flamand de France, established in 1853, and the Félibrige in Provence, which Frédéric Mistral launched the following year.[50] *Eskualduna*, founded by the conservative Basque deputy and local *savant* Louis Etcheverry in 1887, was a reaction to the secularising policies of the French state and aimed to serve, the inaugural number claimed, as a 'passionate defender of the old traditions of the *pays*', in particular the Catholic tradition. It was committed to the safeguarding of farmers' agricultural interests, which were 'cruelly' in jeopardy, and of such traditional authorities as patriarchy, the clergy and 'a stable government' that protected the family and religion.[51] While the format of *Eskualduna* was that of a newspaper, rather than of a scholarly journal, it was inspired by the numerous pro-*fuero* publications that had proliferated in Spain after the abolition of the *fueros* in 1876, such as the *Revista de las provincias euskaras* (1878–81), the *Revista Euskal-Herria* (1880–1918) and the *Revista Euskara* (1878–83), which was the yearly journal of the Asociación Euskara de Navarra. The first number of the *Revista Euskara* introduced the goals of the Asociación, which included 'to preserve and to spread the Basque-Navarrese language, literature and history, to study its legislation and to work towards the moral and material wellbeing of the country'. The Basque people, it added, had preserved its distinct race, genius, customs, personality and virtues throughout the centuries thanks to Euskara. As a result, the Asociación was committed to its protection and propagation.[52] The French Basques looked at the Spanish Basque *savant* production as a source of inspiration and imitation. It was unpatriotic, the *abbé* Adéma claimed in an address in Tardets in 1887, that *Eskualduna* should defend Basque interests all by itself. Spain, he explained, had several such publications and even Germany had recently started publishing a Basque journal, *Euskara*. Yet the French Basque country possessed only *Eskualduna*. Local notables, he argued, must have 'atrophied hearts and minds devoid of all patriotic ideas and noble resolutions'.[53] In this regard, Basque *savants* believed that a sound scholarly publication required a militant, political character.

Scholars similarly promoted Basque folklore through the collection and publication of local songs and poems, legends, proverbs and theatre plays. Basque and non-Basque scholars often worked hand in hand towards the production of local folklore. The comprehensive works by Michel, the British clergyman Wentworth Webster and the French linguist Julien Vinson were complemented by local publications, such as collections of folk songs by Jean-Dominique-Julien Sallaberry, José António Santesteban and José Manterola, and of folk tales by José María de Goizueta and Juan de Araquistain.[54] Scholars believed that folklore solved, at least in part, the problem of the lack of a Basque written literary tradition, as folklore incapsulated the ancestral character of the Basques. Michel, for example, quoted the French writer Charles Nodier to describe proverbs as the 'intimate expression of the spirit of a nation',[55] while Webster argued that the *pastorales*, a form of popular theatre typical of Soule, 'preserved the popular memory and tradition of the great legends and romances, of the *chansons de geste*, of chivalric novels, of the great epic poems of the middle ages'.[56] Finally, Araquistain, the most militant of the folk collectors, wrote in the introduction of his work that popular traditions always included 'the three highest and purest sentiments of humanity': 'love of God, love of family and love of the motherland'.[57] As with any European collection of folklore, those of the Basque country claimed to be revealing some unique cultural features of the people. However, such traits resembled those of many other regions and nations across the continent and awarded Basque culture an increasingly standardised and stereotyped character. In this respect, as Eric Storm and Joep Leerssen have remarked about nations, regional cultures were 'supposed to be unique. Yet they [were] all unique in the same manner.'[58]

While Basque collections of folk tales and songs were similar to many across Europe, though, in the mid-nineteenth century, two French Basque scholars, Augustin Chaho and Antoine d'Abbadie, popularised a Basque-specific form of folk culture: the *bertsolaritza*, a Basque type of improvised sung verse that soon became a symbol of Basque identity. The *bertsolaritza* first emerged as a genre in the late middle ages, but in the nineteenth century Chaho and d'Abbadie, like the Bretons and followed by the *fueristas*, elevated local poets to bards, claiming that their art dated from time immemorial and represented the essence of the Basque nation.[59] Chaho was the first Basque, from either France or Spain, to embrace the Europe-wide Romantic understanding of folklore as the literary depository of the nation and the foundation on which to revive national culture.[60] In October 1844, he founded the newspaper *Ariel* with the aim, among others, of publishing the most renowned folk songs in order to popularise the essence of the Basque spirit among the Basque population.[61] In the first number, he explained that the Basques were distinct among European nations insofar as they were the only people still to possess 'the gift of improvised poetry', which was the result of their historical isolation from other peoples, as well as the preservation of their traditions and of their language.[62] The following April, he added in another article that the Basques had lost their legends and their poems but had preserved 'the songs of their *bardes improvisateurs*'. Improvised poetry represented 'the most indestructible monument' of Basque culture, he explained, because it was passed on across generations and, in the process, it also perpetuated Euskara, a 'virginal and scholarly language'. In this respect, he concluded, improvised poetry was superior to any written book because it represented 'the last harmonies of a destroyed world' and, as '[a] statue exhumated from the ruins', it was 'a monument of the past'.[63] Chaho, in other words, identified the *bertsolaritza* as an intimate and popular connection between the past and the present of the Basque country, as well as an act of defiance against the forces of 'modernity' that were destroying the last vestiges of Basque ancestral culture.

Nine years later, Antoine d'Abbadie invented the *fêtes basques*, which elevated the prestige of the *bertsolaritza*. A friend and collaborator of Chaho,[64] d'Abbadie, the son of an Irish woman and a Basque man, developed a keen interest in Basque culture, and from the moment he moved to the Basque country, worked towards the preservation of its language and culture.[65] Similarly to Mistral's Félibrige movement in Provence, d'Abbadie celebrated Euskara as a symbol of Basque identity and was hostile to anti-clericalism and urbanism, but never challenged the authority of the French state.[66] At the banquet on the occasion of the first *fêtes traditionnelles* of Saint-Jean-de-Luz in the 1890s, for example, an ageing d'Abbadie was quoted reminding his fellow diners that: 'In these times where the strength of things tends to mix up all the things of the past, I would like to believe that my dear Basques will draw closer together in order to resist, to a wise extent, this invasion, to preserve intact their language, sentiment of their honour and their faith.'[67] The Basques, d'Abbadie's speech implied, should resist the annihilation of their language and culture, but only as long as they did not threaten the unity of the French nation-state.

The first sung poetry competition, which took place on the occasion of the first *fêtes basques* in Urrugne in August 1853, reflected d'Abbadie's commitment to popularising Basque improvised poetry. In the months prior to the launch of the festival, he worked closely with such fellow scholars as Louis-Lucien Bonaparte and the linguist Jean-Pierre Duvoisin, as well as a number of local churchmen, such as the above-mentioned *abbé* Inchauspé and *curé* Adéma, the *abbé* Maurice Harriet, author of a Basque dictionary published by Louis-Lucien, the Dominican priest Joannateguy and the *abbé* Pierre Haristoy, author of *Les Paroisses du Pays basque pendant la période révolutionnaire* (1895). In a letter to d'Abbadie in June 1853, Harriet made the case for having improvised sung poetry competitions because, he believed, the genre was inherent to Basque people's identity. '[T]he Basque understands feeling and poetry only when he sings,' he wrote. '[I]t is, after all, the privilege of peoples who still possess the simplicity of primitive poetry; they love, they suffer, they feel pleasure through singing. Would it not be the case that the pieces should be in the form of songs?'[68] D'Abbadie agreed. The first *fêtes basques* in Urrugne hosted an improvised sung poetry competition; the theme was the regrets of the Basques leaving for Montevideo and the prize was an ounce of gold and a *makhila*, a traditional Basque stick that was a standard accessory of the Basque man.[69] The *fêtes basques* became extremely popular in the following decades and were held in French Basque villages every summer. While the original aim was the cultivation of Basque culture, they quickly became a lucrative source of tourist consumption, which contributed to the standardisation of clichés of Basque identity. In this respect, the *bertsolaritza* kept Euskara alive but also contributed to turning the Basque country into a 'living museum'.[70]

In 1879, the Asociación Euskara de Navarra exported the *fêtes basques* to Spain. The transition produced two main results. On the one hand, the Spanish Basque country's adoption of the festivals served as a cultural bridge between the seven Basque provinces. From the start, the Asociación committed to the unity of all Basque peoples. It named d'Abbadie and Duvoisin as honorary associates and had the former distribute several awards, including the one for the best improvised poem.[71] Additionally, d'Abbadie decided to alternate the location of the festivals between France and Spain every year, forging ties between the two Basque communities where there were none.[72] On the other hand, once the Spanish Basque country adopted the festivals, the latter acquired a more political dimension, as the *fueristas* regarded them as an emblem of the Basque cultural renaissance that resulted from the abolition of the *fueros*.[73] Officially, the *fiestas* were apolitical events. On the occasion of the *juegos florales* of Bilbao of 1882, for example, the call for essays about the history, law and successes of Euskal Herria excluded any political theme.[74] At the same time, the principal goal of the *fiestas* was the protection of the Basque language and the creation of a Basque literary tradition, which had inevitable political undertones both in France and in Spain. Commenting on the *fiestas euskaras* of San Sebastián in 1889, for example, *Eskualduna* wrote that the Basque country was witnessing a real literary renaissance, which was a patriotic duty to which the French Basques should contribute too. 'A lot of young, intelligent and educated people know the Basque language from birth,' it argued. '[W]hat are they missing in order to produce literary works? Only a little bit of good will.'[75] As Julian Wright has pointed out, regionalist claims possessed an underlying tension between the 'mystique' and the 'politique', between purely cultural concerns and wider anxieties about state reforms and the prosperity of local communities.[76]

The festivals' improvised poetry contests elevated the *bertsolaritza* as a literary genre, as each competition was scored by a panel of judges, raising the quality of the poems and awarding them further recognition in the literary field.[77] While the most famous songs were Spanish Basque, they included in their narrative the French Basques too, strengthening the notion of the Basque country as one cultural community. José María de Iparraguirre and Felipe de Arrese y Beitia, in particular, became emblems of Basqueness in the second half of the nineteenth century. Iparraguirre, who was known as 'the last Basque bard',[78] became famous for his poem in eight stanzas *Guernicaco Arbola* (later *Gernikako Arbola*), which he composed in 1854 to celebrate the legendary Tree of Guernica, an oak tree that symbolised the liberties of the Basque people. The poem perpetuated many of the clichés of Basque identity. First, it attributed a pervasive religiosity to the Basque country. The Tree of Guernica, the poem sang, was a 'blessed' symbol of the Basque country, a 'sacred tree' planted by God himself. Through it, the Basques possessed a special relationship with God, as well as a unique communication channel with the divine. Second, the poem was a rallying cry against the Spanish state's threat to the *fueros*. The fourth stanza, for example, argued that if the assembly of Vizcaya, supported by the four Basque provinces, defended local liberties, the tree would not fall and the Basque people would continue to live in peace. Further, the seventh stanza sang that the Basques 'do not desire war; / we wish to live in peace with our wise, free and beloved laws'. Third, the poem celebrated the unity of the four Spanish Basque provinces: 'the four of us' in the text.[79] Although the song dealt specifically with the Spanish Basque situation, it became the unofficial national anthem of the Basque country on both sides of the Pyrenees. At the Congress of Basque Tradition in Saint-Jean-de-Luz in 1897, for instance, the fanfare played the song on the first day of the event, ahead of the inaugural speech by Louis de Fourcaud, the spokesman for the French minister of public instruction.[80]

Arrese y Beitia's *Ama Euskeriari azken agurrak (Goodbye to Mother Euskara)*, which won the first prize at the *bertsolari* contest of the first *fiestas euskaras* of Elizondo in 1879, similarly reflected the Spanish Basque country's struggle at the end of the nineteenth century but included the French Basque country too. Together with perpetuating the myths of Basque Iberianism and Basque Cantabrianism, it conceptualised the idea of the Basque country as the combination of all seven Basque provinces: Vizcaya, Álava and Guipúzcoa were the original three, he wrote, with the addition of Navarra, as well as the three French Basque provinces, 'our brothers'. The poem responded to the alleged impending disappearance of the Basque nation after the abolition of the Spanish Basque *fueros*, but its emphasis on Euskara as the essence of Basqueness resonated with the French Basques as well. Referring to Euskara, the verses between the first and the second stanzas sang: 'Mother, you are going to die! / What a wretched feeling it is to see our beloved land Castilianised.' The loss of Basque liberties, the poem continued, was to be imputed to the Basques themselves, because they had not loved their language enough. 'If Euskara had been better protected, our pure and wonderful customs would still live among us,' it cried. One could not hope to preserve the *fueros* without the Basque language, it concluded. If Euskara ceased to exist, the Basques could bid farewell to their liberties.[81] The elegy reflected Basque intellectuals' view that the survival of the Basque country was under threat because the Basque population preferred French and Spanish to Euskara and was not doing enough to protect its language and build a literary tradition that would provide a solid basis for the Basque nation.

Basque culture at the service of France

While some European scholars argued that the only way of providing new life and dignity to such minority languages as Basque and Breton in the nineteenth century was to 'entrust them to the glorious cenotaphs of science',[82] Basque intellectuals believed that tradition could not be simply a token of the past; it had to be embraced as an inherent part of contemporary Basque identity in order to justify the existence of the Basque nation. In 1887, for example, the *abbé* Adéma deplored the fact that foreigners seemed more interested than locals in the preservation of Basque culture and language. While the Basques were lucky to still possess their folkloric *fêtes*, he argued, they should do more to cultivate the Basque language, as Euskara was the real defender of tradition. He wrote in *Eskualduna*:

> Gentlemen, let us defend our populations so proud of their ancient integrity, let us defend them against this modernism that diminishes and degrades their character. Let us watch over the children of our race to make sure they do not degenerate and degrade themselves as a result of their abandonment or ignorance of the Basque language. Let us greet each other in Basque; let us write in Basque; let us encourage the publication of anything that honours this noble language.[83]

Gustave Boucher, the general secretary of the Société d'ethnographie nationale et d'art populaire that sponsored the Congress of Basque Tradition, similarly encouraged the local population to cherish their traditions as part of their Basque identity during his talk at the congress in 1897. 'Never forget that you are Basques,' he told the public. 'In all circumstances, you should think, act and speak in Basque; your games, your dances are yours; your music, your theatre, your literature, everything is Basque. It is not a provisional and artificial reconstruction; it is your spontaneous, everyday life.'[84] At the end of the nineteenth century, then, local *savants* attributed a militant character to Euskara as the protector of Basque tradition from administrative centralisation and cultural uniformity.

In order to legitimise the Basque country's existence within Third-Republic France, Basque intellectuals, similarly to the *fueristas* in Spain,[85] embraced the idea of France as the sum of its regions. According to the notion of unity-in-diversity, adopted by both the right and the left in the last third of the century, the *petite patrie* was not an impediment to national unity but a necessary first step towards the development of national patriotism.[86] Love of the *petite patrie*, in this respect, needed to be fostered in order to engender love of the *grande patrie*. The goal of the Société d'ethnographie, for example, Boucher argued, was 'to react as much as possible against the unification of mores and manners that becomes every day more complete', 'to encourage respect for the thousand objects of local life that have an original character' and 'to popularise the idioms, the songs, the dances, the legends, the music [and] the literature of each province through exhibitions, representations [and] conferences'.[87] Regional culture, Basque intellectuals added, was not a threat to the unity of the nation. Instead, being both French and Basque was convenient to both sides. In February 1902, for example, *Eskualduna* reproduced an article from *La Dépêche* that set out regionalists' demands in the realm of primary education. They did not ask for much, they stated: they only wished to have one hour per week dedicated to 'the teaching of the *petite patrie*', which meant studying its history, historical monuments and, in the case of the Basques, their language. This small addition to the school curriculum, the newspaper argued, would benefit both the *petite patrie* and the *grande patrie*. 'This teaching, far from harming French unity, will strengthen it by providing it with a more solid basis,' it pointed out. 'By first having learnt to love his village and his region, the young Frenchman will learn to love France better.'[88] *Eskualduna* mirrored the claims of such regionalists as Jean Charles-Brun, the founder of the Fédération régionaliste française in 1900, and the conservative intellectual Maurice Barrès, a pro-federalist republican, in arguing that their demands were not reactionary.[89] Rather, the newspaper maintained that it was committed to economic and social progress and hence to the 'grandeur de la France', but that this was possible only if the country was not suffocated by centralisation.[90] As the next chapter will show, while the patriotic pedagogy of the Third Republic, as Thiesse and Jean-François Chanet have argued, included an appreciation for France's regional diversity,[91] it also regarded such regional languages as Basque, Breton and Flemish as impediments to national unity. Such a paradox resulted in a constant dualism between the cultural and political roles of the *petites patries* vis-à-vis the *grande*.

The Congress of Basque Tradition that opened in Saint-Jean-de-Luz in August 1897 reflected such tension. The congress was the second of its kind after an inaugural event had taken place in Niort to celebrate tradition of Poitou and Charentes the previous year. The purpose, the historian Gaston Paris explained at the Sorbonne in 1895, was to restore the national genius, after the defeat of Sedan of 1870, through a celebration of France's regional diversity.[92] From the start, there was an underlying dichotomy between the cultural and the political, which became evident the following year when the congress opened in Saint-Jean-de-Luz. The republican government that supported the event and Basque *savants* had quite different understandings of the idea of France as the sum of its regions. For the French historian Louis de Fourcaud, who was representing Rambaud, the minister of public instruction, at the event, there was a clear distinction between what he called 'intellectual decentralisation' and political 'separatism'. 'We should never let anyone insinuate that intellectual decentralisation could be anywhere, at any time and in any way a form of separatism,' he said during his inaugural address. Basque culture, he added, was an essential part of France and, without its regional diversity, the country would lose its spark and become weaker, more boring and less authentic. At the same time, the cultivation of regional cultures should not have a self-serving purpose. Rather, it was meant to serve the greater good of France and to reveal its full potential when put at the service of the *grande patrie*. He claimed:

> I compare the provinces to different families, collateral or allied, equal in rights and duties, showing solidarity among themselves, inseparably united by an essential bond. In the same way that every family has its name and traditions, its heritage and, so to speak, its appearance, each province has its personality, its means, its resources, its inheritance. Each one has its particularism and all together they are absorbed into the indivisible nation. The nation is not so to the exclusion of others, but is in each individual and simultaneously in all. So is formed an indissoluble organism.

Thus, 'effective decentralisation', he concluded, meant to increase national patriotism and the utility of each region for the nation. '[T]he more you will be Basques, the better you will be French,' he told the crowd. 'You will work with your entire soul towards the advancement of your province. You will provide France – *la douce France*, as the poets of our *chansons de geste* referred to her – with some original elements.'[93]

Fourcaud's speech reflected the position of the republican left, which believed in the key Revolutionary principle of France as one and indivisible. Over the course of the nineteenth century, republicans had come to embrace the value of the country's regional cultures but thought that the only reason for their existence was to be at the service of the nation. Like the radical Revolutionaries of the 1790s, the republican left of the Third Republic disliked the notion of federalism, as they believed that France was more than the sum of its regions. What made it *la grande nation*, the likes of Ernest Renan and Léon Gambetta argued, was that it was based both on a shared past and on men's will to live together and work for the greatness of the country.[94] France, in other words, was not a geographical accident but the realisation of predestined civic genius.[95]

Basque scholars at the congress agreed on the basic principles of Fourcaud's position, insofar as they rejected separatism and believed in the need for France's moral regeneration after 1870. However, they understood unity-in-diversity in conservative terms that mirrored Barrès's federalist stance. Rather than viewing France's 'moral unity' as a combination of a shared history and of a social contract, as left-wing republicans did, they regarded it as the result of common heritage and of the environment, or region, in which people lived: *la terre et les morts*.[96] While Fourcaud placed the emphasis on the abstract unity of the French nation, then, local scholars stressed the concrete significance of the Basque region. In his summary of Fourcaud's speech, for example, Boucher argued: 'Yes, we are all French [and] we love the *grande patrie, la douce France* of the *chansons de geste*; but to love and understand her best, let us all love our *petite patrie*.'[97] While the words that the two men used were almost identical, Fourcaud's emphasis was on being Basque in order to become French, while Boucher stressed the importance of remaining Basque in order to love France. In his own paraphrasing of Fourcaud, moreover, Planté, in his speech on whether or not the Basques had a history, was even more explicit about the importance of preserving Basque identity for the future of the Basque country. He exhorted the Basques to preserve their traditions, by having Fourcaud say: 'Be aware of your traditions. Preserving the teachings of the ancestors is not to return to the past! The more you will be Basque, the more you will be French.' If the Basques continued to love the Basque country, he concluded, they were never going to die.[98] Regionalist scholars, then, rejected left-wing republicans' idea that the French nation should be rebuilt on unity and centralisation. Rather, they made use of the literary and folkloric tradition that was invented in the earlier nineteenth century to maintain that France's moral regeneration could only succeed through the rebuilding of a cult of the ancestors and of provincial tradition.

Conclusion

Western Europeans' preservation of national heritage occurred at the expense of weaker or stateless nations, because stronger nations such as Britain, France and Germany found validation of their historical grandeur in the slow demise of nations without a written literary history. Basque elites were aware of such cultural hierarchy and wary of the fact that outsiders were more interested than locals in the preservation of Basque language and culture. Foreigners, they believed, had the merit of reviving Basque history but treated the Basque country as a heritage site whose value rested exclusively in its past. As a result, local *savants* attempted to produce a literary tradition that would keep the Basque language alive and validate their demands for regional autonomy. As the Basques possessed a limited written tradition, they emphasised the significance of folk literature as the cultural essence of the nation. In this respect, as historians have pointed out, the phrase 'Basque popular literature' became a 'pigeon-holing of anything that has not fitted into the classification of written literature'.[99]

The invention of a Basque literary tradition produced two paradoxical results. On the one hand, it created a transnational Basque culture that the French Basques used within their own national context. The Basque opus strengthened the ties between the French and the Spanish Basque countries, as scholars from the two sides of the Pyrenees worked closely together, imitated each other's artistic productions and, through culture, supported each other's political struggles. The motto 'zazpiak bat', 'the seven [Basque provinces] are one', was born out of the Basques' concerted literary renaissance in the nineteenth century. At the same time, French Basque intellectuals, like their Spanish Basque counterparts, were not seeking separatism. Rather, they regarded the creation of a transnational Basque literary culture as a way of strengthening their position within the French nation. On the other hand, local *savants* celebrated Basque culture as a symbol of the liveliness of the Basque nation but did so in standardised ways that contributed to the creation of Basque cultural stereotypes. The popular *jeux floraux*, in particular, represented regionalists' commitment to the protection of local cultures vis-à-vis state centralisation and a celebration of France's unity-in-diversity. Pride of the culture of the *petite patrie*, local *savants* argued, was essential to foster French citizens' love of the *grande patrie*. In the midst of the celebrations of Basque culture as an essential aspect of French culture, though, Basque tradition was safely kept on display, where it could do no harm to the unity of the nation.

Notes

1 Adrien Planté, 'Les Basques, ont-ils une histoire?', in Gustave Boucher (ed.), *La Tradition au Pays basque* (Paris, 1899), 136–7.
2 Swenson, *The Rise of Heritage*, 334; Astrid Swenson, 'The Law's Delay? Preservation Legislation in France, Germany and England, 1870–1914', in Melanie Hall (ed.), *Towards World Heritage: International Origins of the Preservation Movement, 1870–1930* (Farnham, 2011), 147.
3 *Eskualduna*, 1 October 1887: 'un peuple sans presque pas d'histoire … les monuments de notre passé … on voudrait nous conserver comme un prodigieux monument historique et philologique.'
4 Benoît Mihail, *Le Passé flamand de la France et sa redécouverte de l'époque romantique au régime de Vichy* (Charleroi, 2006).
5 Gerson, *The Pride of Place*, 136.
6 Molina Aparicio, 'La disputada cronología de la nacionalidad'; Molina Aparicio, 'España no era tan diferente'; Agirreazkuenaga, *The Making of the Basque Question*.

7 Nicole Boivin and Michael D. Frachetti, 'Introduction: Archaeology and the "People Without History"', in Nicole Boivin and Michael D. Frachetti (eds), *Globalization in Prehistory: Contact, Exchange, and the 'People Without History'* (Cambridge, 2018), 1–2.

8 Augustin Chaho, *Biarritz entre les Pyrénées et l'océan. Itinéraire pittoresque*, Volume 2 (Bayonne, 1855), 2.

9 Planté, 'Les Basques, ont-ils une histoire?', 112: 'Les Basques sont comme les femmes honnêtes: ils n'ont pas d'histoire.'

10 Frederick M. Barnard, *Herder on Nationality, Humanity, and History* (Montreal, 2003), 161; Swenson, *The Rise of Heritage*, 334.

11 Arturo Campión, 'Amaya ó los bascos en el siglo VIII. Estudio crítico', *Revista Euskara*, 3 (1880), 54: 'Cada vez que en nuestra noble y desgraciada Pátria Euskara se produce una obra literaria, revive en mi corazon alguna amortiguada esperanza … guardadoras de tradiciones, vengadoras de injusticias, y nérvio y sávia de invencibles reivindicaciones'.

12 Stephen Bann, *The Clothing of Clio: A Study of the Representation of History in Nineteenth-Century Britain and France* (Cambridge, 1984), 2 and 165.

13 Richard Bauman and Charles L. Briggs, *Voices of Modernity: Language Ideologies and the Politics of Inequality* (Cambridge, 2003), 143; Jean-Pierre Babelon and André Chastel, *La Notion de patrimoine* (Paris, 1994), 79.

14 Hermilio Olóriz, 'El romance en Euskaria', *Revista Euskara*, 1 (1878), 99: 'es el metro en que el pueblo ha llorado sus desgracias y cantado sus glorias y sus mitos … En sus páginas vive el alma de una raza, en ellas nos describe sus costumbres y sus sentimientos.'

15 See Ian Haywood, *The Making of History: A Study of the Literary Forgeries of James MacPherson and Thomas Chatterton in Relation to Eighteenth-Century Ideas of History and Fiction* (London and Toronto, 1986), 11.

16 See Jon Juaristi, 'El Cantar de Beotibar, ¿un romance noticiero vasco?', *Anuario del Seminario de filología vasca 'Julio De Urquijo'*, 20:3 (1986), 845–56.

17 Juaristi, *El linaje de Aitor*, 53.

18 Wilhelm von Humboldt, 'Berichtungen und Zusätze zum ersten Abschnitte des zweyten Bandes des Mithridates über die Cantabrische oder Baskische Sprache', in Johann Christoph Adelung, *Mithridates oder allgemeine Sprachenkunde mit dem Vater Unser als Sprachprobe in bey nahe fünf hundert Sprachen und Mundarten* (Berlin, 1817), 351–6.

19 Claude Fauriel, *Histoire de la Gaule méridionale sous la domination des conquérants Germains*, Volume 2 (Paris, 1836), 354: 'un chant

de montagnard, un vrai chant primitif, où l'art en est encore aux plus simples inspirations de la nature'.
20 See, for example, Michel, *Le Pays basque*, 231.
21 Haywood, *The Making of History*, 47.
22 [Eugène Garay de Monglave], 'Canto de Altobiscar', Hermilio Olóriz ed., *Revista Euskara*, 1 (1878), 31: 'Bat! Ez da bihiric aghertzcen ghehiago. / Akhabo da.'
23 Jean-François Bladé, *Dissertation sur les chants héroïques des Basques* (Paris, 1866), 9 and 18–19.
24 [Garay de Monglave], 'Canto de Altobiscar', Hermilio Olóriz ed., 28: 'grito de independencia en el que se siente palpitar el noble é indomable espíritu de la raza euskara, ese himno sagrado de nuestras montañas, sencillo y grandioso como las más sublimes concepciones Homéricas.'
25 Bauman and Briggs, *Voices of Modernity*, 143.
26 Arturo Campión, *Orreaga (Roncesvalles). Balada escrita en el dialecto guipuzcoano* (Pamplona, 1880), 8 and 19: 'Nuestro canto nacional'; 'Ese estruendo es el canto de guerra de Basconia, y hoy es el último dia de nuestra gloria.'
27 Ibid., 20: 'Ya no hay extranjeros en Basconia'.
28 Francisque Michel, 'Basque Popular Poetry', *The Gentleman's Magazine*, 5 (1858), 381–3.
29 Michel's main target was George Henry Burrow, who wrote that the Basques possessed a plethora of songs but no real poetry. As such, he regarded the Basques as a nation without popular poetry. See George Henry Burrow, *The Bible in Spain* (Champaign, [1843] 1996), 224–8.
30 Michel, 'Basque Popular Poetry', 381 and 383.
31 Agirreazkuenaga, *The Making of the Basque Question*, 49.
32 Chaho made reference to Aïtor also in *Voyage en Navarre* and in *Histoire primitive*, but in *Ariel* in 1845 he wrote down the whole legend for the first time.
33 *Ariel*, 5 January 1845: 'un Barde inconnu de Cantabrie'.
34 Augustin Chaho, *La Légende d'Aïtor*, Hector Iglesias ed. (Saint-Denis, [1845] 2017), 22: 'le grand ancêtre, le patriarche, le père de la race Indo-Atlantique, et le premier né des Euskariens'.
35 Juaristi, *El linaje de Aitor*, 96–7.
36 José Javier López Antón, *Escritores carlistas en la cultura vasca* (Pamplona, 1999), 87.
37 Francisco Navarro Villoslada, *Amaya o los vascos en el siglo VIII*, Volume 3 (Madrid, 1879), 406: 'nuestro padre Aitor quiere que todos sus hijos reconozcan la ley de Cristo.'
38 Ibid., 402: 'Pájaro de dulce canto, / cántame así de contíno. / Más desdichada que yo, / nadie en el mundo ha nacido. / Perdí á mi madre,

perdí / mi hogar, mi valle nativo... / ¡Nunca, nunca cesarán / de llorar los ojos mios!' Chaho's original stanza was slightly different: 'Oiseau, joli chanteur, chante doucement. Il n'est pas né à ce monde d'autre infortuné que moi. J'étais parti de la vallée natale, et à ce souvenir mes pleurs, qui coulent, ne s'arrêtent point.' See Chaho's original in *Ariel*, 5 January 1845.

39 Stephen Bann, 'History as Romance and History as Atonement: Nineteenth-Century Images from Britain and France', in Stefan Berger, Chris Lorenz and Billie Melman, *Popularizing National Pasts: 1800 to the Present* (New York and London, 2012), 58.
40 Juaristi, *El linaje de Aitor*, 117.
41 Augustin Chaho, 'La leyenda de Aitor', *Revista Euskara*, 1 (1878), 220–30, 241–49 and 281–92.
42 Marianne Heiberg, *The Making of the Basque Nation* (Cambridge, 1989), 48.
43 Campión, 'Amaya', 121: 'los eternos defensores del suelo nacional'.
44 G. Olivier, 'Chants populaires', *Dictionnaire de la conversation et de la lecture*, Volume 13 (Paris, 1834), 14: 'le fils le plus dévoué de la patrie, qui en revêt les mœurs, en garde les coutumes, et se fait l'arche dépositaire de ses plus précieux souvenirs.'
45 Louis Spach, 'Chants populaires', *Encyclopédie des gens du monde*, Volume 5 (1835), 417: 'Chanter, c'est vivre'.
46 Michel, *Le Pays basque*, 211: 'A la différence de la poésie qui naît de la littérature, elle s'inspire par la réalité. Ses productions ont un intérêt historique et pour ainsi dire psychologique; elles révèlent les aventures privées d'un peuple, les allures de son caractère, les attitudes de son esprit: ce sont des mémoires, ou plutôt des confessions, dans lesquelles il s'épanche sans réserve.'
47 Natalie Morel-Borotra, 'Le Chant et l'identification culturelle des Basques (1800–1950)', *Lapurdum*, 5 (2000), 355.
48 Spach, 'Chants populaires', 418: 'la moisson serait plus riche qu'on ne pense ... Les montagnes sont les dépositaires fidèles des vieilles traditions.'
49 Morel-Borotra, 'Le Chant et l'identification culturelle des Basques', 355.
50 Gerson, *The Pride of Place*, 27; Gildea, *The Past in French History*, 200–1 and 208–9.
51 *Eskualduna*, 15 March 1887: 'défenseur passionné de toutes les vieilles traditions du pays ... cruellement ... un gouvernement stable'.
52 Estéban Obanos et al., 'Asociacion Euskara de Navarra. Programa', *Revista Euskara*, 1 (1878), 3–4: 'conservar y propagar la lengua, literatura é historia vasco-navarras, estudiar su legislación y procurar cuanto tienda al bienestar moral y material del país'.

53 *Eskualduna*, 1 October 1887: 'cœurs atrophiés, et des intelligences dépourvues de toute idée patriotique et de tout noble ressort'.
54 Michel, *Le Pays basque*; Julien Vinson, *Le Folk-lore du Pays basque* (Paris, 1883); Wentworth Webster, *Basque Legends* (London, 1877); J.-D.-J. Sallaberry, *Chants populaires du Pays basque* (Bayonne, 1870); José António Santesteban, *Colección de aires vascongados para canto y piano* (San Sebastián, 1878); José Manterola, *Cancionero vasco. Poesías en lengua euskara*, Volume 1 (San Sebastián, 1877); José María de Goizueta, *Leyendas vascongadas* (Madrid, 1851); Juan V. Araquistain, *Tradiciones Vasco-Cántabras* (Tolosa, 1866).
55 Michel, *Le Pays basque*, 29: 'expression intime de l'esprit d'une nation'.
56 Wentworth Webster, 'Les Pastorales basques', in Gustave Boucher (ed.), *La Tradition au Pays basque* (Paris, 1899), 243–4: 'elles ont aussi conservé la mémoire et la tradition toute populaire des grandes légendes et romances, des chansons de geste, des romans de chevalerie, des poèmes épiques du moyen âge'.
57 Araquistain, *Tradiciones Vasco-Cántabras*, 14: 'los tres mas grandes y puros sentimientos de la humanidad, el amor de Dios, el amor à la familia, el amor à la patria'.
58 Eric Storm and Joep Leerssen, 'Introduction', in Joep Leerssen and Eric Storm (eds), *World Fairs and the Global Moulding of National Identities* (Leiden and Boston, 2022), 1.
59 Joxerra Garzia, Jon Sarasua and Andoni Egaña, *The Art of Bertsolaritza: Improvised Basque Verse Singing* (San Sebastián, 2001), 17 and 19; On Brittany, see Thiesse, *Écrire la France*, 41.
60 David Hopkin, 'Regionalism and Folklore', in Xosé M. Núñez Seixas and Eric Storm (eds), *Identity Construction and Movements from 1890 to the Present Day* (London, 2018), 44.
61 Agirreazkuenaga, *The Making of the Basque Question*, 222.
62 *Ariel*, 6 October 1844: 'le don de l'improvisation poétique'.
63 *Ariel*, 27 April 1845: 'une langue vierge et savante'; 'les chants de ses bardes improvisateurs ... des monuments plus indestructibles ... les dernières harmonies d'un monde détruit. Une statue exhumée des ruines est un monument du passé'.
64 Chaho and d'Abbadie co-wrote a philological text. See Antoine d'Abbadie and Augustin Chaho, *Études grammaticales sur la langue euskarienne* (Paris, 1836).
65 Chauvirey, *La Vie quotidienne au Pays basque*, 138–9.
66 Philippe Martel, 'Le Félibrige', in Pierre Nora (ed.), *Les Lieux de mémoire*, Volume 3 (Paris, 1997), 3515 and 3523; Gildea, *The Past in French History*, 208.
67 Charles Petit, 'Antoine d'Abbadie', in Gustave Boucher (ed.), *La Tradition au Pays basque* (Paris, 1899), 557: 'En ces temps où la force des

choses tend à mêler toutes les choses du passé, il me plaît de croire que mes chers Basques se serreront les uns contre les autres pour résister, dans une sage mesure, à cet envahissement, pour conserver intacte leur langue, sentiment de l'honneur et de leur foi.'

68 Quoted in Morel-Borotra, 'Le Chant et l'identification culturelle des Basques', 357: 'le Basque n'entend du sentiment et de la poésie qu'autant qu'il en chante; c'est du reste le privilège des peuples qui en sont encore à la naïveté de la poésie primitive; ils aiment, ils souffrent, ils jouissent en chantant. Ne faudrait-il pas que les pièces fussent des chansons?'
69 *Le Courrier de Bayonne*, 4 September 1853 and 8 September 1853.
70 Ahedo Gurrutxaga, *The Transformation of National Identity in the Basque Country of France*, 41.
71 Comisión de fiestas euskaras, 'Elizondoco Bestac/Fiestas euskaras de Elizondo', *Revista Euskara*, 2 (1879), 155–6.
72 Jean Haritschelhar, 'The Eighteenth and Nineteenth Centuries: Bridges across Borders', in Mari Jose Olaziregi (ed.), *Basque Literary History* (Reno, 2012), 127.
73 Agirreazkuenaga, *The Making of the Basque Question*, 224.
74 Arellano de Galarza et al., 'Fiestas euskaras de Bilbao', *Revista Euskara*, 5 (1882), 118.
75 *Eskualduna*, 28 January 1889: 'Beaucoup de jeunes gens intelligents et instruits connaissent de naissance la langue basque; que leur manque-t-il pour produire des travaux littéraires? Un peu de bonne volonté seulement.'
76 Wright, *The Regionalist Movement in France*, 43.
77 Agirreazkuenaga, *The Making of the Basque Question*, 223.
78 Juaristi, *El linaje de Aitor*, 99.
79 José Maria de Iparraguirre, 'Gernikako Arbola', *Revista Euskara*, 2 (1879), 18–19: 'bedeinkatuá ... Arbola Santua ... Gerrarik nay ez degu, / Pakea betiko, / Gure lege zuzenak / Emen maitatzeko. ... Laurok'.
80 Gustave Boucher, 'Les fêtes', in Gustave Boucher (ed.), *La Tradition au Pays basque* (Paris, 1899), 18.
81 Felipe de Arrese y Beitia, 'Ama Euskeriari azken agurrak', *Revista Euskara*, 2 (1879), 238–43: 'Amatcho, zuaz illtzera! / Zorigaistuan negargarri-ta / Dot sendimendu andia, / Guere lur maite dakustalako / Gaztelatu-ta jarria'; 'Izan bagiña eurak legetche / Euskeriaren zaliak, / ¡ Oso ta garbi gordeko ziran / Oitura aiñ miragarriak!'
82 Adolphe Mazure, *Histoire du Béarn et du Pays basque* (Pau, 1839), 509–12: 'les confier aux glorieux cénotaphes de la science'.
83 *Eskualduna*, 8 October 1887: 'Messieurs, défendons nos populations jadis si fières de leur vieille intégrité, défendons-les contre ce modernisme qui abaisse et avilit leur caractère. Veillons à ce que les enfants de notre

race ne dégénèrent et ne se dégradent par l'abandon ou l'ignorance de la langue basque. ... Saluons-nous en basque; écrivons en basque; encourageons tout ce qui se publie à l'honneur de cette noble langue.'
84 M. Bernadou, 'Compte rendu des fêtes de la tradition basque à Saint-Jean-de-Luz', in Gustave Boucher (ed.), *La Tradition au Pays basque* (Paris, 1899), 55: 'Jamais vous n'oubliez que vous êtes Basques. Dans toutes les circonstances vous pensez, vous agissez, vous parlez en Basque; vos jeux, vos danses sont vôtres; votre musique, votre théâtre, votre littérature, tout est basque. Et il ne s'agit pas là d'une reconstitution provisoire et factice, mais de votre vie quotidienne et spontanée.'
85 Molina, 'España no era tan diferente'.
86 Gerson, *The Pride of Place*, 228–9; Thiesse, *Ils Apprenaient la France*, 8.
87 Bernadou, 'Compte rendu', 12: 'réagir dans la mesure du possible contre l'unification chaque jour plus complète des mœurs et des modes ... inciter au respect pour les mille objets de la vie locale ayant un caractère d'originalité ... faire connaître par des expositions, des représentations, des conférences, les parlers, les chansons, les danses, les légendes, la musique, la littérature de chaque province'.
88 *Eskualduna*, 21 February 1902: 'l'enseignement de la petite patrie ... Cet enseignement, loin de nuire à l'unité française, ne ferait que la fortifier en lui donnant une base plus solide. Pour avoir appris à aimer davantage son village et sa région, le jeune Français apprendra à mieux aimer la France.'
89 Wright, *The Regionalist Movement in France*, 28; Gildea, *The Past in French History*, 179.
90 *Eskualduna*, 21 February 1902.
91 Thiesse, *Ils Apprenaient la France*; Jean-François Chanet, *L'École républicaine et les petites patries* (Paris, 1996).
92 Gaston Paris, 'Discours prononcé à la Sorbonne le 24 mars 1895', in *La Tradition en Poitou et en Charentes: art populaire, ethnographie, folk-lore, hagiographie, histoire. Société d'ethnographie nationale et d'art populaire, Congrès de Niort* (Paris, 1897), iii–vii.
93 Louis de Fourcaud, 'Discours prononcé à Saint-Jean-de-Luz à l'occasion de l'ouverture du Congrès de la tradition basque', in Gustave Boucher (ed.), *La Tradition au Pays basque* (Paris, 1899), 4–7: 'Ne laissons jamais insinuer que la décentralisation intellectuelle puisse être nulle part, à aucun moment, en aucune mesure, une façon de séparatisme'; 'Je compare les provinces à des familles distinctes, collatérales ou alliées, égales en droits et en devoirs, solidaires entre elles, indissolublement unies par un lien essentiel. De même que chaque famille a son nom et ses traditions, son patrimoine et, pour ainsi parler, ses allures, chaque

province a sa personnalité, ses ressorts, ses ressources, ses hérédités. Chacune se particularise et toutes s'absorbent dans l'indivisible nation. Pas une n'est la nation à l'exclusion des autres, mais la nation est à la fois en toutes et en chacune. Tel s'affirme un organisme inviolable en soi'; 'décentralisation efficace'; 'plus vous serez Basques, mieux vous serez Français. Vous travaillerez selon votre âme entière à l'avancement de votre province. Vous fournirez à la France – la *douce France*, comme parlaient les poètes de nos chansons de geste – des éléments originaux.' Partial translation in Ahedo Gurrutxaga, *The Transformation of National Identity*, 21–2.

94 Léon Gambetta, 'Discours prononcés le 1er octobre 1872 à La Roche et à Annecy', in *Discours et plaidoyers politiques de M. Gambetta*, Volume 3, Joseph Reinach ed. (Paris, 1881), 168–70; Ernest Renan, *Qu'est-ce qu'une Nation?*, Philippe Forest ed. (Paris, 1991), 38–9.

95 Girardet, *Mythes et mythologies politiques*, 156–7; Thiesse, *Ils Apprenaient la France*, 4–5; Gerson, *The Pride of Place*, 230.

96 Gildea, *The Past in French History*, 179–80.

97 Bernadou, 'Compte rendu', 20: 'Oui, tous soyons Français, aimons la grande patrie, *la doulce France* des chansons de geste; mais pour la mieux aimer et comprendre, aimons chacun notre petite patrie.'

98 Planté, 'Les Basques, ont-ils une histoire?', 136–7: 'Prenez conscience de vos traditions. Garder les leçons de ses ancêtres, ce n'est pas revenir en arrière! Plus vous serez Basques, plus vous serez Français.'

99 Garzia, Sarasua and Egaña, *The Art of Bertsolaritza*, 15.

6

Euskara or challenges to the French nation

In 1836, the sub-prefect of Bayonne wrote to the *conseil d'arrondissement*, arguing that while Euskara awarded a 'picturesque' character to the Basque country, it also isolated 'a portion of the population from the big family' and caused 'problems from a political and economic standpoint'. He wanted teachers to use French in schools and priests to alternate the two languages in church but, he complained, such an achievement seemed impossible because the *comités d'arrondissement* that were to supervise the schooling system existed only on paper and 'the interest of the Church does not always agree with that of the *pays*'.[1] The sub-prefect's letter was revealing of the difficulties nineteenth-century provincial authorities encountered in the Basque country – as among other linguistic minorities in France – when they tried to reconcile the state's commitment to the propagation of French in the countryside with the complex local realities that revolved around economies of subsistence, archaic traditions and popular religiosity.

The language question was a primary legacy of the French Revolution and resulted from three unresolved issues that defined the relationship between the French state and the Basque country in the nineteenth century. First was the question of national unity and the extent to which Euskara hindered the creation of a unitary national identity. Second was the problem of education. French was associated with notions of enlightenment and progress, which were key for the creation of citizens and patriots, while regional languages like Euskara were linked to backwardness, superstition and national disunity. Finally, the religious conflict remained unresolved. Although the Concordat of 1801 reconciled the rift the Revolution had created between Paris and Rome, declaring Catholicism the religion of the majority of the French until the separation of Church and state in 1905, after the Revolutionary decade such linguistic minorities as the Basques, the Bretons and the Flemish associated the safeguarding of local languages with the perpetuation of a Catholic tradition, as they perceived the clergy to be the defender of local cultures against state centralisation.[2]

The Revolutionaries started to depict Euskara as an obstacle to the Basque country's integration into the nation during the radical phase of the Revolution, when the Convention made language central to the national identity of France. Such an idea of French nation was new. Before then, the *ancien-régime* monarchy had periodically attempted to impose French on the elites but had never forced it upon the population as a whole,[3] and, at the beginning of the Revolution, moderate Revolutionaries remained sympathetic to linguistic plurality. Starting in 1792, however, the Convention came to see multilingualism as an impediment to national unity and patriotism. The main proponent of linguistic uniformity was the *abbé* Grégoire who, two years later, presented the chamber with an influential report on the languages of France, in which he deplored the fact that almost a fifth of the population of France – about six million people – did not understand French and argued for the need to extirpate all *patois*. Two main ideas of the *Rapport Grégoire* proved especially influential. On the one hand, he characterised French as a superior language on account of it being the language of liberty, the Revolution and the Republic. In turn, he associated regional tongues with administrative chaos, religious fanaticism and feudalism. On the other, he claimed that the universalisation of French was key for people to understand and obey the laws and for spreading the republican credo. Multilingualism, instead, he claimed, hindered the smooth administration of the Republic, as had happened in the Basque country in 1792, where 'a great number [of Basques] was susceptible to fanaticism because the [Basque] language was an obstacle to the propagation of enlightened ideas'.[4] The association of Euskara with religious fanaticism led the *représentants en mission* of the Comité de salut public to engage in violent acts of retaliation against the Basque population during the Terror of 1793–94.

From Thermidor until the 1880s, the relationship between the French state and the Basque country in matters of language and religion was benign. Although the Basques, like the Flemish and the Bretons, regarded Catholicism as a means of protecting their independence vis-à-vis state intrusion,⁵ until the 1880s the Basque clergy were not openly defiant of state authority and, except for a few skirmishes between religious and secular *instituteurs*, language was hardly a battleground between the Church and state officials. This was to an extent the result of more tolerant policies toward linguistic minorities, as the regimes that followed the First Republic were committed to the diffusion of French but were not seeking to achieve linguistic uniformity.⁶

Conflict over linguistic pluralism re-emerged in the 1880s when the Third Republic began to promote linguistic homogeneity to put an end to the influence of the Church over education and to create a unitary, secular, French-speaking, republican nation. In the Basque country, the Loi Ferry of 1882 that eliminated religious instruction from public schools and the imposition of French-taught catechism in 1903 especially exacerbated the conflict. As the Basque clergy refused, to an extent, to comply with state measures, Basque conservatives associated Euskara with Catholicism, as they regarded the Church as the defender of tradition and local culture against centralisation, secularisation and the forces of 'modernity'. Importantly, Catholic ultraconservatives were a relative minority in the Basque country and electoral results did not always reflect the alleged conservatism of the Basques. Republicans, for example, won the local elections of 1886, prompting the pro-republican newspaper *Le Réveil basque* to conclude that the Basques were not 'as refractory to ideas of liberty and progress' as too many argued.⁷ Catholic ultraconservatives, though, were extremely influential in perpetuating the conservative definition of Basque identity that had originated in the French Revolution and, in the nineteenth century, had been cultivated by conservatives and liberals alike. As a result, the conflict over the role of language and religion in the school curriculum at the turn of the twentieth century defined the relationship between the French state and the Basque country. It reinforced a conservative definition of Basque identity that had originated in the French Revolution, founded upon the tenets of language, religion and ancestry.

'Fanaticism speaks Basque'

Euskara became synonymous with religious fanaticism for the first time during the radical phase of the French Revolution. The deputy

Bertrand Barère, in his *Rapport du Comité de Salut Public sur les idiomes* of year II (1794), associated counterrevolutionary stereotypes with linguistic minorities, famously claiming: 'Federalism and superstition speak Bas-Breton; emigration and hatred of the Republic speak German; counterrevolution speaks Italian and fanaticism speaks Basque.'[8] While all these 'inferior' languages perpetuated 'the reign of fanaticism and superstition', he argued, Euskara was the worst because the Basques had priests who 'use their idiom to fanaticise them; but they ignore the French language, and the language of the laws of the Republic'.[9] For Barère, as for Grégoire, the national language was a means of legal and moral education against the obscurantism perpetuated by the Catholic Church.

Although the Basques possessed a profound religious tradition, however, the accusations of fanaticism were to a large extent an overreaction. On the one hand, the Basque country did not witness active and armed resistance as the Vendée did. Rather, both the Basque clergy and the local population engaged in acts of passive resistance that caused little disruption. In 1790, only 13 per cent of *curés* and 5 per cent of vicars in the former diocese of Bayonne swore to the Civil Constitution,[10] and given the proximity of the border, a lot of non-juror priests, including the bishop of Bayonne Monseigneur de Villeveille, crossed into Spain, from where they rallied their parishioners to resist.[11] The paranoia that clerical emigration produced among the *représentants en mission*, nevertheless, was largely unfounded. The Basque population responded to the replacement of their *curés* with constitutional priests with dismay but rarely with violence, and only a handful of times was the *gendarmerie* forced to intervene to disperse the crowd.[12] Instead, people revealed their discontent by failing to attend jurors' masses and to welcome the new constitutional bishop, Sanadon, and turned to non-juror priests to receive their sacraments.[13] The villagers of Baïgorry, for example, who were just under 3,500 in 1793, had eighty-five newborns christened in the Spanish parish of Erratzu, across the border with Basse-Navarre, between 1793 and 1804.[14]

On the other hand, the rejection of the constitutional clergy was rarely indicative of people's lack of commitment to the Revolution and its ideals.[15] Rather, it was often evidence of the Basques' uneasiness with the changing order which threatened the precarious economic balance of local communities. Indeed, the *curé*, in the Basque country as in the rest of France, was more than a spiritual guide: he was a support to the family and the first person to be contacted in moments of crisis or difficulty.[16] In October 1791, for example, the mayor of Itxassou, on behalf of his community and the whole Basque country, begged Louis XVI to retract the Civil Constitution, as religion, he explained, was the only joyful distraction for such an unfortunate people as the Basques. 'These people,' he wrote, 'poor because of the poverty of the soil, have only one joy, that is, the Roman, apostolic and Catholic Religion.'[17] For the Basques, then, resistance to the constitutional clergy was not a form of disloyalty to the principles of the Revolution. It revealed their anxiety about both salvation and such material concerns as the fate of their village poor, hospitals and charities.[18]

The Basque notability, furthermore, regarded the religious status quo as a means of preserving order, a view that was shared by most Revolutionaries at the beginning of the Revolution. Indeed, during the Constitutional Monarchy, state officials saw religion as an ally to support and reinforce the authority of the new nation. Even though they did not regard Christianity as a moral and institutional basis for monarchical legitimacy, as they used to under the *ancien régime*, they still believed that Christian morality favoured respect of the hierarchy and of the social order, as well as of the patriarchal authority of the father, the king and, ultimately, God.[19] The mayor of Ciboure, for instance, explained to the government in 1792 that religion was an important means of keeping people calm and united because 'fanaticism, rather than cooling down when it is opposed, increases and heats up against what opposes it, and against its privations; these pressing cries are dictated by necessity and will stop once such needs are satisfied'.[20] The local notability often attempted to prioritise common sense over Revolutionary ideology, warning Jacobin authorities that their paranoia concerning the Basques' religious fanaticism was unfounded or exaggerated.

As the *montagnards* came to regard Christianity as 'a rival cultural system that prevented people from becoming true citizens of the new Republic',[21] however, they associated multilingualism with Catholic counterrevolution, claiming that opponents of the Revolution based their success on the population's ignorance of the French language.[22] In the Basque country, they targeted Euskara as the main reason for the population's indifference to Republican ideas. Ignorance of French, the likes of Grégoire and Barère believed, prevented the propagation of Revolutionary thought and made the Basques easy prey for the enemies of the Revolution and of the Republic, first of all the refractory clergy. In particular, it resulted in people's inability to read and understand laws, which, they argued, priests exploited to spread misinformation and undermine the foundations of the new nation. In the battle 'between the clergy and the Nation', the *directoire* of the Basses-Pyrénées wrote to the National Assembly on 20 December 1790, priests employed religion as 'a weapon against the Law' and excited 'pious terror mixed with desperation in simple and credulous souls, which are the precursors of fanaticism and of all the crimes deriving from it'.[23] As a result, teaching French to the Basque population was the first, essential step to turn them into good French patriots.

The solution, radical Revolutionaries believed, was to improve the primary schooling system, thanks to which France would be able to achieve uniformity of language, which they saw as essential to foster national unity and patriotism. In his report on the idioms of France, for example, Barère complemented his remark that 'fanaticism speaks Basque' with the proposal to send French-language teachers to those areas of France, such as Brittany, Corsica, the *départements* of the Rhine and the Basque country, where the primary language of communication was not French. Instructors should teach French to male and female children, as well as translate to the other members of the community the laws and decrees issued by the Convention. 'To leave citizens ignorant of the national language', he argued, 'is to betray the *patrie*; it is to allow the stream of enlightened ideas to be poisoned or obstructed in its course; it is to disregard the benefits of the printing press, because each printer is a public teacher of language and legislation.'[24] For Barère, the language of the Rights of Man was an 'instrument of public thought' that ensured 'the enlightenment, education, public spirit and democratic government' of France.[25]

The Revolutionaries regarded *l'école* as the propagator of Revolutionary and republican values.[26] *Instituteurs* needed to be supervised, the administration of the Basses-Pyrénées wrote in year VI (1798), because they had the function of 'forming citizens': 'the hopes of the *patrie* lie in [their] hands'.[27] Uniformity of language, moreover, the Revolutionaries believed, would have the merit of weakening priests' influence on the Basque population. The *commissaire* of the *directoire* of the Basses-Pyrénées, for example, alleged in year VII (1799) that priests opposed 'the expansion of enlightened ideas and the Propagation of the principles of regeneration'. Consequently, he invited officials to find ways of convincing parents to send their children to school and to distribute books that countered the ones priests gave to families. Increasing the level of schooling, especially in the rural cantons of the Basque country, he explained, was essential because linguistic difference created an unbridgeable divide between the Basques and their neighbours. Without education, he wrote, 'the Basques will never completely enjoy the advantages of the revolution'.[28]

Authorities believed that investing in the teaching of French was more essential in the Basque country than in the majority of France because Euskara bore no similarities to French and, as a result, mutual incomprehension between French and Basque officials had baleful repercussions on the smooth administration of the *département*. During the Terror, the main target of the *représentants en mission* was religion, as they claimed that priests used Euskara to foster counterrevolutionary feelings. Following France's declaration of war on Spain in March 1793, the deputies became increasingly paranoid about the influence of the French Basque refractory clergy, who lived just across the border with Spain, on the loyalty of the Basque population to the Republican cause. Their paranoia resulted in two main acts of retaliation. On the one hand, mirroring the iconoclasm happening in other parts of the country, the *représentants en mission* replaced Christianity with the cult of Reason and of the Supreme Being, and engaged in the violent destruction of religious symbols, including guillotining a Christ in front of the terrorised population of Saint-Pée.[29] On the other hand, as Chapter 2 described, in February 1794 the deputies deported the entire population of the villages of Labourd bordering Spain to at least sixty miles from the border, ascribing the decision to the bad influence the clergy had on conscription. Indeed, rumour had it that the forty-seven Basque soldiers who had deserted the army were instigated by a refractory priest acting as the emissary of an *émigré* leader, the duc de Saint-Simon. 'Their hearts are closed to the love of the *patrie* and to republican principles,' the *représentants* reported to the Comité de salut public a few days later as a justification for the uniquely severe decision.³⁰ Four thousand Basques primarily from the villages of Sare, Itxassou and Ascain were deported to the neighbouring *départements* of Lot, Gers, Lot-et-Garonne, Landes and Hautes-Pyrénées. They lived in miserable conditions in churches, where hundreds died, until September when, at the end of the Terror, the new administrators of the Basses-Pyrénées, Garrau and Baudor, allowed them to go home. Thus, the Basques' attachment to religion, the *montagnards* believed, made them side with the Spanish enemy and their language precluded their adoption of Republican principles.

After the fall of Robespierre, local authorities largely stopped associating Euskara with clerical counterrevolution but claimed that linguistic difference could cause administrative disruption and threaten public order. According to state officials, the standards of local administration in the Basque country were low because of the village mayors' and their subordinates' ignorance and lack of knowledge of the French language. Indeed, mayors were often illiterate and, although basic literacy was a requirement to hold their post, in the Pyrenean *départements* this was not always the case, causing problems of mutual incomprehension. In 1815, for instance, the prefect d'Antin d'Ars reported that in some communes of the Basque country mayors had no knowledge of French and had to visit the prefecture assisted by an interpreter.³¹ Almost a decade later, the then prefect Dessolle wrote that, in the village of Bassussarry, mayor Garat had been re-elected for five years because, in a village of 300 people, he was the only one who could speak some French.³²

Particularly daunting, authorities argued, was the fact that mayors could not complete birth, wedding and death certificates accurately. There was no such problem in central France, remarked the *conseil général*, with some exaggeration, in the early nineteenth century. But peasants in most villages of the Basses-Pyrénées spoke only Basque or Béarnais and could not do a thorough job. '*Instituteurs*', the *conseil* added, 'cannot remedy this deficiency [either]. Their ability is limited to being able to read and write imperfectly. In general, they are the sons of poor labourers, who prefer a comfortable and almost idle life to working the land.'³³ Failure to provide accurate certificates had serious political consequences. During the Revolutionary decade, the Revolutionaries perceived it as a battle between secularism and religion. In year IX (1800), for example, the sub-prefect of Bayonne accused priests of misleading 'uninstructed people' into believing that the observation of religious ceremonies and religious laws was all that mattered.[34] After the promulgation of the Loi Jourdan in 1798, moreover, birth certificates became essential for conscription quotas. Frustrated by mayors' lack of compliance, the central administration of the Basses-Pyrénées repeatedly blamed 'the ignorance of most mayors of rural villages' as the main cause of desertion and of lack of sense of duty in the *département*.[35]

Officials were also wary that linguistic difference could challenge the preservation of public order in the Basque country. From the outset of the French Revolution, in particular, they worried that the newly established *gendarmerie* could not fulfil its duties because the *gendarmes*, who were recruited nationally, had no knowledge of Basque. In 1791, the *directoire* of the Basses-Pyrénées petitioned the government to have the number of brigades raised from eighteen to twenty-four, on account of the *département*'s size, the length of the border and, especially, the different mores and language of the Basque population. It explained: 'The Basques understand only Basque and no one else understands Basque. It is therefore evident that the troops destined to track down crimes and criminals, and whose officers are in charge of the first procedural acts alone, will miss the precious goal of their appointment in a *pays* where they do not understand the language, and theirs is not understood.' As a result, the *directoire* suggested the addition of two Basque-speaking *gendarmes* to each brigade.[36] Problems of mutual incomprehension between the *gendarmerie* and the Basque population continued throughout the nineteenth century. In 1855, for example, the sub-prefect of Mauléon still complained that *gendarmes* found it difficult to fulfil their duties because they could not understand Euskara and suggested the inclusion of two Basque-speaking *gendarmes* in each brigade, as they knew 'the habits and language of the population'.[37] For much of the nineteenth century, then, state representatives in the Basque country petitioned governing ministers asking for a degree of linguistic exceptionalism in order to ease the performance of their administrative duties.

Mayors' ignorance and the *gendarmes*' linguistic problem should not be exaggerated, though. Their position was uncomfortable, as they often found themselves split between local ties and affections on the one hand and loyalty to the state on the other. The mayor was a member of the local community and served the interests of his fellow villagers first. From his and his community's perspective, such everyday matters as the harvest and the settlement of communal lands were more important than national impositions such as speaking the national language, schooling and conscription. Additionally, mayors and *gendarmes* frequently acted against the will of the state for fear of retaliation from fellow villagers. In 1792, for example, people in Bayonne displayed posters against the mayor, threatening to kill him if he forced the refractory clergy to leave; and a Revolutionary official received an anonymous letter warning him that he would be shot the moment he tried to enter his new home in town.[38] Unlike mayors, moreover, *gendarmes* were outsiders to the community. Villagers tended to treat them as intruders and they were frequently targets of deserters, brigands and contrabanders.[39] The *gendarmerie* did not always find support in the mayor either. In 1834, for instance, two *gendarmes* arrested an armed man and took him to the mayor of La Bastide-Clairance. The drunken mayor told them to release him and to give him back his weapon; upon the *gendarmes'* hesitation, he instigated a group of spectators to assault them.[40] Thus, although issues with mayors' incompetence and lack of knowledge of the French language were real and remained frequent in the nineteenth century, in some cases they were less ignorant than they wished national authorities to believe. Basque communities were based on a complex system of local loyalties that local officials were often forced to accept if they cared for their own safety. At the same time, the French government's inability to appoint competent officials in rural France and to enforce their demands was revealing of the limits of the French state's resources in the first half of the nineteenth century, which prompted state officials to find compromises between governmental measures and local realities.

Education presented a similar picture. There was some truth in authorities' reports that the population's aloofness vis-à-vis primary schooling was due to ignorance of the French language, the influence of religion and the lack of cooperation of local authorities. The majority of parents, in particular, considered primary schooling a pointless luxury and equated education with catechism. Children who attended the local school, then, tended to stop once they had received their first communion,[41] which prompted prefect d'Auribeau to write, in 1868, that '[s]chools would be much less well attended without the children's need to learn catechism'.[42] At the same time,

Basque peasants, like their counterparts in most of France, still lived an economy of subsistence that did not allow them to consider education a priority. Across nineteenth-century France, children helped their parents with the harvest and, in the summer they were too busy to attend school. In the Basses-Pyrénées, the number of children attending school in the summer decreased by one-third compared to the winter,[43] and pupils also tended to miss school for the needs of agriculture in winter because the weather was not very cold.[44] Additionally, Basque villages did not possess sufficient funding to invest into school buildings and the *instituteurs'* salaries, despite the dignification of primary education that followed the Loi Guizot of 1833. Ten years later, almost two-thirds of the *département*'s public schools had insufficient or poor equipment,[45] and in 1879 half of the pupils of the primary school of Bidart still lacked seats.[46]

Teachers, moreover, had to work multiple jobs in order to gain enough money to survive, which led them to neglect their teaching duties, hindered their preparation and compromised the quality of their teaching. As a result, they were often unable to teach French to their pupils and to apply new teaching techniques in class. In 1839, for example, the inspector of the Académie de Bordeaux reported that Basque *instituteurs* did not understand the methods inspectors asked them to implement, and a few of them 'still assume that the new methods are a fantasy, a fashion'.[47] Moreover, an inspector reported in 1890 that in the *arrondissement* of Bayonne many *maîtres* did not use such practices as essay writing at all, because they themselves could not fully understand the meaning of the words.[48] While all of rural France faced similar issues across the nineteenth century,[49] the fact that most Basque pupils understood only Euskara made the *instituteurs'* job almost impossible, as the French-taught curriculum implied a good knowledge of French and the teaching of French hindered progress on any other subject.

Linguistic difficulties prompted officials to be flexible about the use of Euskara in schools through the nineteenth century. Interestingly, before the 1890s, the French state was more sympathetic towards the Basques than towards other linguistic minorities. This was arguably the result of both the lack of an established counterrevolutionary tradition dating back to the Revolution, which made the Basque country less of a political liability than, for example, Brittany, and the European scholarly popularity of the Basque language, which elevated the historical and cultural value of Euskara. In Flanders, for instance, the state allowed the use of Flemish in the teaching of catechism until 1903 but forbade it in schools from the 1850s onwards.[50] In the Basses-Pyrénées, moreover, the *Règlement* of 1874 forbade the use of *patois* in Béarn but allowed translations in Basque schools.[51] Still in 1890, school inspector Carré conceded that *instituteurs* needed to use Euskara to a certain extent in class to help children learn French. He recommended that teachers should not use it when a French word corresponded to a concrete object and could be explained by means of visual aids, but they could use it to translate abstract words. He was happier to make linguistic concessions in the Basque country than in Brittany, he added. Basque children, in his view, seemed brighter than the Bretons, *instituteurs* were less likely to take advantage of the special permission to start teaching whole classes in Euskara and, crucially, while he saw no inconvenience to the disappearance of Breton in France, he believed it was useful for French Basques to be able to communicate with their Basque neighbours in Spain.[52]

Thus, except for the years of the Terror, across the nineteenth century state authorities tolerated the use of Euskara in education and in the administration of the Basque country. Until the 1880s, moreover, officials never seriously challenged the Church's monopoly of education. The relationship changed after the promulgation of the Lois Ferry of 1881–82 and especially after the decree of 1903, which imposed French-taught catechism in Brittany, Flanders and the Basque country. Basque Catholic conservatives denounced the secular policies of the Third Republic as a perpetuation of the anti-clerical persecution of the First Republic and, like their Breton and Flemish counterparts, they viewed the Catholic faith as a means of protecting Euskara from disappearance.

'The war against Euskara'

At the turn of the twentieth century, Euskara became a battleground between two opposite ideas of France. On the one hand, there was the republican idea, which was positivist, secular and founded upon the principles of progress and 'civilisation'. On the other, there was a conservative idea of France, which was Catholic, rural and rooted in traditional cultures and the cult of ancestry. While the republican idea of nation was monolingual and centralised, the conservative one was plurilingual and decentralised. The former presented itself as the heir of the moderate phase of the French Revolution and of the Rights of Man. The latter aimed at a revival of the provinces of the *ancien régime* and of an organic form of society, which conservatives opposed to the individualism of republican ideology.[53] Partisans of each of the 'two Frances' believed that it was their duty to save the country from the threat posed by the opposite camp, and education was the primary battlefield where they faced each other. When radical republicans began to secularise primary schooling and to impose the use of French on religious education, such linguistic minorities as the Basques portrayed themselves as martyrs of the Republic and elevated their local language to the protector of religion and tradition.

Similarly to the First Republic, the radical republicans of the Third Republic were concerned with the compatibility between plurilingualism and national unity. They regarded the national language as the primary vehicle for the spreading of republican values and morals and condemned minority languages for undermining the republican project.[54] The issue, they believed, especially concerned such linguistic minorities as the Basques, the Bretons and the Flemish. There, the clergy exploited regional languages to preserve their control over education, which in turn produced weak, superstitious and unpatriotic citizens, the likes of whom had led France to the defeat of Sedan in 1870.[55] Paul, the prefect of the Basses-Pyrénées, for example, wrote to the minister of worship, Émile Combes, in 1896 that the almost exclusive use of Euskara in Basque churches was the main cause of illiteracy and poor knowledge of French in the Basque country. This, he argued, generated a 'triple inconvenience: an obstacle to the diffusion of education, the strength of the clergy [and] a threat to the idea of the French *patrie*'.[56] The consolidation of a republican national identity, then, depended on the disappearance of regional languages and *patois*.

Basque conservatives disagreed that multilingualism hindered national unity. On the one hand, they did not believe that there was an inherent incompatibility between love of the *grande patrie* and attachment to the *petite patrie*. There was no conflict, they claimed, between their loyalty to France and their devotion to the Basque country. In a letter to prefect Francière in 1902, for example, three self-proclaimed representatives of the Basque *pays* argued that they were offended by the accusation of 'an incompatibility of sorts between our deep Bascophile sentiments and our sincere love for France, our dear *Patrie*'. They listed the Basque men who had fought honourably in the French army, including the leader of the Revolutionary *chasseurs basques*, Marshal Harispe, and Admiral Bernard Jauréguiberry, who had distinguished himself in the Crimean and Franco-Prussian wars, asking rhetorically: 'Are there better *French* soldiers than our mountaineers? ... were they not excellent patriots?'[57] The following year, Renaud d'Elissagaray, the director of the conservative Basque newspaper *Eskualduna*, responding to the new decree imposing religious education in French, wrote that, naturally, 'we love our *grande patrie, la France*; but we also have a cult of our *patrie basque*, which, we can say with pride, honours the other one.'[58] As Chapter 5 showed, for Basque conservatives, the *grande patrie* and the *petite patrie* were not only compatible; the *petite patrie* was an essential part of the nation, which contributed to its defence and to its military greatness.

On the other hand, Basque conservatives rejected the notion that 'the faithful and the citizen'[59] were irreconcilable political stances. Catholics were not the enemy of the French nation, they claimed. France's one and only enemy was the Republic itself, which was essentially evil because it was in antithesis with the sacred principles of Christianity. The Republic, they argued – employing a similar rhetoric to the one used by the far-right nationalist movement Action française and the anti-Dreyfusards at the turn of the twentieth century[60] – was run by freemasons, Jews and foreigners, enemies to real, Catholic France. *Eskualduna*, for example, wrote in 1888 that La Ligue de l'enseignement, which the freemason pedagogue Jean Macé had founded in 1866 to promote compulsory, free and secular primary schooling, was 'a masonic enterprise' whose goal was to 'dechristianise France' and develop a 'savage plan of godless teaching'.[61] The following year, the *curé* of Ossès warned the population from the pulpit that 'our current governments are the Jews and the freemasons, the same ones who crucified our Lord Jesus Christ'.[62] In the aftermath of the decree imposing the teaching of catechism in French in 1903, moreover, *Eskualduna* reported an article from the liberal *La République nouvelle* that called prime minister Combes, himself a freemason, a 'foreign satrap' whose brain was 'shut to the most elementary notions of liberalism'.[63] Thus, the real enemies of France, Basque conservatives claimed, were all those perceived foreign elements in contemporary society, such as freemasons, Jews, protestants, socialists, communists and radical republicans themselves.[64]

The survival of Basque culture and language, conservatives believed, depended on the fall or at least the weakening of the Republic. As a result, in the first few decades of its existence, they engaged in three main activities that disrupted its stability: they meddled in elections, compared radical republicans to the Jacobin terrorists of the 1790s and refused to comply with the government's secularisation of education.

The clergy's meddling in local elections was not an exclusively Basque phenomenon: similar episodes were recorded among other linguistic minorities. Timothy Baycroft, for example, has detailed the powerlessness of the government in tackling priests' influence on elections in French Flanders.[65] Like in the Nord, in the Basque country the anti-republican clergy preached sermons in favour of conservative candidates and presented the Republic as the enemy of religion and of the people. The *desservant* of Arcuit, for example, on the occasion of the election of the *conseil général* of the Basses-Pyrénées in 1886, prompted his faithful to choose the candidate 'who loved God and religion', pointing out that to vote for republican candidates was 'to vote for the Devil'.[66] The conservative press similarly contributed to the portrayal of the Republic as the enemy of Christianity. In 1888, for instance, *Eskualduna* wrote that its goal for the upcoming municipal election was to combat the influence of freemasonry on 'the souls of our children' and 'the wind of atheism' that blew over public schools.[67] The message that Basque conservatives tried to pass, in other words, was that voting for republican candidates meant voting for the enemies of Christianity, and voting for the enemies of Christianity equalled voting for the enemies of the Basque country.

Basque conservatives drew parallels between the radical phase of the First Republic and the contemporary Third Republic as a scare tactic to convince the population of the oppressive and violent nature of republicanism. They reminded people of the persecution of priests, the acts of iconoclasm and the deportation of the Basque population during the Terror, and warned them that the primary targets of the Third Republic were the same as the First's: Catholicism and the Basque language. The *curé* of Ossès, for one, alleged in 1889 that 'our statesmen, like the revolutionaries of 1789, expel religion, catechism, crucifixes from schools'.[68] Current republicans, like the ones of the First Republic, *Eskualduna* added, abused the 'liberty, equality, fraternity' motto, which was in fact a 'triple lie'.[69] Conservatives claimed that they were witnessing a Basque martyrdom and drew parallels between the sufferings of the Basque population during the Revolutionary Terror and the current war that they argued radical republicans were waging against Basque priests and Euskara. Local scholars produced the first Basque histories of the French Revolution, in which they portrayed the Republic as a criminal enterprise and stressed the suffering of the local lay and clerical population. The most famous text was the *abbé* Pierre Haristoy's *Les Paroisses du Pays basque pendant la période révolutionnaire*, published in 1895, where he described the Basques' experience of the French Revolution as 'tyrannical, cruel and bloody'.[70] The book, which was the first to make use of local archives, emphasised the suffering of the refractory clergy and their parishioners, the hardship of forced emigration and deportation, as well as the cruelty of the *représentants en mission*. Set against the 'anti-Christianism' and 'anti-patriotism' of the Jacobin deputies, he portrayed the Basque people not only as Revolutionary victims but also as Christian martyrs.[71]

The most celebrated story of martyrdom was that of Madeleine Larralde. According to the legend, in 1793 teenager Larralde, from the French Basque village of Sare, defied the law that forbade the crossing of the border and walked to the Spanish Basque village of Bera to seek confession. On her way back, she was arrested and faced trial. The soldiers who captured her took pity on her and recommended that she told the Revolutionary tribunal that she went to Spain to visit an acquaintance, rather than for religious purposes. Larralde, however, refused to lie, as lying was a sin, and was sentenced to death. Her sacrifice made her the ultimate Basque martyr of the Revolution. Although historical documents suggested that the real Madeleine Larralde was an older woman who was guillotined for cross-border smuggling,[72] the legend of the teenage martyr was popularised by many local scholars at the end of nineteenth century.[73] These included Antoine d'Abbadie, who made Larralde the subject of a *bertsolari* contest he organised in Saint-Jean-de-Luz in 1894. The poem that won the competition drew parallels between Larralde and the Virgin Mary, 'the queen of martyrs', and invited fellow Basques to continue to live always according to divine truth.[74] The selective memorialisation of the French Revolution in the Basque country at the end of the nineteenth century, then, opposed republicanism to Christian morality and challenged the Third Republic by reminding people of its original sin: the Terror of the First Republic.

The third challenge to the Republic was the Basque clergy's protection of religious education from secularisation and their commitment to the teaching of catechism in Euskara. While the Catholic Church still held considerable authority over private schools and especially the teaching of catechism, its influence over public schooling had undergone a relentless decline since the promulgation of the Lois Ferry of 1881–82. Basque conservatives were especially opposed to Article 2 of the Loi Ferry of 1882, which eliminated religious education from the public-school curriculum. They adopted the classic Catholic position according to which, while secular education was good because intelligence, as one of God's gifts, had to be cultivated, religious education was more important because God judged people on the basis of their moral conduct, not of their culture.[75] *Eskualduna*, for example, wrote in 1887 that although secular education was 'a good thing', religious education was an even better one because it taught people the most indispensable lesson: 'to live well and to die well'.[76] Four years later, a letter to the newspaper signed by 'un basque' made a similar point, explaining that the education of the masses was important but that its most important element was 'religious morals, catechism'.[77] While radical republicans considered *l'école* the place to teach civic morality, Catholics believed that there could be no moral teaching without a religious foundation.[78]

When in 1903 the government passed an unpopular decree imposing the teaching of catechism and the preaching of mass in French in Flanders, Brittany and the Basque country, Basque conservatives' focus shifted from the teaching of religious education per se to the teaching of religious education in Euskara. The argument that clergymen in all three regions presented for the teaching of catechism in the local language was simple. The primary purpose of catechism was for children to learn and understand the word of God. Since most pupils' level of French was low, French-taught catechism defied the purpose of religious education.[79] Things were not so simple, though. Basque children's knowledge of French was disputed and often a matter of interpretation, and some clergymen were more honest than others about the linguistic difficulties of their pupils. As a result, the language of catechism became a tug of war between the prefect and Basque clergymen. Prefect Francière was a sensible man. He warned Combes that a sudden and intransigent imposition of the new decree would unnecessarily antagonise people and acknowledged that the Basque population understood French only imperfectly. At the same time, he believed that, unlike the elderly, most primary school children did have the necessary level of French to understand catechism. Thus, while he suggested that mass should continue to be preached in Euskara for the time being, he claimed that catechism should be taught in French.[80] Exceptions were at his discretion. He was sympathetic, for example, to those *curés* who continued to teach in Euskara to pupils close to the first communion, and hence to the completion of their religious studies, as well as to those whose claims that their students could not understand French matched the findings of the inspectors of the Académie. However, he deemed unacceptable that some *curés* taught in either French or Euskara according to the will of their pupils' parents, as well as those, of course, who opposed French-taught catechism on principle.[81] Among them, Francière and his successor Gilbert denounced the *desservant* of Musculdy who taught catechism in French only to the *instituteur*'s son,[82] the *desservant* of Lacarry who forced his students to study two catechisms, one in French and one in Basque,[83] and the *desservant* of Arbonne who referred with scorn to French-taught girls as the 'Parisiennes', and in church separated pupils attending the *école laïque* from the other children, referring to public schools as the 'schools of the devil'.[84]

While the prefects deemed *curés*' resistance to French-taught catechism a mere question of 'ill will',[85] however, many Basque conservatives perceived the decree as part of a broader government attempt to control the way in which they conducted their private religious life.[86] As a result, preventing the state from meddling in the language of catechism was a symbolic act of resistance to avert both further state intrusion into citizens' private lives and the complete annihilation of regional languages. In 1902, for example, *Eskualduna* published a poem that the Breton songwriter Théodore Botrel had written against French-taught catechism in Brittany, which suggested that such an imposition was the first step for the state to penetrate the sacredness of the household and prevent Bretons from communicating in their local language altogether. The first few verses of the third stanza read:

> Someday soon, in your homes,
> They will forbid you, young sons,
> To speak with your grandmothers
> The dear language of your ancestors...[87]

Ceasing to speak their respective regional languages, Basque and Breton conservatives believed, would end the connection between the current generation and its glorious ancestors that had preserved their culture and race almost unscathed throughout the centuries. It meant, in other words, the death of the Basque and Breton civilisations.

Conservatives adopted Basque historical myths to defend their language and culture from the perceived attacks of the state in three main ways. They argued for the traditional independence of the Basques against accusations of fanaticism; they employed theories of ethnogenesis and the myth of Basque Cantabrianism against attacks on Euskara; and they tried to protect the language of their ancestors by reminding the Basque population of the antiquity and glory of their race.

In the aftermath of the Lois Ferry, *Eskualduna* resented the fact that republican authorities portrayed Basque resistance to secular education as religious fanaticism. In an infamous report to the government, indeed, prefect Deffès had described the Basques as 'peasants, naïve, credulous, superstitious', while the *directeur des cultes* Charles Dumay had depicted them as having 'a violent and obstinate nature, defiant of all that does not emanate from their land'.[88] *Eskualduna* rejected such portrayals as mischaracterising the identity of the Basques. What republicans called fanaticism, it argued, was mere religious faith and love of the Church; what they perceived as resistance to authority was the Basques' quintessential love of liberty and independence.[89] In 1891, the paper responded to the affirmations of Deffès and Dumay, republishing excerpts from a famous statistical report that General Serviez, who was prefect of the Basses-Pyrénées in 1801–2, had written for Napoleon during his time in office.[90] Serviez, *Eskualduna* wrote, described the Basques as a people whose '*independence was invincible*' and whose '*perpetuity of mores and language*' was due especially '*to their love of independence*'. Thus, it argued, 'what Monsieur Dumay calls violence, obstinacy, exclusivism, General Serviez called: love of liberty, honour of ambition, purity of race, attachment to religion'. This, the paper concluded, was the portrayal that the Basques still deserved and expected from republicans in the present day.[91] Such war of stereotypes revealed the extent to which, for both French authorities and the local conservative press, Basque myth-making was a matter of interpretation, circumstance and ideology. Paradoxically, nation and region depended on each other as they built their identities in emotional opposition to each other.[92]

Basque conservatives further relied on the historical myth of Basque Cantabrianism and on studies of comparative philology to demand respect for the Basques and their language. They employed Basque Cantabrianism to remind the Basques of the glorious military tradition of their ancestors and republicans of Basque soldiers' contribution to French military history. In 1888, for example, *Eskualduna* summarised the military glories of the Basques to attack Martial-Henri Berdoly, the director of the rival Basque republican newspaper *Le Réveil basque*, who had argued that ignorance of French was the main cause of the high rates of desertion in the Basque country. The Basques, *Eskualduna* narrated, had provided soldiers to Hannibal, who then defeated the Romans. They halted Julius Caesar and Charlemagne. They contributed to William the Conqueror's conquest of England and to Spain's *Reconquista* against the Saracens. They provided the Revolutionary and Napoleonic armies with courageous soldiers, the *chasseurs basques*, under the command of General Harispe. Finally, they had fought with conviction in the recent Franco-Prussian War. 'And here is the reward for so many centuries of valour,' the article concluded with scorn: 'the Republic gives you a Berdoly to sing your military glories!'[93] A few years later, *Eskualduna* further portrayed the entire history of the Basques as a history of resistance to oppression and the Third Republic's secularism as its swan song. It was the Basques' actions, it warned its readers, that were to decide their fate. If they were ready to fight and prove to be the 'rightful descendants' of their ancestors, who 'managed

Euskara or challenges to the French nation 167

to have their traditions and their independence respected with energy and valour', the Basque race would survive. If instead they complied with the government's rules, it would be 'the end of a glorious people'.[94] The conservative press, then, revived the myth of Basque Cantabrianism to rally the Basque population to resist the state's hostility to plurilingualism.

Additionally, conservatives employed the myths of ethnogenesis that Chapter 4 analysed in order to distinguish between the Basque language and lesser important *patois*, hoping to convince republicans to spare Euskara on the basis of its antiquity and superiority. An affronted 'bascophile', for example, defended Basque-taught catechism in 1903 by arguing that Euskara was not 'a vulgar *patois*' but a 'matrix language', whose origin dated back 'to the cradle of humankind' and had preserved intact its purity and beauty, 'like a precious repository left to us by our ancestors'.[95] In an article reported by *Eskualduna*, moreover, the republican newspaper *Le Temps* expressed its doubts about French-taught catechism in Brittany and the Basque country because Breton and Basque were two scientifically 'inestimable treasures'. 'By ceding a tiny part of this patrimony', it argued, 'we shall foolishly impoverish ourselves.'[96] Protecting Euskara meant protecting the heritage of both the Basque country and France.

Basque conservatives also tried to rally the population to stand up to the state by portraying Euskara as the idiom of religion and tradition. Language, religion and ancestry, they believed, constituted the three tenets of Basque identity and, by speaking Euskara, the Basques protected religion and the traditions of their ancestors. The conservative press praised Lower Brittany's armed resistance against the Law on Associations of 1901 and French-taught catechism two years later, and exhorted the Basques to imitate it.[97] Basques and Bretons, *Eskualduna* wrote in 1904, safeguarded 'the monopoly of faith, of the loyalty to the examples of our fathers'. It was essential that, like the Bretons, the Basques continued to be good Christians, as it was a quality that 'the children of *Vasconie*' had always shared.[98] Only by preserving Christianity could the Basques preserve the traditions of their ancestors and save their identity. One crucial means through which to preserve their Christian roots, conservatives argued, was to persevere in speaking Basque instead of French, the language of Christianity against the tongue of the godless Republic. In a poem published in *Eskualduna* in 1903, for example, the author exhorted readers to unite and '[p]reserve the language and Faith of our fathers' by rejecting the edict that banned them both.[99] Ultimately, to defend Euskara was to defend religious freedom and to defend religious freedom was to defend Euskara.

Conclusion

The French Revolution turned Euskara into an obstacle to national unity by associating French with the language of the Enlightenment, the Rights of Man and the *mission civilisatrice*, and regional languages with clericalism, superstition and backwardness. Such Revolutionaries as Grégoire and Barère were the first to equate Basque identity with religious fanaticism, a connection that had short- and long-term consequences. In the short term, accusations of fanaticism prompted the *représentants en mission* to develop a paranoid fear of the counterrevolutionary potential of the Basque clergy, leading them to commit terrorist acts of retaliation against both non-juror priests and the lay population. In the long term, radical republicans at the turn of the twentieth century, seeing themselves as the heirs of the First Republic, associated clericalism and multilingualism with national division and targeted the influence of the Church on education as a major impediment to national unity and patriotism. Basque conservatives responded to the perceived war on religion by turning Euskara into the ultimate defender of their Catholic faith and their ancestral traditions against the *République sans Dieu*.

The battle between the Basque clergy and radical republicans for the control of schooling was revealing of two opposite understandings of both the value of education and what constituted French identity. On the one hand, republicans understood schools as the place to teach pupils the republican credo and to form future citizens. Instead, Basque conservatives, like their ultra-Catholic counterparts across France, believed that there could be no education without religion. On the other hand, while republicans regarded clericalism and multilingualism as enemies of national unity and of the Republic, Basque conservatives portrayed the Republic as the enemy of the real nation – what Action française called *le pays réel* – which was pluralistic, multilingual and religious. They portrayed their fight against state secularisation as a battle for the identity of France, which was Catholic – as was the majority of the country's population. Thus, the clash over schools strengthened a conservative definition of Basque identity which developed a symbiotic relationship with Catholicism and was founded upon the principles of rural culture, respect for ancestry and religion.

Notes

1 A.N., F/1cVII/46, The sub-prefect of Bayonne to the *conseil d'arrondissement* of Bayonne, 1836: 'une partie de la population de la grande famille ... n'est pas non plus sans incovéniens sous le rapport politique et économique ... l'intérêt de l'église n'est pas toujours d'accord avec celui du pays'.
2 Ford, *Creating the Nation in Provincial France*, 24–5.
3 Michel de Certeau, Dominique Julia and Jacques Revel, *Une Politique de la langue. La Révolution française et les patois: l'enquête de Grégoire* (Paris, 2002), 11.
4 Henri Grégoire, 'Rapport sur la nécessité et les moyens d'anéantir les patois et d'universaliser l'usage de la langue française', in Michel de Certeau, Dominique Julia and Jacques Revel, *Une Politique de la langue. La Révolution française et les patois: l'enquête de Grégoire* (Paris, 2002), 336: 'un grand nombre était accessible au fanatisme, parce que l'idiome est un obstacle à la propagation des lumières'.
5 Robert Gildea, *Education in Provincial France, 1800–1914: A Study of Three Departments* (Oxford, 1983), 3–4.
6 Ford, *Creating the Nation in Provincial France*, 15.
7 *Le Réveil basque*, 14 November 1886: 'réfractaire aux idées de liberté et de progrès'.
8 Bertrand Barère, 'Rapport du Comité de Salut Public sur les idiomes', in Michel de Certeau, Dominique Julia and Jacques Revel, *Une Politique de la langue. La Révolution française et les patois: l'enquête de Grégoire* (Paris, 2002), 326: 'Le fédéralisme et la superstition parlent bas-breton; l'émigration et la haine de la République parlent allemand; la contrerévolution parle l'italien, et le fanatisme parle le basque.'
9 Ibid., 324: 'le règne du fanatisme et de la superstition ... se servent de leur idiome pour les fanatiser; mais ils ignorent la langue française et la langue des lois de la République'.
10 Alan Forrest, *The Revolution in Provincial France: Aquitaine, 1789–1799* (Oxford, 1996), 171–2.
11 M. Sacx, *Bayonne et le Pays basque. Témoins de l'histoire* (Bayonne, 1968), 110.

12 Forrest, *The Revolution in Provincial France*, 172.
13 Laharie, *La Révolution dans les Basses-Pyrénées*, 161; Sacx, *Bayonne et le Pays Basque*, 111–12.
14 Mayi Castaingts-Beretervide, *La Terreur et la déportation des Basques du Labourd, 1794* (Sare, 1994), 30.
15 Timothy Tackett, *Religion, Revolution, and Regional Culture in Eighteenth-Century France* (Princeton, 1986), 288.
16 Timothy Tackett, *Priest and Parish in Eighteenth-Century France. A Social and Political Study of the Curés in a Diocese of Dauphiné, 1750–1791* (Princeton, 1977), 152–3 and 157.
17 A.N., F/1cIII/Basses-Pyrénées/8, The mayor of Itxassou to the king, 26 October 1791: 'Ce peuple, pauvre par l'ingratitude de son sol, n'a des jouissances, que celles de la Réligion Catholique, apostolique et romaine.'
18 Castaingts-Beretervide, *La Terreur et la déportation des Basques du Labourd*, 29.
19 Suzanne Desan, *Reclaiming the Sacred: Lay Religion and Popular Politics in Revolutionary France* (Ithaca, 1990), 3–7.
20 A.N., F/19/461, The mayor and the municipality of Ciboure to [the *directoire* of the Basses-Pyrénées], 31 January 1792: 'le fanatisme, bien loin de s'attiédir par la resistance, fermente et s'echauffe au contraire en raison de celle qu'on lui oppose, et des privations qu'il éprouve, ses cris importuns sont ceux des besoins, qui cessent, dès que ces besoins sont satisfaits.'
21 Desan, *Reclaiming the Sacred*, 7.
22 Goldstein Sepinwall, *The Abbé Grégoire and the French Revolution*, 133.
23 A.N., F/19/461, Register of the deliberations of the *département* of Basses-Pyrénées, 20 December 1790: 'entre le clergé et la Nation ... une arme contre la Loi ... dans des ames simples et credules de pieuses terreurs melées du desespoir, avant-coureurs prochains du fanatisme et de tous les crimes qui marchent à sa suite'.
24 Barère, 'Rapport', 328: 'Laisser les citoyens dans l'ignorance de la langue nationale, c'est trahir la patrie; c'est laisser le torrent des lumières empoisonné ou obstrué dans son cours; c'est méconnaître les bienfaits de l'imprimerie, car chaque imprimeur est un instituteur public de langue et de législation.'
25 Ibid., 328: 'l'instrument de la pensée publique'; 'les lumières, l'éducation, l'esprit public et le gouvernement démocratique'.
26 François Furet and Jacques Ozouf, *Lire et écrire: l'alphabétisation des français de Calvin à Jules Ferry* (Paris, 1977), 97.
27 A.D., E dépôt/Came/2D6, The administration of the Basses-Pyrénées to the administrations of its cantons and communes, 21 *ventôse* VI

(11 March 1798): 'de former les citoyens'; 'c'est entre ses mains qu'est remise l'espérance de la patrie'.
28 A.N., F/1cIII/Basses-Pyrénées/7, The *commissaire* of the *directoire* of the Basses-Pyrénées to the minister of the interior, 28 *nivôse* VII (17 January 1799): 'à l'accroissement des Lumieres et à la Propagation des principes régénérateurs ... les Basques ne jouiront jamais completement des avantages de la révolution'.
29 Léon Basterreche, *Dénonciation des crimes de Monestier, de Puy-de-Dôme, aux membres composant les comités de gouvernement* (Bayonne, [1795]).
30 Aulard, *Recueil des actes du Comité de Salut Public,* Volume 11, 398–9: 'Leurs cœurs sont fermés à l'amour de la patrie et aux principes républicains.'
31 A.N., F/7/9171, The prefect to the director of police, 11 February 1815.
32 A.N., F/1bII/Basses-Pyrénées/9, The prefect to the minister of the interior, 14 June 1822.
33 A.N., F/1cV/Basses-Pyrénées/1, The *conseil général* of the Basses-Pyrénées to the government, [c. 1800]: 'Les instituteurs des écoles primaires ne suppléent pas à cette incapacité. Leur science se réduit à lire et écrire imparfaitement. Ce sont en général des fils des laboureurs pauvres, qui ont préféré aux travaux de la terre une vie plus commode et presque oisive.'
34 A.D., E dépôt/Came/2D10, Register of the *arrêtés* of the sub-prefect of Bayonne, 26 *frimaire* IX (16 December 1800): 'les personnes peu instruites'.
35 A.N., F/9/236, The *directoire* of the Basses-Pyrénées to the government, 7 *brumaire* VIII (28 October 1799); A.N., F/9/236, The *directoire* of the Basses-Pyrénées to the minister of the interior, 12 *brumaire* VIII (2 November 1799); A.N., F/9/236, The prefect to the minister of war, 5 *nivôse* XI (25 December 1802); A.N., F/9/312, The minister of the interior to the prefect, 11 *floréal* IX (30 April 1803); A.N., F/9/236, Ordinance concerning the conscripts of years XIII and XIV, 9 *frimaire* XIV (29 November 1805): 'l'ignorance de la plupart des maires des communes rurales'.
36 A.N., F/9/325, The *directoire* of the Basses-Pyrénées to the minister of the interior, 15 April 1791. See also, A.N., F/9/325, The *directoire* of the Basses-Pyrénées to the minister of the interior, 9 July 1791: 'Les basques n'entendent que le basque, et personne qu'eux n'entend le basque. Il est pourtant bien évident qu'une troupe destinée à suivre la trace des crimes et des criminels, et dont les officiers auront souvent a faire seuls les premiers actes de procedure, manquera nécessairement le but précieux de son institution dans un païs, dont elle n'entendra pas la langue, et ou la sienne ne sera pas plus entendue.'

37 A.N., F/1cVII/46, The sub-prefect of Mauléon to the *conseil d'arrondissement*, 1855: 'connaissant les usages et la langue des habitants'.
38 A.N., D/XL/15, The *directoire* of the district of Ustaritz and the municipality of Bayonne to the *directoire* of the Basses-Pyrénées, 25 May 1792.
39 Forrest, *Conscripts and Deserters*, 203; Louis Bergès, *Résister à la conscription, 1798–1814. Le cas des départements aquitains* (Paris, 2002), 338–9.
40 A.N., F/1bII/Basses-Pyrénées/10, The minister of war to the minister of the interior, 17 December 1834.
41 Antoine Prost, *Histoire de l'enseignement en France, 1800–1967* (Paris, 1968), 101.
42 A.N., F/17/9375, The prefect to the minister of education, 1868: '[l]es écoles seraient bien moins suivies sans la nécessité pour les enfants d'apprendre le catéchisme'.
43 Pierre Hourmat, 'L'Enseignement primaire dans les Basses-Pyrénées au temps de la Monarchie Constitutionnelle 1815–1848 (suite)', *Bulletin de la Société des sciences, lettres et arts de Bayonne*, 127 (1972), 101.
44 A.N., F/17/9306/1, Report of the Académie de Pau, 1838–9.
45 Hourmat, 'Enseignement primaire', 99. See also, A.N., F/1cV/Basses-Pyrénées/2, The prefect to the *conseil général* of the Basses-Pyrénées, 1836.
46 A.D., E dépôt/Bidart/1R1, The sub-prefect of Bayonne to the mayor of Bidart, 4 November 1879.
47 A.N., F/17/9306/1, Report of the Académie de Bordeaux, 1838–9: 'supposent encore que les nouvelles méthodes sont une fantaisie, une mode'.
48 A.N., F/17/9251, The *inspecteur général* to the *directeur* of French teaching in the Basque country, 19 March 1890.
49 Prost, *Histoire de l'enseignement en France*, 99, 113 and 134–5.
50 Timothy Baycroft, *Culture, Identity and Nationalism: French Flanders in the Nineteenth and Twentieth Centuries* (Woodbridge, 2004), 91–4.
51 Furet and Ozouf, *Lire et écrire*, 343.
52 A.N., F/17/9251, The *inspecteur général* to the *directeur* of primary education, 19 March 1890.
53 Tombs, *France* 138–9; Rod Kedward, *La Vie en Bleu: France and the French Since 1900* (London, 2005), 11 and 45.
54 Baycroft, *Culture, Identity and Nationalism*, 89–90.
55 Tombs, *France*, 139 and 141.
56 A.N., F/19/5502, The prefect to the minister of worship, 22 April 1896: 'En somme, triple inconvénient: empêchement de la diffusion de l'instruction, puissance du clergé, atteinte à l'idée de la patrie française'.

57 A.N., F/19/5502, Letter reported by the prefect to the minister of worship, 17 November 1902: 'une incompatibilité quelconque, entre nos sentiments profondément bascophiles et notre sincère amour pour la France, notre chère Patrie. Existe-t-il de meilleurs soldats Français que nos montagnards? ... étaient-ils d'excellents patriotes?'
58 *Eskualduna*, 9 January 1903: 'nous aimons notre grande patrie, la France; mais nous avons également un culte pour notre patrie basque qui, nous pouvons le dire avec orgueil, honore l'autre.'
59 Jacques Limouzy, *Émile Combes. Le fondateur spirituel de la laïcité. Du séminaire de Castres à la loi de 1905* (Toulouse, 2019), 25: 'du fidèle et du citoyen'.
60 Kedward, *La Vie en Bleu*, 47.
61 *Eskualduna*, 24 February 1888: 'une entreprise maçonique'; 'déchristianiser la France'; 'plan sauvage de l'enseignement sans Dieu'.
62 A.N., F/19/5784, Summary of the sermon made in Basque by the *curé* of Ossès during the two masses of 2 June 1889, June 1889: 'nos gouvernements actuels sont les Juifs et les francs-maçons, ceux-là même qui ont crucifié notre Seigneur Jésus-Christ.'
63 *Eskualduna*, 6 February 1903: 'fermé aux notions les plus élémentaires du libéralisme'.
64 Kedward, *La Vie en Bleu*, 47.
65 Baycroft, *Culture, Identity and Nationalism*, 132–4.
66 A.N., F/19/5784, The mayor of Arcuit to the sub-prefect of Bayonne, 27 September 1886: 'qui aimait Dieu et la religion ... c'était voter pour le Diable'.
67 *Eskualduna*, 1 June 1888: 'le vent d'athéisme ... l'âme de nos enfants'.
68 A.N., F/19/5784, Summary of the sermon made in Basque by the *curé* of Ossès during the two masses of 2 June 1889, June 1889: 'nos gouvernants, comme les révolutionnaires de 1789, chassent la religion des écoles, le catéchisme, les crucifix'.
69 *Eskualduna*, 20 February 1888 and 21 September 1888: 'triple mensonge'.
70 Pierre Haristoy, *Les Paroisses du Pays basque pendant la période révolutionnaire*, Volume 1 (Pau, 1895), 38: 'tyrannique, cruelle et sanguinaire'.
71 Ibid., 116.
72 Jean Goyhenetche, 'Deux cas historiographiques des guerres de la Convention: l'évacuation des communes du Labourd et l'exécution de Madeleine Larralde', in Jean-Baptiste Orpustan (ed.), *La Révolution française dans l'histoire et la littérature basques du XIXe siècle* (Saint-Étienne-de-Baïgorry, 1994), 163–88.
73 On Basque primary sources on Madeleine Larralde, see Jean-Baptiste Orpustan (ed.), *La Révolution française dans l'histoire et la littérature basques du XIXe siècle* (Saint-Étienne-de-Baïgorry, 1994), 279–93.

74 Haristoy, *Les Paroisses du Pays basque*, 300–1: 'la reine des martyrs.'
75 Prost, *Histoire de l'enseignement en France*, 156.
76 *Eskualduna*, 6 August 1887: 'une bonne chose ... à bien vivre et à bien mourir'.
77 *Eskualduna*, 20 January 1888: 'la morale religieuse, le cathéchisme'.
78 Jean-Noël Luc, Jean-François Condette and Yves Verneuil, *Histoire de l'enseignement en France, XIXe–XXIe siècles* (Malakoff, 2020), 106; Prost, *Histoire de l'enseignement en France*, 159 and 196; Mona Ozouf, *L'École, l'Église et la République, 1871–1914* (Paris, 1963), 81.
79 Baycroft, *Culture, Identity and Nationalism*, 123.
80 A.N., F/19/5502, The prefect to the minister of worship, 17 November 1902.
81 A.N., F/19/5502, The prefect to the *directeur des cultes*, 5 April 1903.
82 A.N., F/19/5502, The prefect to the *directeur des cultes*, 5 April 1903.
83 A.N., F/19/5502, The prefect to the minister of worship, 5 July 1903.
84 A.N., F/19/5502, Inquiry of the special commissary of Biarritz on the *desservant* of Arbonne, 15 October 1903: 'écoles du diable'.
85 A.N., F/19/5502, The prefect to the *directeur des cultes*, 5 April 1903; A.N., F/19/5502, The prefect to the minister of worship, 9 January 1904: 'mauvaise volonté'.
86 Prost, *Histoire de l'enseignement en France*, 197.
87 *Eskualduna*, 21 November 1902: 'Et quelque jour, en vos chaumières, / On vous défendra, petits fieux, / De parler avec vos grand'mères / Le cher langage des aïeux...'
88 Quoted in *Eskualduna*, 16 January 1891: 'paysans naïfs, crédules, superstitieux'; 'natures violentes et obstinées, rebelles à tout ce qui n'émane pas de leur propre terre'.
89 *Eskualduna*, 31 January 1890.
90 Emmanuel-Gervais Roergas de Serviez, *Statistique du département des Basses-Pyrénées* (Paris, 1801).
91 *Eskualduna*, 16 January 1891: '*indépendance était invincible ... perpétuité de mœurs et de langue ... à leur amour pour l'indépendance ...* ce que M. Dumay appelle violence, obstination, exclusivisme, le général Serviez l'appelait: amour de la liberté, honneur de l'ambition, pureté de race, attachement au culte.'
92 Michael Jeismann, 'Nation, Identity, and Enmity: Towards a Theory of Political Identification', in Timothy Baycroft and Mark Hewitson (eds), *What Is a Nation? Europe 1789–1914* (Oxford, 2006), 19 and 22.
93 *Eskualduna*, 26 October 1888: 'Et voilà la récompense de tant de siècles de vaillance: la République te donne un Berdoly pour chanter tes louanges militaires!'

94 *Eskualduna*, 1 January 1903: 'les dignes descendants ... surent avec énergie et vaillance faire respecter leurs traditions et leur indépendance ... la fin d'un peuple glorieux'.
95 *Eskualduna*, 9 January 1903: 'un patois vulgaire ... une langue mère ... au berceau du genre humain ... comme un dépôt précieux transmis par nos ancêtres'.
96 *Eskualduna*, 7 November 1902: 'trésors inestimables ... Céder une obole de ce patrimoine ... c'est s'appauvrir inutilement, sottement.'
97 Ford, *Creating the Nation in Provincial France*, 137–8.
98 *Eskualduna*, 8 July 1904: 'le monopole de la foi, de la fidélité aux exemples de nos pères'; 'les enfants de Vasconie'.
99 *Eskualduna*, 10 April 1903: 'Gardons la langue et la Foi de nos pères'.

7

'The other within': ideas of progress and decline in Basque travel writing

In the nineteenth century, western European travellers regarded the Basque country as a testing ground for ideas of 'civilisation', progress and decline. They 'orientalised' the Basques in a similar fashion to the Spaniards and eastern Europeans, portraying them as a picturesque and primitive people who was unable to embrace 'modernity' and hence lived at the margin of 'civilised' western Europe.[1] In their imagination, the Basque was the embodiment of the myth of vanishing primitivism. On the one hand, he represented Jean-Jacques Rousseau's ideal of the primitive man, later called the 'noble savage',[2] who lived according to the laws of nature and was free from the chains of civil society. On the other, he was one of the last bearers of classical antiquity in western Europe, succumbing to the pressure of 'modernity'. Writers voiced their sadness at the disappearance of Basque culture but also believed it to be a necessary step to set the Basques on the historical path of progress that, thanks to the gradual improvement of both scientific knowledge and moral virtue, led to the perfectibility of humankind.[3]

Travel writing popularised a series of stereotypes that came to characterise both the way in which Europeans perceived the Basque country and the manner in which, to an extent, the Basques presented themselves to outsiders. Basque stereotypes, in this respect, said more about the western Europeans who put them in writing than about the Basques themselves. As historians of imagology have pointed out, a people's definition of a different community always reflects back on the identity of the former, as identity is to an extent defined in comparison with and especially in contrast to an 'other'.[4] The *littérateurs* who travelled to and wrote about the Basque country in the nineteenth century were a heterogeneous group of people for gender, nationality and political affiliation, who nevertheless largely shared a liberal view of politics and a series of concerns about the present and future of 'modern' commercial society.[5] Influenced by the dominant Enlightened view of progress from the previous century, they held unconditional faith in the superiority of western European culture and were fascinated by the scientific and technological discoveries that led to the advancement of society and to the mastery of nature and of the human mind. As many of them identified with the Romantic movement, however, they were equally suspicious of the excesses of reason, science and industrialisation. They worried about the inequality and greed that resulted from a commercial society and deplored the perceived moral corruption that came with the luxury and opulence of a capitalist economy.

The Basque country was the perfect embodiment of such tension. By the mid-nineteenth century, it possessed a rural interior still largely untouched by 'modernity' and coastal towns and mountainous spas exposed to tourism, technological advances and a cosmopolitan culture. There, upper-class visitors inundated the growing tourist resorts with wealth and riches, modifying the habits and behaviours of the local population. Although *littérateurs* frequently belonged to such elite society and spent the majority of their time on the beaten track, they contrasted the two seemingly incompatible worlds to expose the paradoxes of contemporary western Europe and its two contradictory yet interconnected interpretations of history: an optimistic linear view of history from barbarism to 'civilisation' and the perfectibility of mankind, as expressed by Turgot, Nicolas de Condorcet, Henri de Saint-Simon, Auguste Comte, Georg Hegel and Karl Marx, and a more pessimistic cyclical idea of history, as detailed by Thomas Malthus and Edward Gibbon, where times of progress were followed by inevitable periods of decline.[6]

The 'noble savage' of the Pyrenees

Travellers were enthusiastic about visiting the Basque country because they considered it the only remaining vestige of a 'primitive' people living at the heart of Europe. Their representation of the Basques was complex. On the one hand, they considered them an 'Oriental' other and described them with such adjectives as 'savage', 'primitive' and 'uncivilised' that mirrored the rhetoric that travellers employed when they depicted the non-European peoples of the colonies.[7] When the writer Prosper de Lagarde arrived in the Basque country in the mid-1830s, for example, he compared the indigenous Basque population with the Native American tribes of the Iroquois and the Mohicans. 'What a pleasure to be in the middle of these savages without leaving France', he wrote.[8] Similarly, the naturalist Armand de Quatrefages wrote in the mid-1850s that 'there is definitely something strange about finding a society of the middle ages in the middle of the nineteenth century, so close to France'.[9] On the other hand, as the Basques were a European people, scholars and travellers believed that, by interacting with them, they were coming as close as possible to an encounter with one of Europe's ancient civilisations. In this respect, the experience that visitors sought to have in the Basque country was more similar to the journeys they undertook to Greece and Italy, where they hoped to get a taste of ancient Greece and Rome, than to the ones in the colonies.[10] The original character of the ancient Basques, they believed, was still visible in their contemporary mores. The naturalist Vincent de Chausenque, for example, remarked in 1854 that the Basque still possessed 'the proud and independent soul of his fathers' and an 'energetic character' that made him superior to all other nations 'for his activity, love of war and of bold strokes'.[11] The grammarian Louis-Marie-Hyacinthe Fabre, moreover, observed that the Basques were the descendants of the Cantabrians, who still formed a separate people within France and Spain for 'their customs, their mores, their oriental language'.[12] These were the characteristics of a primitive people but also the mores of European 'civilisation' at its purest.

Travellers admired the Basques for their alleged preservation of 'patriarchal mores',[13] 'patriarchal habits'[14] and 'patriarchal traditions'.[15] The principal bearers of such values were women and, by extension, the family, which was women's primary duty and responsibility.[16] While writers' depiction of Basque women's southern European beauty bore similarities to their 'Orientalist' portrait of Spanish women, they did not describe them as temptresses and passionate lovers, as they did in Spain.[17] Basque women were pious and lived according to Christian principles and traditional values that shielded them and their families from the corruption of 'modern civilisation'. In his history of Bayonne of 1836, for example, the editor-in-chief of *La Sentinelle des Pyrénées*, Félix Morel, praised local women for their attachment to tradition and the family, which was a virtue that he believed was disappearing in contemporary France and western Europe. A 'lawful wife', he elaborated, was to be 'a sweet and patient companion [to the man], without jealousies or whims'.[18] Three decades later, Fabre similarly praised the traditional values of the family of Ascain that hosted him. They preserved the same 'patriarchal and pure' mores of the past, he explained: 'naïve, simple, honest, whole-hearted [manners] ... the poison of corruption still had not penetrated this peaceful retreat'. The man, as the chief of the family, he added, led by example, while the woman dedicated her life to her husband and her children.[19] Travellers' idealised portrayal of the Basque woman as 'the angel of the hearth'[20] revealed their anxiety that 'modernity' triggered moral impoverishment by eroding faith and tradition.[21]

While visitors also praised men for their display of civility in their treatment of their wives and in their care for the family, they especially pointed out their physical prowess, fierceness and bravery. Such depictions of the Basque man combined the idealised model of physical strength of the ancient Greek and Roman warrior, which derived from the Enlightenment and the Grand Tour, with the chivalric ideal of the medieval knight typical of Romanticism, which travellers believed characterised both the ancient Cantabrian and the contemporary Basque. Relying on Voltaire's alleged characterisation of the Basques as 'a people who dance at the foot of the Pyrenees', travellers remarked on the agility of the Basques, which, as for the Greeks and the Romans, was especially evident in their games, which required remarkable physical strength and endurance. The 'Euskarian race',[22] they wrote, presented remarkable 'strength' and 'flexibility', which derived from their habit of climbing the mountains;[23] it was 'robust, strong, flexible, agile', and possessed a 'springy gait'.[24] Basque men's appearance was 'quick and elegant' and their 'agility [was] unparalleled' as a result both of their running up and down the hills and of the *jeu de paume*, which developed an athletic body.[25] The Basque man, in other words, was the surviving ideal of the ancient warrior.

Physical prowess, though, was not an end in itself; it was the bodily embodiment of high moral standards, which writers contrasted with the risk of softness and effeminacy inherent in the excessive opulence and comfort of contemporary commercial society.[26] Such moral superiority, they argued, was evident in the Basques' 'fierce gaze'[27] and in the special attachment to liberty that characterised their race. Travellers made use of the myth of Basque Cantabrianism to remind readers that the Basques' bravery and fierceness had resulted in the defence of their homes throughout the centuries. Lagarde, for example, explained that the Basques were ready to sacrifice 'everything for that freedom that they love more than life itself',[28] while Morel described the Basque country as 'a vast fortress guarded by a valiant and courageous nation, and still unspoiled by the contamination of a conqueror'.[29] It was thanks to their attachment to liberty that the Basques had preserved the high moral standards of their ancient 'civilisation'.

The myth of the Basque warrior was not without contradiction. In particular, travellers had to make sense of the paradox between their claim of the innate combative nature of the Basques and evidence of their resistance to conscription in contemporary France. Their conclusion was similar to the one that military authorities employed during the Revolutionary and Napoleonic Wars when dealing with the *chasseurs basques*: the Basques were excellent soldiers but their attachment to their homeland made them unsuitable for long-distance deployment. An English visitor, Louisa Stuart Costello, for example, reported in the 1840s that '[t]he Basque is bold and brave, and the French armies never had finer soldiers,' but that he was also especially prone to the *'maladie du pays'*.[30] The dramatist Étienne de Jouy, moreover, writing a few years after the fall of Napoleon, wrote specifically about Marshal Harispe's *chasseurs basques*, who, he argued, had engaged in 'prodigious acts of valour' in 1793 only to desert their battalion the following day to travel home to their families. A few days later, however, he wrote apocryphally, they were back to camp, where Harispe was waiting for them 'unconcerned', as he trusted their combative nature and sense of duty.[31] The myth of the Basque warrior, despite the evident high desertion rate, served not only to protect the exceptionalism of the Basques within the French army but also to corroborate the claim of the survival of their ancient character within France.

Although the relationship between the Basques and conscription was complicated, *littérateurs* claimed that contemporary Basques' military prowess was evident in the violence of their cross-border contraband activities. While some writers acknowledged that, given the endemic poverty of the region, the Basques smuggled primarily to make ends meet,[32] the majority argued that it was a natural consequence of their combative character. Stuart Costello, for example, wrote that the Basque 'is very adventurous, and fond of excitement; it is not, therefore, singular that he should be a hardy smuggler, so cunning and adroit that he contrives to evade the officers of the excise in a surprising manner'.[33] Additionally, the editor of the *Gazette des Eaux*, Germond de Lavigne, argued in 1856 that the Basques smuggled because they loved the danger and glory that came with it.[34] The acclamation of the Basque smuggler mirrored liberal elites' romanticisation of the figure of the contrabander, who became a symbol of liberty in the first half of the nineteenth century.[35] The Basque smuggler embodied such portrayal perfectly and came to represent a model of virtue and morality. In his widely read ethnographic study of the Basque country of 1857, for example, Francisque Michel wrote that many of the Basque chief contrabanders were men of honesty and integrity, defined by 'loyalty, righteousness, chivalric devotion'.[36] The ideal of the noble smuggler, he and others suggested, was Ganix of Macaye, who, as we saw in Chapter 3, had helped Don Carlos's fiancée, the princess of Beira, cross the border into Spain in 1838.[37] With his physical beauty and his probity, Michel explained, Ganix was 'the real type of noble contrabander, such as a novelist would desire'.[38] The ideal of the Basque contrabander equalled that of the noble warrior, whose moral, masculine rectitude was at odds with the corruption of contemporary urban life.

'I would like Biarritz to remain Biarritz'

Travellers worried that despite the strength of their ancestral mores, the Basques were at risk of being corrupted by 'modernity' like the rest of France and western Europe. They identified the culprit in the development of early spa tourism, which, as the next chapter will show, had reached the Basque country in the aftermath of the Napoleonic Wars and had introduced in the region such alleged evils of 'modern' commercial society as luxury, materialism, greed, selfishness and immorality. Writers, then, took their visit to the Basque country as an opportunity to reflect on the state of western

European 'civilisation', to engage with the declinist threat inherent in the idea of progress and to express their fears about the consequences of urbanism, industrialisation and what Malthus had called the 'accelerated velocity' of commercial society.[39]

The introduction of 'modern' infrastructure into the Basque coast inevitably marred the experience of naturalist Romantics, who travelled to the region to experience unblemished natural landscapes and their culturally virginal populations. Indeed, for them, sublimely beautiful nature had unique moral significance and was the physical representation of their inner feelings.[40] When Victor Hugo visited Biarritz in the 1840s, for example, he compared his experience of listening to a local girl singing on the beach to Ulysses listening to the mermaids.[41] Similarly, Hippolyte Taine, visiting the Basque coast a decade later, was charmed by the 'primitive' solitude of the seaside and of the movement of the waves and of the clouds, which reminded him of 'the souls of Dante, standing still in ecstasy at the entrance of paradise'.[42] The 'authenticity' of the Basque people and their landscape, however, they and others complained, was slowly succumbing to the needs and imperatives of the developing tourist industry, which took the form of Pyrenean spas and seaside resorts.

While many travellers journeyed to the western Pyrenees to escape 'modern' urbanism and retreat into an idealised pre-modern world, they complained, they were disappointed to discover there the same amenities of western European capitals. At Eaux-Bonnes, one of the most fashionable mountain spa towns in neighbouring Béarn, Taine was irritated at encountering, instead of a rural village, 'Parisian street and the promenades of the Bois de Boulogne'. He added: 'No countryside was ever less pastoral. ... It is grotesque that a bit of hot water should have brought the *cuisine* and civilisation to these caves.'[43] The aristocrat Marie Montaran, at Eaux-Bonnes in the late Second Empire, also recalled her disappointment at escaping 'Paris and its febrile agitation', only to 'run into what I escape' in the Pyrenees,[44] while the English writer Charles Richard Weld noted that fashion styles on the beaches of Biarritz were 'displayed here as if their owners were on the Champs Élysées'.[45] At Pasajes, once a customs post on the Franco-Spanish border, Hugo denounced the 'bitter derision' of 'escaping Rue de Rivoli' to find it in Guipúzcoa.[46] Describing similar feelings about Irún, one of the first Basque villages across the Pyrenean border, he exclaimed: 'Oh prettified villages, how ugly you are becoming! Where is history? Where is the past, where is poetry? Where are the memories? Irún looks like [the Parisian district of] Batignolles.'[47] Fabre was similarly saddened that the picturesque costume of the Basque country had been replaced by 'modern innovations that have effaced the local character',[48] while the writer Paul Perret, reporting on Biarritz in the early 1880s, wrote with sarcasm of his disappointment at being *en route* for paradise and then, upon arrival, finding what? The door of the Café Helder', the most famous coffeehouse of the town.[49] While travellers journeyed to the Basque country and its Pyrenean neighbours in order to escape urbanism and industrialisation and to recapture a glimpse of an idealised pre-modern past, then, they perceived the presence of 'modernity' there as the ultimate confirmation of the inevitability of progress and of its destruction of the preceding phases of 'civilisation'.

The transformation of the beach from a place of meditation and medical cure to a place of leisure, travellers believed, had corrupted the simplicity, 'authenticity' and morality of Basque mores. Romantics and their successors deplored the fact that commercial society was tearing apart pre-modern cultures that were based on religion, simple manners and community values, replacing them with materialism, individualism and greed. While they believed that the emergence of refined manners and polite society were positive inputs of 'modern civilisation', the excesses of aristocratic and commercial luxury led to superficiality, corruption and immorality.[50] Perret was especially damning in his depiction of the dissoluteness of high society. The seaside resort, he wrote in 1882, was 'a corrupting agent' that introduced in modest villages 'all the miseries of civilisation: luxury, elegant furniture, ridiculous fashions, sophisticated food, expensive life, adulterated wine, reading rooms and a piano on all floors'. He contrasted such luxurious lifestyles with the simplicity of small hamlets, defined by 'rest, daydreaming, *far niente*, silence, unsophisticated life, simple clothing, waking up at the first light of day, going to sleep at the last light of the sun'. He warned that Biarritz was becoming like such popular seaside towns as Dieppe, Boulogne, Trouville, Le Tréport and Étretat: 'places of perdition where beautiful women drench their silk dresses, where handsome men singe their finely polished shoes in the hot sand'.[51] While in their accounts of southern Europe travellers often contrasted southerners' perceived *ozio* and *dolce far niente* to the superior work ethic of northern Europe,[52] in the Basque country they used the same attributes to eulogise a slower, simpler and healthier rural lifestyle against the uncontrollable speed, overly sophisticated manners and prudish morality of the urban elites.

Nowhere in the Basque country was the transformation more startling than in the seaside town of Biarritz, which became one of France's most popular seaside resorts during the Second Empire. As changes to its landscape and cityscape transformed it beyond recognition, writers began to idealise the old Biarritz, and to distinguish between the Romantic and pure experience of travelling and the mundane and corrupted experience of tourism. In the 1840s, for example, when the popularity of Biarritz was just starting to emerge, Hugo wrote that he hoped that Biarritz would be spared the same fate as other seaside resorts in northern France such as Dieppe, Le Havre and Le Tréport. Becoming like the other resorts, he argued, meant that the Basque town would lose its 'authenticity' and would become but a pale imitation of Paris. If Biarritz became fashionable, he wrote, the 'rural', 'rustic' and 'still honest' village would be caught up in the 'bad appetite for money'. It would become 'prudish and rapacious' and build theatres and reading rooms. Ultimately, he lamented, 'Biarritz will cease to be Biarritz. It will be something colourless and fake like Dieppe and Ostend. Nothing is greater than a fishing village, full of ancient and simple mores ... Nothing is smaller, more wretched and more ridiculous than a fake Paris.'[53] In their criticism of 'modernity', then, Romantics distinguished between what Eric Hobsbawm has called customs – which were immemorial, based on a pre-existing lifestyle and reflective of the pre-modern world – and tradition, which was recent, invented to inculcate specific values and norms of behaviour, and, as such, perceived as fake.[54]

Travellers idealised Biarritz as it had been before it became *à la mode*, when the majority of visitors were the local middle classes and the town still possessed its local character. Such characterisation of old Biarritz was not necessarily realistic, but it reflected writers' discomfort with the growing industrial and capitalist economy. While, on the one hand, they were fascinated by the mastery of nature that industrialisation displayed, on the other, they abhorred the exploitation, materialistic vulgarity and desecration of landscape that came with it. Their idealisation of the past, in this respect, was a rejection of industrialisation and a longing for what they perceived as simpler and healthier times.[55] The physician P.-R. Affre, for example, recalled in 1856 the time when travellers in Biarritz were hosted in private houses, rather than in hotels, and entered a symbiotic relationship with their hosts, living, like them, according to the laws of nature, not the rules of urban life: they were awake during the day and asleep at night, instead of dedicating a part of the night to work and a part of the day to restless sleep; they ate four times a day like fishermen instead of two like the urban population; and they wore simple clothes that reflected locals' simple lifestyle, where luxury was banned. In the present day, he added with sadness, 'civilisation' had penetrated Biarritz, turning it into a town.[56] Although Biarritz, or any French town in the mid-nineteenth century, could not compare with the scale of industrialisation witnessed by English towns such as London, Liverpool or Leeds, French Romantics shared with their British counterparts like William Blake and William Wordsworth a sense of alienation from their own time and an understanding of 'modern civilisation' as philistine, corrupt and decadent.[57]

The problem with 'civilisation', they believed, was that it had spun out of control and had pushed such Enlightened virtues as the refinement of manners and politeness to an extreme. They shared Rousseau's view that respectability, science and reason led to moral decline and, while they did not believe that the state of nature was better, they portrayed it as more authentic and sincere. It was 'modern' society's strive for progress and perfection, they claimed, that was responsible for the creation of a world of false appearances, measured exclusively by commerce and money.[58] An anonymous account of Biarritz, for example, recounted during the Second Empire that in earlier decades, when the main visitors to Biarritz were only the middle classes of Bayonne, the prudish yet lavish manners of the French elites had not yet arrived in the Basque country and, as a result, the 'preoccupations of the *toilette*' did not cross people's minds. It was only the 'tyrannical emblem of civilisation' that brought them along, making men and women succumb to the pressure of etiquette. 'There is an abyss of at least two centuries between the demands of then and now,' they summarised. 'Then we lived for ourselves and for what we had inside, whereas now we live a lot for others and for the outside; we did not worry like today about the approbation or disapprobation of the crowd, and were we not happier then!'[59] The binary opposition between living for others and living for oneself mirrored Rousseau's distinction, in his *Discours sur l'origine de l'inégalité parmi les hommes*, between 'the savage', who lived for himself, and 'the social man', who lived for the opinion of others.[60]

The corruption of local mores, like their preservation, lay primarily with women. Morel, for one, distinguished between two types of Basque woman: the *grisette*, or working-class woman, and the bourgeoise. The *grisette*, with her dark eyes and hair, her energy, coquetry, youthfulness and 'elegant simplicity', was the embodiment of the local character. The bourgeoise, on the contrary, a 'cosmopolitan goddess' enveloped in expensive fabrics and jewellery, devoted to 'disgraceful luxury' and the *toilette*, was essentially a Frenchwoman: 'like all those who draw on the lessons of our modern civilisation,' he wrote, 'their life is all external, all *resonant*'.[61] Women's extravagant and expensive clothing and complicated hairstyles, travellers believed, were the emblem of the decadence that the corrupted urban lifestyle had introduced in the Basque country. For Fabre, for instance, the sophisticated clothes that visiting women sported on the beaches of Biarritz and at the town's endless *soirées* were 'an assault of luxury' that looked unnatural in a rural environment where 'simplicity and liberty' should prevail.[62] Weld, moreover, noted in 1859 that 'fashion had run mad at Biaritz [sic], so out of character were the dresses of the women with the surrounding scenery.' He was then not surprised, he added, that priests had begun to condemn 'extravagance in dress' from the pulpit, seeking 'to impress upon the ladies that, while their gowns are very wide, the gates of Paradise are very narrow'.[63]

The *grisettes*, on their part, were slowly succumbing to urban fashion, too. Not only did they observe upper-class women's clothes with envy,[64] but, as Perret noted, their hairstyle was losing its picturesque character to 'modern industry'. All the new 'gears and pins' imported into the Basque country to fix women's hair made it lose some of its 'cockiness', he complained, while the replacement of the simple madras with the hat was banal. Basque girls looked like 'a dressed-up monkey' under those 'stupid' hats, he argued, adding: 'I accuse progress, this universal leveller. When it is complete, no one will be stupid, but no one will have a mind; no one will be ignorant, but no one will be educated. No woman will have a sickly ugliness any more, but no one will possess the original beauty either.'[65]

Thus, travellers shared with Rousseau the idea that polite society and 'modern' education were directly responsible for moral decline and for a world of insincere pretence. The lavishness that travellers witnessed in the spa and seaside resorts of the Basque country, moreover, worried them, as they regarded it as a symptom of the weakness, effeminacy and degeneracy of the French race. Such fears of decline reflected France's demographic concerns about low fertility rates compared to the rest of Europe, as well as Rousseau's prediction that the excessive luxury of commercial society would lead to a nation of weak and effeminate men.[66] While political concerns linking low population growth with the loss of military power became a leitmotif of the early Third Republic, during the Second Empire anxiety about physical and moral degeneration reflected the widespread criticism of the lavish lifestyle of Napoleon III's court. Visiting the Basque spa town of Cambo in 1867, for example, Fabre complained that patients were more interested in the comfort of its baths than in recovering their good health. The over-attachment to luxury, he warned, led to an 'excessively effeminate life', which had baleful repercussions, both physical and moral. '[I]f society does not stop on the slope where it is sliding,' he wrote, 'luxury and softness will soon make our race degenerate to the point that in half a century there will not be able-bodied men any more.'[67] As a result, writers feared that commercial society's inherent drive for growth would soon reach a tipping point from which, as with previous civilisations, an inexorable phase of decline would ensue.

The Basques vis-à-vis the inevitable march of progress

While travellers despised the alleged 'effeminacy' and softness of elite society, they equally condemned the lack of social evolution of the Basques. They praised their idleness as an antidote to the frenzy of urban industrialisation but worried that it hindered economic, political and cultural progress, which in turn undermined the foundations of the unitary nation. They regarded the history of humankind as a process of national perfectibility from antiquity to 'modernity', which had a temporal as well as a spatial dimension: it represented a geographical move from the ancient civilisations of southern Europe to the 'modern' civilisations of north-western Europe. In this respect, portrayals of the 'primitiveness' of the Basque country were a self-congratulatory affirmation of the superiority of the work ethic of the people of the north as opposed to the indolence and laziness of the people of the south.[68]

Basque 'primitiveness', then, had two opposite connotations. On the one hand, it had a positive meaning, as it indicated that the Basques were the last descendants of an ancient civilisation that had survived the natural evolution from southern Europe's classical antiquity to northern European 'modernity'. Lagarde, for example, remarked in the 1830s the 'incontestable traces' of an 'extremely advanced previous civilisation' in the Basque country.[69] Additionally, the writer Marie d'Abbadie d'Arrast noticed in 1909 that, albeit declining, the presence of a 'primitive civilisation' was still evident in the mores and mentality of the Basque population. In particular, she designated the Basques' attachment to the family as the place where local traditions were perpetuated, as well as the single-inheritance rule, which had been defying the Napoleonic Code for nearly a century.[70] On the other hand, 'primitiveness' had a negative meaning that suggested that the Basques were not yet civilised. 'Civilisation', in this context, did not refer to ancient culture but to 'modernity' and its three key attributes: reason, progress and liberty.[71] Lagarde, for example, argued that Euskara insulated the Basques 'in the middle of civilisation that encroached upon them from all sides'.[72] At the beginning of the Third Republic, moreover, Vinson praised the antiquity of the Basque language and the historical independence of its speakers, but equally argued that it was clear that the Basques had lived for centuries in 'the most rudimentary state of civilisation'. They were 'the unknown remains of the Troglodytes of the stone age', he explained, who, 'without civilisation, without history', had been left unscathed by the passage of other European peoples throughout the centuries. In the present day, nevertheless, he added, 'choosing themselves to follow the fatal law of progress, ... they have mingled with the great Latin civilisation, which henceforth carries them forward with its incessant and implacable evolution.'[73] It was only a question of time, writers predicted, before the Basques became fully integrated into 'modern civilisation'.

Littérateurs were convinced that the Basques' embrace of 'modernity' was a historical necessity. Influenced by such theorists of progress as Hegel, Saint-Simon, Comte, Marx and Engels, they regarded history as the natural progress of civil society from backwardness to 'civilisation', finding its fulfilment in the bureaucratic, technological and commercial nation-state.[74] In 1849, for example, Friedrich Engels addressed the question of the Basques directly in an article published in Marx's *Neue Rheinische Zeitung*, in which he argued that such ahistorical peoples as the Basques were unable to participate in the 'march of history' and, as a result, were condemned to be fully denationalised and assimilated into bigger nations. Every country in Europe, he wrote, possessed 'remnants of an earlier population, repressed and subjugated by the nation that later became the bearer of historical development'. The ruins of ancient peoples, he added citing Hegel, were being crushed by 'the march of history' until full extinction was achieved. These peoples included the Celts in Scotland, the Bretons in France and the Basques in Spain.[75] By failing to embrace the principles of 'modernity', then, the Basques defied the laws of nature and were destined to disappear. *Littérateurs* shared a similar view. Humboldt, for instance, noted already at the turn of the nineteenth century that it seemed a pre-determined outcome of the progress of human culture that minorities must disappear into larger societal 'masses'.[76] Hugo, moreover, despite praising the sublimity of the Basque landscape and of its population, acknowledged a few decades later: 'The big States have to absorb the small ones; it is the law of history and of nature.'[77] Similarly, after Spain's abolition of the Spanish Basque *fueros* in 1876, the liberal newspaper *L'Avenir des Pyrénées et des Landes* claimed to support the decision, insofar as 'the world marches on and, at risk of perishing, every people has to conform to the general standard.'[78] Finally, writing a handful of years later, Vinson claimed that progress was 'the only necessary condition for the existence of modern peoples' and that the Basques' glorious tradition was 'from now on incompatible with the necessary conditions of life'.[79] Thus, travellers regarded the Basques as being stuck at an earlier stage of 'civilisation', which made them more similar to the peoples of the colonies than to western Europeans. The transition from the 'waiting-room' of history to 'historical time' was a necessary step for the Basques' full integration into the political nation, their enjoyment of the benefits of the 'modern' world and the full development of their potential.[80]

The strength of Basque culture, travellers and scholars believed, could be an obstacle to the creation of a unitary French nation. As a result, cultural diversity, like plurilingualism, had to be eliminated in order to strengthen the national project. The historian Jules Michelet voiced this view in 1846 in one of his most famous works, *Le Peuple*, where he wrote: 'This sacrifice of the different internal nationalities within the big nationality that contains them all strengthens the latter, without any doubt. It perhaps eliminates the remarkable, picturesque detail that characterises a people in the eye of a superficial observer; but it strengthens [the nation's] genius and allows it to manifest it.'[81] *Littérateurs* echoed Michelet as they discussed the Spanish Basques' defence of the *fueros* during the three Carlist Wars of the nineteenth century. Similarly to the legitimist press that was analysed in Chapter 3, travellers used the *fueristas'* fight against centralisation to discuss the French Basques and their place within France. While for legitimists the preservation of the *fueros* was a symbol of resistance to liberal and Revolutionary principles, for the *littérateurs* the *fueros* were a hindrance to progress and national unity.

On the one hand, they viewed them as the cradle of clericalism, which, according to the Revolutionary tradition, impeded social advancement and the spreading of Enlightened ideas. Vinson, for example, writing at the beginning of the Third Republic, believed that the *fueros* had kept the Basques prisoners of 'the clerical and ultramontane spirit', as during both the First and Second Carlist Wars the Basques were not only shouting 'long live the *fueros*' but also 'long live religion'. He compared the Carlist Wars to the French Revolution of 1789, when French Basque priests refused to swear the civil oath and emigrated to the other side of the Franco-Spanish border, 'preaching to their parishioners contempt for national authorities and disobedience to the law'. Thus, he argued, regional tradition failed to produce good liberals and, in the case of France, good republicans.[82]

On the other hand, writers, including Vinson, acknowledged that the *fueros* contained ideas of liberty and equality not dissimilar to the ones preached in the Rights of Man. However, they believed that, in their contemporary world, a localised system of government was outdated, and liberalism could be fully implemented only within such bigger nations as France and Spain. Chausenque, for example, writing in the aftermath of the First Carlist War, argued that the Basques had misunderstood María Cristina's new liberal regime, but that he was confident that one day they would understand it and would find liberty not in local institutions but 'in the tight unity of the *grande patrie*, as modern civilisation, better understood and better applied, will finally be able to produce results there peacefully'.[83] Commenting on the suppression of the *fueros* at the end of the Third Carlist War in 1876, moreover, *L'Avenir des Pyrénées et des Landes* wrote that it supported their elimination because, 'tying more closely the Basque provinces to the rest of Spain, [the abolition] will consolidate the bundle of national forces and will make it impossible for the odious insurrections that these provinces have witnessed for the past fifty years to repeat themselves'.[84] Only as part of their bigger nation, then, could the Basques fulfil their potential and not endanger the unity of the *grande patrie*. As Fabre pointed out at the end of the Second Empire, thanks to the contact with 'a civilised nation', such 'a backward people' as the Basques could learn 'the benefits of enlightened ideas, of fair laws, or moral institutions, of pure mores'.[85] Ultimately, writers believed that the suppression of Basque particularism was necessary to strengthen the identity of the *grande patrie*, which was based on Enlightened principles, civic patriotism and, after 1870, republican ideals.

Conclusion

Nineteenth-century writers were obsessed with the idea of progress. Whether they celebrated or criticised it, they measured the places and peoples they saw according to their stage of development and considered western Europe the pinnacle of world 'civilisation'. The Basque country, with its 'noble' yet 'savage' people and its 'modern' yet 'corrupted' tourist industry, represented perfectly the tensions that *littérateurs* felt between 'civilisation' and 'barbarism' and progress and decline. On the one hand, writers elevated the 'primitiveness' of the Basques to an expression of ancient virtue and morality, which they contrasted with the dissolution of morals of contemporary commercial society, as they witnessed it on the beaches of Biarritz and the spa towns of the Basses-Pyrénées. On the other, they condemned the Basques' same 'primitiveness' by associating it with notions of barbarism, anti-historicism and lack of 'modernity'. The fact that the Basques failed to embrace progress, they argued, was not only unnatural but was also a threat to the unity of the French nation, which was the utmost expression of history's onward march. The innumerable texts that were published on the Basque country and its people in the nineteenth century, then, revealed more about their writers than about the Basques themselves. They were travellers' own reflections on ideas of France and western Europe, of nation, progress and 'civilisation', rather than anthropological and ethnographic studies of the Basque country. While travellers treated the indigenous population merely as a means to an end, however, the Basques were not simple observers of such a process of stereotyping. Similarly to the way in which modern Greeks dealt with western European philhellenes,[86] the Basques retained their influence on their own image by, to an extent, adopting and adapting such clichés to their advantage. As the next chapter will show, the staging of 'authenticity' became an inherent part of the tourist industry and a crucial source of revenue in the Basque country in the second half of the nineteenth century.

Notes

1 On Spain, see Andreu Miralles, *El descubrimiento de España*. On eastern Europe, see Wolff, *Inventing Eastern Europe*.
2 On Rousseau and the invention of the 'noble savage', see Ter Ellingson, *The Myth of the Noble Savage* (Berkeley, 2001).
3 Robert Nisbet, *History of the Idea of Progress* (New York, 1980), 4–5.
4 Andrei Oişteanu, *Inventing the Jews: Antisemitic Stereotypes in Romanian and Other Central-East European Cultures* (Lincoln and London, 2009), 2–3; Klaus Heitmann, *Das Rumänenbild im deutschen Sprachraum, 1775–1918* (Cologne, 1985), 5–8.
5 On *littérateurs'* journeys to provincial France and the creation of a certain idea of unitary France, see Stéphane Gerson, 'Parisian Litterateurs, Provincial Journeys and the Construction of National Unity in Post-Revolutionary France', *Past and Present*, 151 (1996), 141–73.
6 Arthur Herman, *The Idea of Decline in Western History* (New York, 1997), 27–35 and 39–43.
7 On the notion of 'Orientalism', see Edward W. Said, *Orientalism* (New York, 1978).

8   Prosper de Lagarde, *Voyage dans le Pays basque et aux bains de Biaritz* (Paris, 1835), 31–2: 'Quel plaisir d'être au milieu de ces sauvages sans sortir de France'.
9   Armand de Quatrefages, *Souvenirs d'un naturaliste*, Volume 2 (Paris, 1854), 236: 'il y a certes quelque chose d'étrange à retrouver en plein XIXe siècle, à deux pas de la France, une société du moyen âge.'
10 Fleming, 'Philhellenism', 872.
11 Vincent de Chausenque, *Les Pyrénées, ou Voyages pédestres dans toutes les régions de ces montagnes depuis l'océan jusqu'à la Méditerranée*, Volume 1 (Agen, 1854), 204: 'l'âme fière et indépendante de ses pères, … caractère énergique … supérieurs à toutes les nations pour l'activité, l'amour de la guerre et des coups hardis'.
12 M. H.-L. Fabre, *Lettres labourdines ou lettres sur la partie du Pays basque appelée le Labourd* (Bayonne, 1869), 5–6: 'ses usages, ses mœurs, sa langue orientale'. Fabre was known as Louis-Marie-Hyacinthe, but his initials were inverted in his published book.
13 Ibid., 152: 'mœurs patriarcales'.
14 Paul Perret, *Les Pyrénées françaises: le Pays basque et la Basse-Navarre*, Volume 2 (Paris and Poitiers, 1882), 64: 'habitudes patriarcales'.
15 Quatrefages, *Souvenirs d'un naturaliste*, 154: 'traditions patriarcales'.
16 Julien Vinson, *Les Basques et le Pays basque: mœurs, langage et histoire* (Paris, 1882), 78.
17 Andreu Miralles, *El descubrimiento de España*, 93.
18 Félix Morel, *Bayonne, vues historiques et descriptives* (Bayonne, 1836), 382–3: 'une femme légitime … une compagne douce, patiente, sans jalousies, ni caprices'.
19 Fabre, *Lettres labourdines*, 152: 'mœurs patriarcales et pures'; 'naïve, simple, franche, tout cœur … le poison de la corruption n'avait point pénétré dans ce paisible réduit'.
20 Morel, *Bayonne*, 382–3: 'la gardienne du foyer domestique'.
21 Peter Wagner, *Modernity: Understanding the Present* (Cambridge and Malden, 2012), 19.
22 Quatrefages, *Souvenirs d'un naturaliste*, 242.
23 Chausenque, *Les Pyrénées*, 206: 'force … souplesse'.
24 Vinson, *Les Basques et le Pays basque*, 71: 'trapus, forts, souples, agiles … la démarche élastique'.
25 Lagarde, *Voyage dans le Pays basque*, 57: 'alertes et souples … agilité est sans pareille'.
26 Herman, *The Idea of Decline in Western History*, 43.
27 Chausenque, *Les Pyrénées*, 206: 'regard fier'.
28 Lagarde, *Voyage dans le Pays basque*, 55–6: 'tout pour la liberté qu'ils aiment plus même que l'existence'.

29 Morel, *Bayonne*, 495: 'une vaste forteresse gardée par une nation vaillante et courageuse, et vierge encore de la souillure d'un conquérant'.
30 Louisa Stuart Costello, *Bearn and the Pyrenees: A Legendary Tour to the Country of Henri Quatre*, Volume 2 (London, 1844), 248.
31 De Jouy, *L'Hermite en province*, 153: 'sans inquiétude'.
32 Michel, *Le Pays basque*, 119.
33 Stuart Costello, *Bearn and the Pyrenees*, 250.
34 Germond de Lavigne, *Autour de Biarritz. Promenades à Bayonne, à la frontière et dans le Pays basque* (Paris, 1856), 107.
35 Todd, *L'Identité économique de la France*, 163.
36 Michel, *Le Pays basque*, 120–4: 'une fidélité, une droiture, un dévouement tout chevaleresque'.
37 Ibid., 120–4; Perret, *Les Pyrénées françaises*, 170.
38 Michel, *Le Pays basque*, 124: 'le vrai type du contrebandier noble, tel que peut le désirer un romancier'.
39 Thomas Malthus, *First Essay on Population* (London, [1798] 1926), 2.
40 Guillaume De Syon, 'French Romanticism: Its Literary Legacy', in Christopher John Murray (ed.), *Encyclopedia of the Romantic Era, 1760–1850*, Volume 1 (New York and London, 2004), 386.
41 Victor Hugo, *Voyage vers les Pyrénées*, Francis Claudon ed. (Paris, [1845] 2001), 71.
42 Hippolyte Taine, *Voyage aux Pyrénées* (Paris, 1860), 41: 'aux âmes de Dante arrêtés en extase à l'entrée du paradis'.
43 Ibid., 127–8: 'une Rue de Paris et les promenades du bois de Boulogne. ... Jamais campagne ne fut moins champêtre ... On trouve grotesque qu'un peu d'eau chaude ait transporté dans ces fondrières la cuisine et la civilisation.'
44 Marie Constance Albertine Montaran, *Mes Pensées en voyage: excursions dans les Pyrénées* (Paris, 1868), 201: 'Paris et son agitation fébrile ... je rencontre ce que je fuis'.
45 Charles Richard Weld, *The Pyrenees, West and East* (London, 1859), 51.
46 Hugo, *Voyage vers les Pyrénées*, 114: 'amère dérision ... fuir la rue de Rivoli'.
47 Ibid., 97: 'Ô villages qu'on embellit, que vous devenez laids! Où est l'histoire? où est le passé, où est la poésie? où sont les souvenirs? Irun ressemble aux Batignolles.'
48 Fabre, *Lettres labourdines*, 136: 'Des innovations modernes ont effacé le cachet local.'
49 Perret, *Les Pyrénées françaises*, 40: 'en route pour le paradis, et de trouver devant soi, à l'arrivée, quoi? la porte du café du Helder'.

50 Herman, *The Idea of Decline in Western History*, 22–3 and 41–2.
51 Perret, *Les Pyrénées françaises*, 89–90: 'un agent corrupteur; il introduit partout, brutalement, toutes les misères de la civilisation: le luxe, les meubles élégants, les toilettes folles, la table recherchée, la vie chère, le vin frelaté, le cabinet de lecture et le piano à tous les étages. ... le repos, la rêverie, le *far niente*, le silence, la vie sans recherche, le costume sans façon, le réveil aux premières lueurs du jour, le coucher aux derniers feux du soleil ... des lieux de perdition où les belles dames reçoivent les coups de mer sur des robes de soie, où les beaux messieurs brûlent dans le sable leurs fins souliers vernis'.
52 Andreu Miralles, *El descubrimiento de España*, 91–2; Patriarca, 'Indolence and Regeneration', 389.
53 Hugo, *Voyage vers les Pyrénées*, 71: 'agreste ... rustique ... honnête encore ... mauvais appétit de l'argent ... pudique et rapace ... Alors Biarritz ne sera plus Biarritz. Ce sera quelque chose de décoloré et de bâtard comme Dieppe et Ostende. Rien n'est plus grand qu'un hameau de pêcheurs, plein de mœurs antiques et naïves ... Rien n'est plus petit, plus mesquin et plus ridicule qu'un faux Paris.'
54 Hobsbawm, 'Introduction: Inventing Traditions', 1–14.
55 William Burns, 'Industrial Revolution', in Christopher John Murray (ed.), *Encyclopedia of the Romantic Era, 1760–1850*, Volume 1 (London, 2003), 558.
56 P.-R. Affre, *Manuel du baigneur, ou Notice médicale sur les bains de mer de Biarritz (Basses-Pyrénées)* (Paris, 1856), iv–v.
57 Herman, *The Idea of Decline in Western History*, 41–2.
58 Frank M. Turner, *European Intellectual History from Rousseau to Nietzsche*, Richard A. Lofthouse ed. (New Haven and London, 2016), 7 and 9.
59 Anonymous, *Une Saison d'été à Biarritz. Biarritz autrefois, Biarritz aujourd'hui* (Bayonne, 1859), 32–3: 'préoccupations de la toilette ... tyrannique emblème de la civilisation ... il y a un abîme de dix siècles au moins entre les exigences d'alors et celles d'aujourd'hui ... Alors on ne vivait que pour soi et pour son intérieur, tandis que maintenant on vit beaucoup pour les autres et pour le dehors; on ne se préoccupait pas comme aujourd'hui des approbations ou des improbations de la foule, et n'est-ce pas qu'on devait être bien plus heureux ainsi!'
60 Jean-Jacques Rousseau, 'Discours sur l'origine de l'inégalité parmi les hommes', in *Œuvres complètes de J.-J. Rousseau*, Volume 6, Louis Barré ed. (Paris, [1754] 1856–7), 273.
61 Morel, *Bayonne*, 373–5, 376–7 and 379: 'déesse cosmopolite ... un luxe disgracieux ... comme toutes celles qui puisent aux leçons de notre moderne civilisation, leur vie est toute extérieure, toute *résonnante*'.

62 Fabre, *Lettres labourdines*, 64: 'un assaut de luxe ... la simplicité et la liberté'.
63 Weld, *The Pyrenees*, 51–2.
64 Morel, *Bayonne*, 374.
65 Perret, *Les Pyrénées françaises*, 8–10: 'l'industrie moderne'; 'd'engins et d'épingles'; 'crânerie'; 'stupides'; 'un singe habillé ... C'est le progrès qui s'accuse, c'est le nivellement universel. Quand ce sera fait, personne ne sera bête, mais personne n'aura d'esprit; personne ne sera ignorant, mais personne ne sera instruit. Aucune femme n'aura plus la laideur chétive, mais aucune n'aura plus la beauté originale.'
66 Rousseau, 'Discours sur l'origine de l'inégalité', 244 and 282.
67 Fabre, *Lettres labourdines*, 224: 'vie trop efféminée ... si la société ne s'arrête pas sur la pente où elle glisse, le luxe et la mollesse auront tellement fait dégénérer la race, que dans un demi-siècle il n'y aura plus d'hommes valides.'
68 Andreu Miralles, *El descubrimiento de España*, 91–2.
69 Lagarde, *Voyage dans le Pays basque*, 43–4: 'traces incontestables ... d'une civilisation antérieure extrêmement avancée'.
70 Marie d'Abbadie d'Arrast, *Causeries sur le Pays basque. La femme et l'enfant* (Paris, 1909), 4: 'civilisation primitive'.
71 Andreu Miralles, *El descubrimiento de España*, 70.
72 Lagarde, *Voyage dans le Pays basque*, 40–1.
73 Vinson, *Les Basques et le Pays basque*, 31 and 36: 'l'état de civilisation était des plus rudimentaires'; 'sans civilisation, sans histoire'; 'restes inconnus des Troglodytes de l'âge de pierre ... cédant eux-mêmes à la loi fatale du progrès, ... ils se sont mêlés à la grande civilisation latine qui les emporte désormais dans son incessante et implacable évolution'.
74 Herman, *The Idea of Decline in Western History*, 31–5.
75 Friedrich Engels, 'Der magyarische Kampf', in Karl Marx and Friedrich Engels, *Werke*, Volume 6 (Berlin, [1849] 1959), 172: 'Überbleibsel einer früheren Bewohnerschaft, zurückgedrängt und unterjocht von der Nation, welche später Trägerin der geschichtlichen Entwicklung wurde ... Gang der Geschichte.'
76 Wilhelm von Humboldt, *Die Vasken, oder Bemerkungen auf einer Reise durch Biscaya und das französische Basquenland im Frühling des Jahrs 1801, nebst Untersuchungen über die Vaskische Sprache und Nation, und einer kurzen Darstellung ihrer Grammatik und ihres Wörtervorraths* (Berlin, [1801] 1920), 10: 'Massen'.
77 Hugo, *Voyage vers les Pyrénées*, 103: 'Les grands États doivent absorber les petits; c'est la loi de l'histoire et de la nature.'
78 *L'Avenir des Pyrénées et des Landes*, 23 May 1876: 'le monde marche et, sous peine de périr, chaque peuple doit se mettre au niveau général'.

79 Vinson, *Les Basques et le Pays basque*, viii and 30: 'seule condition nécessaire pour l'existence des peuples modernes'; 'incompatibles désormais avec les conditions nécessaires à la vie'.

80 The terms are borrowed from Chakrabarty, *Provincializing Europe*, 7 and 9.

81 Jules Michelet, *Le Peuple* (Paris, 1846), 259: 'Ce sacrifice des diverses nationalités intérieures à la grande nationalité qui les contient, fortifie celle-ci, sans nul doute. Elle efface peut-être le détail saillant, pittoresque, qui caractérisait un peuple aux yeux de l'observateur superficiel; mais elle fortifie son génie, et lui permet de le manifester.'

82 Vinson, *Les Basques et le Pays basque*, 48 and 57–8: 'l'esprit clérical et ultramontain'; '"vivent les fueros!" ... "vive la religion!"'; 'prêchant à leurs paroissiens le mépris des autorités nationales et la désobéissance aux lois'.

83 Chausenque, *Les Pyrénées*, 206: 'dans l'unité compacte de la grande patrie lorsque la civilisation moderne mieux jugée et mieux conduite, pourra enfin y porter en paix ses fruits'.

84 *L'Avenir des Pyrénées et des Landes*, 23 May 1876: 'rattachant plus étroitement les provinces basques au reste de l'Espagne, consolidera le faisceau des forces nationales et rendra pour jamais impossibles les insurrections odieuses dont ces provinces ont été depuis cinquante ans le théâtre'.

85 Fabre, *Lettres labourdines*, 133: 'une nation civilisée ... un peuple arriéré ... les bienfaits de ses lumières, de ses lois justes, de ses institutions morales, de ses mœurs pures'.

86 David Roessel, *In Byron's Shadow: Modern Greece in the English and American Imagination* (Oxford, 2002), 15.

8

Reversing the 'tourist gaze'

While the travel writers analysed in the previous chapter portrayed the Basques as passive observers of the transformations that tourism caused to their landscape and culture, the local population affected by it played a key role in building and projecting a Basque identity that was appealing to tourists yet respectful of pre-existing mores and traditions. When visitors began to travel to the Basque country for scholarly, medical and, later, leisure purposes in the aftermath of the Napoleonic Wars, municipal officials and local elites were the first to foresee the economic potential of the developing tourist industry and to invest public and private resources in the spa business. As the popularity of the Basque coast increased during the Second Empire and the *années folles* of the Third Republic, the number of ordinary citizens who worked in and benefited from the tourist industry also grew, creating a system of mutual dependence between hosts and guests. The involvement of the Basque population in the tourist industry should not be exaggerated, as it was limited in terms of both geography and number of people. It concerned mostly the Basque coast, though tourists occasionally travelled to the interior both to reach spa towns and to attend the *fêtes basques*. Additionally, it affected primarily the elites, although workers, shopkeepers and artists contributed to the industry too. Despite the relatively small number of locals involved in tourism, tourist hosts nevertheless played a crucial role in the commodification and standardisation of Basque culture. Their efforts resulted in the codification of Basque cultural stereotypes that came to define the French Basque country as a whole in public imagination.

Visitors travelled to the Basque coast mainly from other parts of France, Spain and Great Britain, as well as from Russia, central

Europe and, in time, even the United States. Spanish visitors were especially numerous because, as a result of the Carlist Wars, the aristocracy was forced to migrate from San Sebastián, one of Spain's main seaside resorts, to Biarritz. British visitors, on their part, had been residing in Pau, the *chef-lieu* of the Basses-Pyrénées, since the beginning of the century and were quick to turn their attention to the Basque coast. While the Spaniards used to spend the summer season in Biarritz, the British enjoyed spending the winter season there too. In Basque spas and seaside towns, visitors looked for 'modern' infrastructure and standardised amenities, but also for an 'authentic' experience of Basque culture. While Romantics believed that 'modernisation' and 'authenticity' were to a large extent mutually exclusive, Basque hosts made their fortune on such dualism, which Adam Rosembaum has called 'grounded modernity'.[1] Their reconciliation of nostalgia and progress, nature and technology, local and cosmopolitan was especially evident in their organisation of recreational activities and folk festivals, which merged traditional Basque dances, songs and games with such European upper-class pastimes as regattas, horseraces and balls. These activities produced two main results. On the one hand, while the local population performed for tourists, they also acted like tourists themselves, joining the divertissements and consuming European culture as much as visitors consumed Basque culture. For guests and hosts alike, the experience of tourism was a mutual cultural discovery. On the other, by staging their 'authenticity',[2] Basque hosts contributed to the crystallisation of Basque stereotypes, turning them into a source of revenue. From the early stages of the tourist industry, the Basque population were aware of visitors' intrusive gaze into their private lives and instinctively reacted to it by crafting what social scientists now call ethnic or cultural forms of tourism. They exploited their externally perceived exoticism and primitiveness as a tourist attraction, presenting a touristic version of their culture, history and traditions as authentic. Ironically, while Romantics distinguished between their own search for 'authenticity' and the upper classes' cosmopolitan amusements, the 'authenticity' that they claimed to be experiencing in the Basque country was equally staged.

The tale of Basque hosts' active participation in the tourist industry contributes to a growing body of literature that challenges the traditional view that local populations were passive witnesses to the dislocations produced by tourism.³ For one thing, the active role that local elites and ordinary citizens played in the reconfiguration of the Basque coast rejects Jean-Didier Urbain's and Alain Corbin's view of the touristic beach as a 'decontextualised' space.⁴ Rather, with the arrival of tourism, Basque hosts worked towards the recontextualisation of the local space, modifying it to their advantage, as much as to the advantage of tourists. Additionally, Basque cultural practitioners' presentation of their heritage had both an entertaining and an educational role that was not necessarily diminishing or destructive of the value of their culture. On the contrary, as Susan Pitchford has argued in her anthropological study of contemporary Wales, it contributed to the re-evaluation of some forms of Basque tradition that were otherwise disappearing and to infusing in tourists further understanding of and respect for the culture they were consuming.⁵ The process through which tourist hosts perpetuated and strengthened tradition in the context of 'modern' tourism was what Philip Frick McKean has called 'cultural involution'.⁶ Finally, by selling their culture, traditions and history as commodities and by accentuating the folklorist and 'primitive' character of their festivals and habits, Basque hosts revealed that they were both aware of what John Urry has famously called the 'tourist gaze' and ready to reverse it to their economic advantage.⁷ In this respect, the view that hosts and guests held of each other was equally distorted and stereotyped.⁸ The gaze was not one-sided but mutual.⁹

Building a cosmopolitan future

Local administrators understood investment in tourism to be a way of bringing progress and 'civilisation' to the Basque country. The future, they believed, was French and cosmopolitan, not Basque and local. The turning point for the development of the tourist industry was the appointment of Pierre Boisaumarié, a former high-ranking official of the First Empire, to the prefecture of the Basses-Pyrénées in 1832. The new prefect foresaw the potential of Biarritz to become a seaside resort like such northern spas as Dieppe in Normandy and Ostend in Belgium and, as a result, he promoted a series of investments to improve the infrastructure and safety of the beaches and to create spa baths. In order to fund the works, the administration of Biarritz convinced the population to sell its communal land in exchange for an inalienable annuity and contributed to the liquidity with an increase in the consumption tax.[10] Over the next twenty years, Biarritz underwent a stunning transformation from a poor fishing village to an affluent upper-class resort. With the financial help of the town of Bayonne and of the *département*, the municipality improved the safety of the coastline, draining the swamps, filling the ravines, stabilising the soil with terracing and blowing up some of the big rocks that constellated the beach. In 1863, moreover, Napoleon III signed two decrees for the construction of the dykes of the Vieux Port, Socoa and Artha, off the coasts of Biarritz and Saint-Jean-de-Luz, in order to bring under control the dangerous ocean currents.[11] The townscape of Biarritz was also rebuilt according to the government's new standards of hygiene and sanitation: the municipality added trees and a fountain to the two squares, enlarged streets and created promenades along the coast. Later, it issued decrees renaming roads and explaining traffic rules to locals and visitors.[12] As a result of the changes, the editor-in-chief of *La Sentinelle des Pyrénées*, Félix Morel, claimed in 1836 that 'Biarritz largely takes part in the civilisation of the eighty-six *départements*,'[13] while the *conseil municipal* of the town argued in 1852 that Biarritz had entered 'a wide road of progress and welfare'.[14] Thanks to tourism, local elites believed, Biarritz had finally joined the rest of France in the path towards 'modernity'.

While Romantic visitors presented the Basques as helpless witnesses to, in the words of Louis Turner and John Ash, a 'golden horde' of luxurious upper classes who turned their sublime coastline into a 'pleasure periphery',[15] Basque elites were proactive in their promotion of and investment in the tourist industry. In Biarritz, private enterprises worked incessantly to build new hotels, which became, according to Alfred Vigreux in *L'Illustration* in 1858, 'real monuments amidst these lilliputian houses'.[16] As the town's popularity and wealth began to increase, the notability of such neighbouring villages as Saint-Jean-de-Luz, Guéthary and Hendaye also started financing the tourist industry, acquiring similar amenities such as houses and hotels, pavilions, omnibuses, roads and, later, rail lines, and inviting creditors to invest in the Basque coast.[17] Similarly, attracted by the new source of wealth, many fishermen in need of a second source of income after the decline of the Basque fishing industry since the eighteenth century also took advantage of the coast's changing fortunes to reinvent themselves. The owners of old chalets along the coast, for instance, renovated them and turned them into rental property for visitors,[18] while others used their boats for fishing in the winter and for coastal tours in the summer.[19] Additionally, some sailors began new jobs on the beach, working as security guards or helping visitors take baths.[20] While tourism and industrialisation challenged the fishing industry and displaced fishermen from the beach, then, the former also offered new job opportunities that locals were often proactive in taking. The percentage of Biarrots working in the hotel business, for example, double from 6 to 12 per cent between 1856 and 1891.[21]

The local administration also invested in the security and respectability of the beaches in order to meet visitors' expectations of finding standardised amenities and services in Biarritz. Given the danger of the Basque coast as a result of floods, for instance, it became imperative to improve the safety of the coastline. As a result, local elites joined tourists in pressuring the *conseil municipal* to create a *société de sauvetage*, which deployed three brigades of lifeguards along the beach and stored emergency medical equipment nearby in case of accident.[22] The municipality, moreover, was quick to comply with visitors' requests for stricter rules on the appropriateness of bathing clothes. Traditionally, the Basques used to bathe on the beaches of Biarritz on Sunday practically naked, a practice that Romantics associated with the purity and naivety of Basque mores.[23] The arrival of upper-class urban visitors, though, required the imposition of new rules of decency and respectability. Indeed, while some scholars have distinguished between nineteenth-century tourists' search for 'authenticity' and twentieth-century visitors' striving for everyday familiarity,[24] early tourists did not appreciate having their social conventions challenged either.[25] As the *conseil municipal* explained in 1852: 'Foreigners, and the Spaniards in particular, began to visit Biarritz and to admire its picturesque atmosphere, but they were disgusted at the idea of bathing the way local bathers did.'[26] The administration satisfied visitors' requests for modesty, building tents and toilets on the beach and imposing a strict dress code. As in other touristic locations like Arcachon,[27] men were to wear a knee-length vest, women a non-transparent vest and children under fourteen a pair of trousers. By 1852, bathers in Biarritz were forbidden from changing clothes outside of the appropriate areas and were asked to leave if they were not appropriately dressed.[28] The 'modern' corruption that Romantics associated with the cosmopolitan identity of Biarritz, in this respect, was largely initiated by local elites themselves.

After Napoleon IIII's proclamation of the Second Empire in December 1852 and his wedding to the Spanish aristocrat Eugénie de Montijo the following month, members of the Basque press committed to publicising the Basque coast in anticipation of an imperial visit, as Louis-Napoleon was interested in the 'modernisation' of the spa towns he visited. Over the course of the 1850s and 1860s, for example, he transformed the cityscapes of Plombières, Saint-Sauveur and Vichy, awarding them new churches, bridges, parks and dykes, and increasing exponentially the number of visitors. In Vichy, in particular, the latter grew from 7,000 in 1852 to 16,000 in 1861.[29] *Le Messager de Bayonne* especially adulated Eugénie, presenting her almost like a member of the Basque family, insofar as she used to visit Biarritz as a child during the First Carlist War. The paper expressed delight in Napoleon III's wedding to Eugénie and hoped that the new empress would soon pay a visit to the Basque country. It argued that shopkeepers in Bayonne still remembered the 'brillante Espagnole' and claimed special knowledge of the empress's true character. 'As in Paris, we know her grace, her spirit; but we also know something that Paris does not know,' the paper wrote: 'her boldness, her courage, both on horseback when she devoured distances, and at sea when, as a brave swimmer, she faced the most furious waves of our shores.'[30] Basque elites, in this sense, did not simply welcome Eugénie to the Basque country; they welcomed her home. Their wish soon became true. The imperial couple visited Biarritz for the first time in 1854 and built a villa there the following year. They resided at the Villa Eugénie almost every summer during the eighteen years of the Empire, boosting the popularity of the town and turning it into a primary aristocratic destination in Europe.

While the preparation for an imperial visit was demanding for town officials, Basque elites equally took advantage of the imperial presence to promote the Basque country and its growing tourist industry. The emperor's interest in the region had obvious economic advantages. His most significant contribution was the inauguration of a rail line from Bordeaux to Bayonne in 1854, three decades earlier than in most of rural France, which immediately increased the number of visitors. At the end of the summer season of 1856, for example, prefect Laity reported that 'this *pays* so far from Paris' was already feeling the positive effect of the railway because the capital was now only twenty-four hours away.[31] The region also took advantage of the network of *routes thermales* that Napoleon III launched to link together the Pyrenean spas, as well as of the *lignes de montagnes* that linked the Basque coast to the interior. The project was inaugurated with some delay in 1905 and had the double intent of uniting the three Basque *pays* and of providing tourists with an easy way of travelling across the Basque Pyrenees.[32] Additionally, during the Second Empire, the presence of the imperial couple in Biarritz provided the town with an aristocratic identity that the Biarrots exploited for tourist purposes. When Charles Richard Weld compared Arcachon to Biarritz to the owner of the Hôtel de France in Biarritz, for instance, the latter was offended. Arcachon, he explained, 'could not be ranked for a moment with Biaritz [sic], which enjoyed Imperial patronage', and whose upper classes came from Paris, not from Bordeaux.[33] In this respect, although Napoleon III's interest in 'modernising' rural France and in networking with local elites was part of his propaganda machine, it was a double-edged sword: provincial elites increasingly expected monetary compensation in exchange for their loyalty to the Empire.[34]

As tourism became increasingly popular and profitable at the turn of the twentieth century, a number of local cultural societies appeared with the aim of promoting the Basque coast. Local notables, like their counterparts across Europe, attracted visitors by emphasising the uniqueness of their region's cultural traditions. Interestingly, at a time when the Basque coast was slowly losing its local character as a result of tourism, local cultural practitioners placed increasing emphasis on its cultural uniqueness, borrowing and compiling folkloric traditions from the entirety of the Basque country. By means of such work of simplification and standardisation of Basque culture, they turned the Basque country into a brand.[35] Although the Basques did not possess as many *syndicats d'initiative* as, for example, eastern and south-eastern France, its associations worked on a similar voluntary basis, shared the goal of cultivating local tourism and, like the *syndicats*, their success depended on the enthusiasm and proactivity of their volunteers.[36] The Comité des fêtes et de publicité, for example, opened in Biarritz in August 1904 with the purpose of persuading an ever-greater number of tourists to visit the town.[37] That December, Monsieur Roland-Gosselin founded the Mimosa Club in Cambo, by then Cambo-les-Bains, hoping that it would become the 'rendezvous point for all foreigners'. Patrons of the club included Edmond Rostand, who built his neo-Basque Villa Arnaga there between 1903 and 1906, and Princess Frederika of Hanover.[38] Henry O'Shea, a British-educated Irish philanthropist and Bascophile, moreover, founded in Biarritz the British Club, which became a point of reference for all British visitors, the Biarritz-Association, a leisure and scientific organisation, as well as the Société d'acclimatation du golfe de Gascogne and the Société des amis des arts de Bayonne-Biarritz, which promoted Basque culture and scientific research.[39] Finally, in 1904 the Club alpin français opened its Basque section and prompted its committee to launch the Syndicat d'initiative du Pays basque, which aimed 'to increase the reputation and prosperity of the Basque country' in the domains of 'hygiene, therapeutics, tourism, alpinism and archaeology'.[40]

The local press prompted the new societies to be bolder and more vocal in their advertisement of Biarritz and the Basque coast, as journalists and readers believed that investing in tourism meant investing in the future of the region as a whole. A letter signed by 'a friend of Biarritz', published in *Le Petit Courrier de Biarritz* in 1907, for example, complained that the recreational activities that the Comité des fêtes organised failed to convince new tourists to visit the town in the first place. At a time when Nice overused advertising and the names of Trouville, Dieppe, Ostend and Arcachon were on everyone's lips, the letter complained, Biarritz went unnoticed.[41] While the remark was exaggerated, as the popularity of Biarritz was greater than ever at the turn of the twentieth century, it revealed two main features of early tourism on the Basque coast as elsewhere. First, it showed the constant pressure and uncertainty that went hand in hand with touristic success, which has prompted Hal Rothman to call tourism a 'devil's bargain'.[42] Second, it highlighted the extent to which local elites were involved in the promotion of tourism. As Eric Zuelow has remarked in his study of tourism in Ireland, a town could not become a successful touristic location without the support, commitment and labour of its population.[43]

Something borrowed, something new

A second aspect of tourism that *littérateurs* misunderstood was the idea that there was a clear-cut separation between activities for tourists and activities for the Basque population. In fact, Basque leisure societies, like their Breton counterparts,[44] consciously organised events that were a mixture of old and new, of French and Basque, and that attracted both tourists and locals. Cosmopolitan activities, on the one hand, included international regattas and horse races, theatre plays and concerts, balls and parties, which caught the attention of visitors and locals alike.[45] *Eskualduna*, for example, pointed out in 1887 that the races in Biarritz in early September were the time of year that drew the highest number of locals from the Basque countryside to town, as the Basques had begun to share tourists' passion for the beach, music and shops.[46] Patrick Young has identified a similar phenomenon in Brittany, which became a tourist attraction in the final decade of the nineteenth century.[47]

Basque activities, on the other hand, included pelota and other traditional games, local dances such as the fandango and the jota, and local music, and were organised by Basque villages every summer for both locals and visitors. *Eskualduna* reported that the pelota match that took place during the *fête* of Urrugne in 1887 witnessed '[b]ig crowds' of foreigners coming from Biarritz, Saint-Jean-de-Luz, Guéthary and Hendaye, who then spent the rest of the day in the village consuming local folklore.[48] In 1909, moreover, *Le Journal de Saint-Jean-de-Luz* noted that Basque folk festivals saw the intermingling of 'mountaineers from Zugarramurdi [and] sailors from Socoa with the elegant cohort of Grand-Dukes of Biarritz'.[49] Additionally, the commercialisation of folk culture was a quintessentially 'modern' phenomenon because it was supported by the nineteenth-century technological advances of the transport network. On the occasion of the pelota match organised for the *fête* of Saint-Jean-de-Luz in 1875, for example, *L'Avenir des Pyrénées et des Landes* pointed out that the reason why the town had 'the monopoly of these great Cantabrian fights' was because of its central location, which could be easily reached by both coach and train.⁵⁰ Thus, local organisers incorporated such 'modern' phenomena as technological development and cultural homogenisation into local culture, prompting an evolution and rethinking of tradition without weakening or destroying it.⁵¹

The preservation of the Basque country's local character was an active concern of Basque elites. While, on the one hand, the adjective 'Basque' was an inherent part of the touristic local brand that needed to be preserved for economic reasons, on the other, safeguarding Basque cultural distinctiveness was local hosts' way of maintaining a sense of local independence and agency vis-à-vis the overwhelming transformative power of tourism. Basque elites, for one thing, advertised the Basque coast as Basque because they were aware that the consumption of folk culture was an inherent aspect of the experience tourists wished to have in the Basque country. In 1907, for example, the Basque notability opposed the idea of renaming as Côte d'Argent the portion of France's Atlantic coast from Royan in the Gironde to Hendaye on the Basque border with Spain – an area which included the whole Côte Basque – because the name was not evocative enough of Basque identity. A letter to *Le Petit Courrier de Biarritz* claimed that changing the coast's name was a mistake because the Basque coast from the Adour to the Bidassoa rivers had to preserve its 'so peculiar and so picturesque' character.⁵² Further, a Parisian woman who signed her letter with the initial M. argued that the coast should preserve its local name because its most representative town, Biarritz, was a Basque town.⁵³ Significantly, moreover, a response to M.'s letter stated that while there may not have been many Basques left in Biarritz, the latter remained a Basque town because tourists saw it as such. The Spaniards, the letter argued, 'sojourned all summers in Biarritz and in Biarritz alone', rather than in any other French seaside town, because the Basque country, of which Biarritz was the touristic centre, represented 'the bridge' between Spain and France. Likewise, the letter added, British visitors also perceived Biarritz as a Basque town. As a result of recent scholarly studies about Basque history and culture, it explained, British visitors had developed great admiration and curiosity for Basque culture and a desire to visit both Biarritz and the Basque country. Although they may not actually know where either Biarritz or the Basque country were on a map, the letter concluded, they wished to visit them both and the name Côte Basque encouraged that purpose.[54] In this respect, as Eric Storm has pointed out, tourists had as much of a say in the branding of regional identities as locals did.[55]

The notabilities of smaller touristic locations also emphasised Basque identity in order to advertise their towns as 'authentically' local vis-à-vis the cosmopolitan identity of Biarritz. Similarly to the *littérateurs*, the notability of aspiring touristic resorts criticised Biarritz for losing its Basque character and portrayed their towns as the true bearers of Basque identity. The small village of Guéthary, in particular, presented itself as a modest version of Biarritz, a description that contained an undisguised moral judgement. Guéthary, local notables implied, did not suffer from the same moral decline as Biarritz and it was ideal for anyone wishing to avoid both the luxury and crowding of the resort. Scholarly visitors responded positively to Guéthary's self-crafted image. Armand de Quatrefages, for example, wrote that 'the cheap price of life, the calm and the isolation of the village, attract all those who abhor the luxury of Biarritz, and who come to ask to the sea relief from real suffering',[56] while Paul Perret pointed out that Guéthary had preserved 'that simple and picturesque character, and that primitive coquetry, which is the charm of the old "Euskarie"'.[57]

While the Biarrots rejected the allegation of being an exclusively elite resort, some were also wary that the tourist industry had spun out of control and that the town's reliance on upper-class tourism had transformed its identity beyond recognition. At the end of a successful summer season in October 1906, for example, *Le Petit Courrier de Biarritz* published an article by V. Riger entitled 'Biarritz s'en va' ('Biarritz is leaving'), which referred to the departure of high society, who used to spend especially the month of September in the Basque resort. By metonymically associating the name of the town with its guests – 'Biarritz is leaving' meant 'the *colonie étrangère* is leaving' – the author suggested that the real Biarritz was that 'apotheosis of light, of perfumes, of flowers, of happiness and of pretty women' that could be witnessed there during the summer. Yet, he added, there was also another Biarritz that emerged after the tourists left: 'the deserted Biarritz, the simple and really beautiful Biarritz, Biarritz the French town'. This version of Biarritz was lovely in 'its serious and serene grace' and attracted 'the dreamers and the artists' who travelled to Biarritz 'to see the Ocean'.[58] The melancholic ending of the article revealed a paradox inherent in local elites' perception of their town: the 'authentic' Biarritz was the silent and beautiful town of the quiet months, yet the real Biarritz was the noisy and superficial resort of the summer season.

Overturning the 'tourist gaze'

While visitors wished to find standardised infrastructure and services on the Basque coast, they also wished to consume local Basque culture. As a result, local hosts commodified their heritage, presenting tourists with a version of their culture that they claimed was 'authentic' but was in fact staged for an external audience. Tourists, in this sense, were not the only ones who gazed; the Basques gazed too and presented tourists with a Basque identity that was a mixture of what guests expected to see and what hosts wished to share with them. The process of staging 'authenticity' perpetuated stereotypes on both sides. Cultural practitioners' marketing of Basque identity reinforced tourists' preconceptions about Basque culture and its people's character. Locals' understanding of which aspects of their identity their guests wished to see, in turn, was equally based on their own simplified view of the average tourist. In this respect, Basque hosts invented 'Basqueness' for tourism. At the same time, by commodifying their culture, the Basques actively crafted an identity for themselves that they shared with the rest of the world. Such a version of Basque culture was based on a simplification and homogenisation of pre-existing traditions, strengthening local pride and producing an empowering version of Basque history that had an educational purpose for visitors and locals alike. The touristic invention of 'Basqueness' was the Basques' way of taking an active part in 'modernity'.

The Basques' staging of their culture began in the aftermath of the Napoleonic Wars, when most visitors were scholars and Romantic travellers. Although at the time 'staged authenticity' was not as standardised as it later became and did not have committees supervising cultural activities, hosts had an instinctual understanding of what visitors were looking for and of how to accommodate it in exchange for money. An early example of 'staged authenticity' was the trips that locals organised for visitors to the Chambre d'Amour, a grotto on the coast north of Biarritz that had been mentioned in Pierre de Lancre's *Tableau de l'inconstance des mauvais anges et démons* in the seventeenth century.[59] According to the legend, two young lovers, Sabaude and Laorens, used to meet there after dark against their parents' wishes; one night the tide surprised them and they drowned after swearing eternal love to each other. The grotto was subsequently named the Love Chamber in their honour.

The experience that locals offered to visitors there was both a form of re-enactment of the legend and a Romantic fabrication of a Basque identity that responded to visitors' expectations and imagination. The day unfolded in three phases. First, male visitors were met at the Porte d'Espagne in Bayonne by young and attractive female guides who served as their *cicerone* for the rest of the day. Second, the guide and her guest travelled to the Chambre d'Amour on the *cacolet*, an uncomfortable wooden bench set on the back of a mule, on which the host and her visitor balanced precariously in close physical proximity. Finally, once at the grotto, the guide recounted the story of Sabaude and Laorens and the pair rested by the sea, in imitation of the two lovers' secret encounters. The visits to the Chambre d'Amour were a lucrative activity through which local hosts presented visitors with the latter's own idealised Romantic vision of the Basque country. The use of young female guides, in particular, had several meanings. For one, it symbolised the survival of an uncorrupted rural world vis-à-vis the immorality of towns. Prosper de Lagarde, for example, mentioned in 1835 that his guide, a young woman with a pretty waist, beautiful eyes and dark hair, had contracted nothing of 'the corruption of the town'.[60] Basque women's exotic self-representation, moreover, characterised a sexually fluid environment that invited male visitors to leave behind the standards of behaviour of upper-class urban life.[61] Although visitors never made explicit reference to sexual encounters in their writings, Corbin has argued that the journeys to the Chambre d'Amour included a 'latent eroticism' that allowed male guests to take liberties with their female guides.[62] As the evolution of the transport network prompted the disappearance of the *cacolet* and its replacement with more comfortable coaches and omnibuses, male travellers elevated the memory of their journeys to a near-mythical status, nostalgically contrasting the simplicity and 'authenticity' of earlier decades to the overly sophisticated and insincere manners of contemporary urban society. As a result, they contributed to the 'sensual mythology' of the Basque country as an exotic place.[63] In the 1850s, for instance, Quatrefages regretted that 'the progress of civilisation' and the new means of transport put an end to 'these picturesque journeys',[64] while an anonymous writer similarly expressed their sadness at the disappearance of the *cacolet* because it symbolised 'the remains of the traditions and mores of past times' and 'the smell of *terroir* that I would have liked to survive the merciless invasions of industry'.[65] Interestingly, travellers' idealisation of the Basque country reflected, to an extent, local hosts' own interpretation of what their guests found attractive in the Basque country.

As the retelling of the legend of the Chambre d'Amour reveals, guides were instrumental in spreading tales about the Basque country. Storytelling was an important means of educational self-representation that allowed the Basques to tell visitors their own version of Basque history.[66] Guides' stories tended to revolve around three themes that became key to Basque stereotyping: Romantic love, military desertion and pelota. The guide who took Louisa Stuart Costello to Roland's Breach in 1844, for example, told her the love story of a deserter, which, she believed, was emblematic of the Basques' *mal du pays*. The protagonist was drafted in Napoleon's Grande Armée and fought valiantly in the wars but as soon as he got the chance, he deserted and travelled home. He lived in hiding but one day he took the risk of appearing at a local *fête* in order to dance with the woman he loved. As a result, he was arrested but was eventually released because his fellow villagers protected him and refused to identify him as the culprit.[67] The most famous desertion story, moreover, was that of the pelota player Parkain or Parquins, which locals recounted in various forms across the nineteenth century. Parkain was a Revolutionary soldier who deserted the army and was forced to flee to Spain. One day, he heard that his pelota rival was organising a match in the border village of the Aldudes and decided to risk his life to cross the frontier and challenge him. He won and, upon the authorities' arrival, he was escorted to the border as a hero by the local population.[68] By means of these stories, the Basques contributed to the standardisation of visitors' views of the Basque country as the land of virile men, outlaws and fierce lovers. Such stereotyping was similar to the one Romantics developed in Spain and, like the latter, placed the Basque country at the crossroads between 'civilisation' and 'barbarism'.[69]

Guides also embodied, and at times enacted, the stereotype of the local man or woman. Female guides, as we have just seen, personified the cliché of the southern European woman. They had dark eyes and long black hair, had simple and pious manners yet also excited male visitors' sexual imagination. Male guides, on their part, displayed strength and agility that were reminiscent of both their ancestors and the protagonists of the stories they recounted. Additionally, they often wore what visitors perceived as traditional clothing as their uniform. Lagarde, for instance, wrote in 1835 that his guide, a young boy aged fifteen who took him from Hendaye to Hondarribia, wore 'his *espadrilles* [and] ran and jumped like a real little Basque'.[70] In 1882, moreover, Perret remarked that the guides at Eaux-Bonnes, in neighbouring Béarn, wore 'the costume of the Val d'Ossau, slightly adjusted to the modern taste: a red shirt, white wool gaiters, brown velvet trousers, the whip strapped to their shoulders'.[71] In turn, visitors seemed to suggest that it was enough for them to dress up 'à la basquaise' and act according to Basque stereotypes to turn into Basques themselves. As he strolled through Béhobie, for example, Lagarde recounted: 'I did not walk; I ran, without paying attention to the place I was crossing. I had become a Basque.'[72] Marie d'Abbadie d'Arrast, moreover, suggested that her vivid portrait of the Basque country would make the tourist arrive in the region as a Frenchman and leave 'as a Basque-acting Basque [Basque basquisant], *makhila* in his hand, beret on his head, red belt tight around his waist, *espargattes, espadrilles or alpargattes* at his feet'.[73] As Patrick Young has observed in his study of Brittany, what visitors understood to be an authentic costume was in fact 'the stylised clothing' worn by the better-off of a particular village on special occasions.[74] In this respect, the *costume traditionnel* was a 'modern' invention that served as a 'visual marker'[75] of the Basque country as a place of tradition and immutability.[76]

Locals staged their authenticity primarily at Basque folk festivals, which, as Chapter 5 explained, were invented by Antoine d'Abbadie in the 1850s. At the *fêtes basques*, the local population entertained visitors with folk dancing, singing and improvised poetry performances, traditional games and, most of all, pelota, which in the nineteenth century came to be known as the Basque national game.[77] Played all over Europe in the early modern period, pelota disappeared everywhere but in the Basque country, where its popularity among both the Basque population and visitors turned it into a quintessential symbol of Basque identity. Event organisers and the local press contributed to fuelling visitors' perceptions of pelota as the embodiment of the Basques' ancestral character. In its advertisement of a game on the occasion of the *fête* of Saint-Jean-de-Luz of 1876, for example, *L'Avenir des Pyrénées et des Landes* wrote that pelota was a noble game, whose 'vigorous gymnastics' had represented the Basques' 'agility, flexibility and strength' since the earliest times.[78] Additionally, they attributed an educational character to the games tourists attended, through which organisers hoped both to attract more visitors and to strengthen the ties between the contemporary Basques and their ancestors, the glorious Cantabrians. During the *fête* of Urrugne of 1890, for example, they set up three different styles of pelota games, which, *Eskualduna* explained, were meant to satisfy all tastes and to provide visitors with a comprehensive understanding of 'the old game of the Iberians'.[79] At the *fête* of Itxassou of 1902, moreover, players engaged in a game with old *chisteras* (the gloves used in pelota). The choice was meant to attract more visitors, as locals understood them to be interested in learning more about the old game.[80] Thus, locals conceptualised pelota as a medium through which to convey a stereotyped image of Basque identity and its genealogy over time.

Avoiding the 'tourist gaze'

While these recreational activities were meant for tourist consumption and hence invited visitors to gaze at the life of the local population, they equally protected hosts from the 'tourist gaze'. Indeed, as Simone Abram has pointed out in her anthropological study of the Auvergne, the same performance could have different meanings for a foreign and a local audience, insofar as locals possessed inside knowledge that allowed them to understand and appreciate recreational activities in ways that tourists' superficial views failed to do. Performances for tourists and for locals, then, did not differ as much in style as in meaning.[81]

A case in point was pelota. For visitors, the game was a form of entertainment and an integral part of the archetype of the Basque man. Lagarde, for example, wrote that pelota was 'the favourite occupation of the whole of the population. This taste manifests itself from childhood, and it would be as rare to find a small child without a pelota ball in the pocket of his vest as it is to find a Normand without an apple or a small Italian *bambino* without his rosary.'[82] For the local population, instead, pelota had multiple overlapping meanings. It was a source of collective enjoyment, of temporary detachment from the difficulties and boredom of everyday life and a source of rivalry within French Basque communities and between French Basques, Spanish Basques and diasporic Basques. *Le Courrier de Bayonne*, for instance, reported on a Franco-Spanish Basque game in Irún in 1853, where the hero of the French Basque team 'came to support the honour of France, together with three young men as vigorous as him. National pride [*L'amour-propre national*] was at stake.'[83] The game that the French Basque Dongaitz from Urrugne and the Spanish Basque Pistia d'Azcoïtia played in Saint-Jean-de-Luz in 1909, moreover, was, according to *Le Journal de Saint-Jean-de-Luz*, 'a real championship match, France versus Spain'.[84] In 1902, a pelota game in Saint-Palais even bypassed the geographical boundaries of the Basque country, as organisers invited the Spanish Basque team to play against an Argentinian Basque team. The Spanish Basque champions Chiquito d'Azcoïtia and Urcelay faced the Argentinian Basque champions Goñi and Soudre in neutral French Basque territory.[85] Thus, while in the summer visitors and locals often attend the same pelota matches, the different meaning that they attributed to the games shielded the local population from the 'tourist gaze'. Since tourists could not understand the deep meaning of what they were witnessing, their gazing was only superficial.

Additionally, although visitors claimed to be looking for 'authenticity', they frequently searched for confirmation of their pre-existing stereotypes about the Basque country. On those occasions when they were faced with 'authentic' outbursts, they did not appreciate them, as the resulting performances were often too hermetic, archaic, overwhelming and unpredictable. It could be off-putting for visitors, for one thing, to see the 'real fury'[86] with which the Basques engaged in and responded to pelota matches. Vincent de Chausenque, for instance, who attended a game in Saint-Jean-de-Luz in 1854, recalled: 'In the middle of this crowd, speaking an unknown language, I felt as foreign as in the depths of Russia.'[87] Similarly, visitors enjoyed Basque music and dance performances when they possessed a homogenised folk character, but they were more lukewarm when the latter lost their standardised and archetypal character and became mere local shows. The writer Pierre Loti, for instance, remarked in 1897 that, during an old man's pan flute and dance performance in Saint-Jean-de-Luz, 'we could hear well, here and there, some idiotic laughs escaping from under [visitors'] elegant hats,' though he admitted that, even 'the most vulgar tourists' were quite charmed. The local population, on the contrary, followed the ceremony in religious silence.[88] When locals performed only for themselves and did not try to meet visitors' expectations, they erected a symbolic wall that separated them from outsiders.

The Basques equally adopted and exaggerated their own archetypes of identity in order to engage in performances that were actively disruptive of tourists' routines. The most renowned of these activities occurred in Cambo on the feast day of St John the Baptist – the *fête de la Saint-Jean* – on 24 June and in Biarritz the weekend following Assumption Day in mid-August. On those two days, the Basques re-enacted their pre-modern custom of drinking the waters of Cambo and of bathing at Biarritz as a protection from illness,[89] and used tradition as a justification for acts of passive resistance against tourists' appropriation of Basque space and culture. In Cambo, on the eve of the Saint-Jean, the Basques descended from the mountains and entered the spa town, singing loudly and playing their traditional instruments, and disrupted the daily routine of the establishment in order to drink the waters.[90] In Biarritz, the Basque population similarly arrived in great numbers from neighbouring villages, singing and dancing, blocking traffic and invading the beaches, where they bathed several times during the day. They wore a special white costume and flower- and ribbon-decorated headgear that replaced the traditional hat. Their actions were purposely disruptive, forcing visitors to make long detours to reach their destinations. 'On that day, the Basque, who is kind and respectful by nature, acts with a certain malice,' an anonymous writer wrote in 1859 about Biarritz;

'but we forgive him because we know that that day is his day.'[91] That Sunday, the author added, was known as the 'Dimanche des Basques' and it was the day when 'the Basques are kings in Biarritz'.[92] The remark was revealing of two aspects of Basque tourism. First, given that Biarritz was a Basque town, the fact that the Basques had a designated day in which they were allowed to take back control and be themselves was emblematic of how much Biarritz and its neighbouring touristic locations had changed in the nineteenth century as a result of tourism. Second, the acts of mockery, masquerading and general disruption were reminiscent of the early modern practice of the *charivari*, which still survived, albeit weakened, in the nineteenth century.[93] As the mock carnivals of the previous centuries were often hidden forms of contestation of secular or religious authorities, the days of the Basques in Biarritz and Cambo represented a temporary form of reappropriation of the spa towns that the local population felt were overwhelmed by tourism.

Conclusion

Basque hosts played an active role in the touristic transformation of the region in the second half of the nineteenth century. On the one hand, local elites promoted the 'modernisation' of Basque spa towns and the standardisation of services and manners, as they believed that the future of the Basque country was cosmopolitan and French-speaking, not local and Euskara-speaking. On the other, they commodified local culture and sold it to tourists as a crucial element of their experience in the Basque country. The cosmopolitan and the local, the 'modern' and the 'archaic' were not at odds with each other. Event organisers embraced the 'modernity' that came with tourism as an opportunity to reconceptualise and strengthen Basque tradition, crafting an archetypal identity that was a valuable economic enterprise, as well as a significant political defence vis-à-vis the homogenising pressure of the nation-state.

The arrival of tourism in the Basque country, then, was a story of local empowerment – at least for those involved in it – not of disappearance of local culture. The traditions that the host population offered to visitors, though, did not necessarily correspond to the 'authenticity' that the latter searched for. As Erve Chambers has argued, a tradition was not authentic only because locals had control over it.[94] In fact, quite the opposite was true. Basque hosts retained their autonomy because they shared with outsiders only those traditions that they wished them to gaze upon. The result was that both hosts and guests understood each other through mutual clichés of identity. Basque cultural practitioners exploited tourists' pre-existing stereotypes of Basque culture in order to attract them to their communities, where their impersonation of an archetypal Basque identity reinforced those same received ideas. While some scholars have argued that the marketing of local culture led to its inevitable impoverishment, Basque elites exploited outsiders' interest in Basque culture to revive locals' pride in it and craft their own interpretation of local history. In this respect, Basque elites' cultivation of regional culture was not a form of conservatism. Rather, it represented their participation in 'modernity' and their contribution to the multifaceted identity of the French nation.

Tourism, however, also played a role in deepening the divide between French-speaking coastal and industrial elites and Euskara-speaking ordinary Basques. This was evident in party divisions at the turn of the twentieth century, when the region became split primarily between two political factions: the Catholic, conservative *xuriak* (whites), which defended traditional values and gained support especially in the rural areas of the Basque country, and the republican, secular *gorriak* (reds), which were in favour of 'modernisation' and met the favour of the touristic coast and the industrial areas of the interior.[95] Although they supported opposite values, they both made use of Basque mythology and stereotypes to define their political programme and win over the electorate. Conservatives adopted Basque ethnic symbolism in order to gain the support of the religious areas of the Basque country, against the process of 'modernisation' and secularisation of the French Republic. Liberals, on their part, cultivated local folklore for touristic purposes and positioned Basque culture within a French cosmopolitan cultural network. Although conservatives often accused liberals of weakening the 'authentic' character of Basque culture, intellectuals across the political spectrum from the French Revolution to the Third Republic reinvented Basque identity at a time when the community, both the local and the national, was reimagined. The position of the *petite patrie* within the *grande patrie* began at the local level with an intense work of ideological negotiation within the region itself.

Notes

1. Adam T. Rosenbaum, *Bavarian Tourism and the Modern World, 1800–1950* (Cambridge, 2016), 2–3.
2. MacCannell, 'Staged Authenticity', 589–603.
3. See, for example, Johan Vincent, *L'Intrusion balnéaire. Les populations littorales bretonnes et vendéennes face au tourisme (1800–1945)* (Rennes, 2007); Patrick Young, *Enacting Brittany: Tourism and Culture in Provincial France, 1871–1939* (Farnham, 2012).
4. Alain Corbin, *Le Territoire du vide. L'Occident et le désir de rivage (1750–1840)* (Paris, 1988), 283–317; Jean-Didier Urbain, *Sur la Plage. Mœurs et coutumes balnéaires (XIXe–XXe siècles)* (Paris, 1996), 19.
5. Pitchford, *Identity Tourism,* 84–5 and 87.
6. Philip Frick McKean, 'Towards a Theoretical Analysis of Tourism: Economic Dualism and Cultural Involution in Bali', in Valene L. Smith (ed.), *Hosts and Guests: The Anthropology of Tourism* (Philadelphia, 1977), 98–104.
7. Urry, *The Tourist Gaze.*
8. Pitchford, *Identity Tourism*, 98.
9. Darya Maoz, 'The Mutual Gaze', *Annals of Tourism Research,* 33:1 (2006), 221–39.
10. A.D., E dépôt/Biarritz/1D6, Session of the *conseil municipal* of Biarritz, November 1852.
11. Chauvirey, *La Vie quotidienne au Pays basque*, 133 and 135; Jean Laborde, 'L'Impératrice Eugénie à Bayonne et à Biarritz (suite et fin)', *Bulletin de la Société des sciences, lettres et arts de Bayonne,* 75 (1956), 7.
12. A.D., E dépôt/Biarritz/1D6, Session of the *conseil municipal* of Biarritz, November 1852; De Chausenque, *Les Pyrénées,* 184; *Le Courrier de Bayonne,* 10 April 1855; *Le Courrier de Bayonne,* 13 June 1852.
13. Morel, *Bayonne*, 431: 'Biarritz prend largement sa part de la civilisation des quatre-vingt-six départemens.'
14. A.D., E dépôt/Biarritz/1D6, Session of the *conseil municipal* of Biarritz, November 1852: 'dans une large voie de progrès et de bien être'.
15. Louis Turner and John Ash, *The Golden Hordes: International Tourism and the Pleasure Periphery* (London, 1975), 14.
16. Alfred Vigreux, 'Biarritz en 1858', *L'Illustration,* 32:2 (1858), 165: 'véritables monuments parmi ces lilliputiennes habitations'.

17 A.D., E dépôt/Saint-Jean-de-Luz/3R1, Monsieur Jolivet to the mayor of Saint-Jean-de-Luz, 30 September 1854; *Le Courrier de Bayonne*, 18 April 1856.
18 Anonymous, *Une Saison d'été à Biarritz*, 62.
19 Ibid., 147.
20 Laborde, *Histoire du Tourisme*, 35.
21 Ibid., 77–8.
22 A.D., E dépôt/Biarritz/1D5, Session of the *conseil municipal* of Biarritz, November 1845; A.D., E dépôt/Biarritz/1D6, Session of the *conseil municipal* of Biarritz, November 1852.
23 See, for example, Hugo, *Voyage vers les Pyrénées*, 69–70.
24 George Ritzer and Allan Liska, '"McDisneyization" and "Post-Tourism": Complementary Perspectives on Contemporary Tourism', in Chris Rojek and John Urry (eds), *Touring Cultures: Transformations of Travel and Theory* (London and New York, 1997), 99.
25 For a similar argument about Brittany and the Vendée, see Vincent, *L'Intrusion balnéaire*, 136.
26 A.D., E dépôt/Biarritz/1D6, Session of the *conseil municipal* of Biarritz, November 1852: 'L'étranger, les espagnols surtout commençaient à visiter Biarritz, à admirer sa pittoresque situation, mais il répugnaient à se livrer au bain, comme l'avaient fait les baigneurs du pays.'
27 Alice Garner, *A Shifting Shore: Locals, Outsiders, and the Transformation of a French Fishing Town, 1823–2000* (Ithaca, 2004), 109.
28 A.D., E dépôt/Saint-Jean-de-Luz/3R1, Ordinance of the mayor of Saint-Jean-de-Luz, 1 September 1857; A.D., E dépôt/Saint-Jean-de-Luz/3R1, Decree of the mayor of Saint-Jean-de-Luz, [1840s]; Laborde, *Histoire du Tourisme*, 35.
29 Armand Wallon, *La Vie quotidienne dans les villes d'eaux, 1850–1914* (Paris, 1981), 79–80.
30 *Le Messager de Bayonne*, 1 February 1853: 'On connaît ici comme à Paris sa grâce, son esprit; mais on y connaît ce que Paris ignore: sa hardiesse, son courage, soit à cheval, quand elle dévorait l'espace, soit à la mer, quand, hardie nageuse, elle affrontait les plus furieuses vagues de nos grèves.'
31 A.N., F/1cIII/Basses-Pyrénées/7, The prefect to the minister of the interior, 20 October 1856: 'ce pays si éloigné de Paris'.
32 *Eskualduna*, 15 September 1905.
33 Weld, *The Pyrenees*, 50.
34 On the propaganda machine of the Second Empire in provincial France, see Matthew Truesdell, *Spectacular Politics: Louis-Napoleon Bonaparte and the* Fête Impériale, *1849–1870* (Oxford, 1997), 121–9 and 159–69.

35 Eric Storm, 'Tourism and the Construction of Regional Identities', in Xosé M. Núñez Seixas and Eric Storm (eds), *Regionalism and Modern Europe: Identity Construction and Movements from 1890 to the Present Day* (London, 2018), 100.
36 Julie Manfredini, *Les Syndicats d'initiative. Naissance de l'identité touristique en France* (Tours, 2017), 24 and 36–7.
37 *Le Petit Courrier de Biarritz*, 14 August 1904.
38 *Le Petit Courrier de Biarritz*, 18 December 1904: 'point de rendez-vous de tous les étrangers'.
39 *Le Petit Courrier de Biarritz*, 10 September 1905 and 1 October 1905.
40 *Le Petit Courrier de Biarritz*, 13 March 1904: 'd'augmenter la réputation et la prospérité du Pays Basque ... l'hygiène, de la thérapeutique, du tourisme, de l'alpinisme et de l'archéologie'.
41 *Le Petit Courrier de Biarritz*, 1 September 1907.
42 Hal Rothman, *Devil's Bargain: Tourism in the Twentieth-Century American West* (Lawrence, 1998).
43 Eric G. E. Zuelow, *Making Ireland Irish: Tourism and National Identity since the Irish Civil War* (Syracuse, 2009), xvii.
44 Young, *Enacting Brittany*, 75.
45 *Le Petit Courrier de Biarritz*, 14 August 1904 and 13 August 1905.
46 *Eskualduna*, 10 September 1887.
47 Young, *Enacting Brittany*, 1.
48 *Eskualduna*, 10 September 1887: 'Grande affluence'.
49 *Le Journal de Saint-Jean-de-Luz*, 12 September 1909: 'des montagnards de Zugarramundi, des marins du Socoa avec l'élégante cohorte des Grands-Ducs de Biarritz'.
50 *L'Avenir des Pyrénées et des Landes*, 4 September 1875: 'le monopole de ces grandes luttes cantabres'.
51 For a similar argument in contemporary Scotland, see Sharon Macdonald, 'A People's Story: Heritage, Identity and Authenticity', in Chris Rojek and John Urry (eds), *Touring Cultures: Transformations of Travel and Theory* (London and New York, 1997), 160.
52 *Le Petit Courrier de Biarritz*, 7 June 1907: 'si particulier et si pittoresque'.
53 *Le Petit Courrier de Biarritz*, 7 July 1907.
54 *Le Petit Courrier de Biarritz*, 4 August 1907: 'séjournaient tous les étés à Biarritz et à Biarritz seulement'; 'pont'.
55 Eric Storm, *The Culture of Regionalism: Art, Architecture and International Exhibitions in France, Germany and Spain, 1890–1939* (Manchester, 2010), 2.
56 Quatrefages, *Souvenirs d'un naturaliste*, 163: 'Le bon marché de la vie, le calme et l'isolement du village, y attirent tous ceux qu'effraie le

57 Perret, *Les Pyrénées françaises*, 62: 'ce caractère simple et pittoresque, et cette coquetterie primitive, qui est le charme de la vieille "Euskarie"'.

58 *Le Petit Courrier de Biarritz*, 14 October 1906: 'apothéose de lumière, de parfums, de fleurs, de gaîté et de jolies femmes'; 'le Biarritz désert, le Biarritz simple et vraiment beau, le Biarritz ville française'; 'avec sa grâce grave et sereine ... les rêveurs et les artistes ... pour y voir l'Océan'.

59 Pierre de Lancre, *Tableau de l'inconstance des mauvais anges et démons, où il est amplement traicté de sorciers et de la sorcellerie* (Paris, 1613), 41.

60 Lagarde, *Voyage dans le Pays basque et aux bains de Biarritz*, 76: 'la corruption de la cité'.

61 Nigel Morgan and Annette Pritchard, *Tourism Promotion and Power: Creating Images, Creating Identities* (Chichester, 1998), 193.

62 Corbin, *Le Territoire du vide*, 99: 'érotisme latent'.

63 Morgan and Pritchard, *Tourism Promotion and Power*, 193.

64 Quatrefages, *Souvenirs d'un naturaliste*, 151–2: 'Le progrès de la civilisation ... ces voyages pittoresques'.

65 Anonymous, *Une Saison d'été à Biarritz*, 35: 'un reste de traditions et des mœurs simples d'autrefois ... d'une odeur de terroir que j'aurais voulu voir survivre aux impitoyables envahissements de l'industrie'.

66 Macdonald, 'A People's Story', 160–1.

67 Stuart Costello, *Bearn and the Pyrenees*, 248–50.

68 Jouy, *L'Hermite en province*, 149–50; Lavigne, *Autour de Biarritz*, 127; *Eskualduna*, 21 October 1904.

69 Andreu Miralles, *El descubrimiento de España*, 21.

70 Lagarde, *Voyage dans le Pays basque et aux bains de Biarritz*, 119–20: 'ses *spardilles*, courait et sautillait comme un vrai petit Basque'.

71 Perret, *Les Pyrénées françaises*, 408: 'le costume du val d'Ossau, légèrement approprié au goût moderne: chemise rouge, guêtres de laine blanche, culotte de velours brun, le fouet en bandoulière'.

72 Lagarde, *Voyage dans le Pays basque et aux bains de Biarritz*, 157–8: 'Je ne marchais pas, je courais, sans faire attention au pays que je traversais, j'étais devenu Basque.'

73 D'Abbadie d'Arrast, *Causeries sur le Pays basque*, 11: 'Basque basquisant, le makhila au poignet, le béret sur le chef, les reins serrés dans la ceinture rouge, les pieds chaussés d'espargattes, espadrilles ou alpargattes'.

74 Young, *Enacting Brittany*, 137.
75 Ibid., 140.
76 Jean-Pierre Lethuillier, 'Costumes régionaux, objets d'histoire', in Jean-Pierre Lethuillier (ed.), *Les Costumes régionaux entre mémoire et histoire* (Rennes, 2009), 11.
77 *Le Journal de Saint-Jean-de-Luz*, 12 September 1909; Jouy, *L'Hermite en province*, 150–1.
78 *L'Avenir des Pyrénées et des Landes*, 4 July 1876: 'la gymnastique vigoureuse ... l'agilité, la souplesse et la force'.
79 *Eskualduna*, 5 September 1890: 'le vieux jeu des Ibères'.
80 *Eskualduna*, 15 August 1902.
81 Simone Abram, 'Performing for Tourists in Rural France', in Simone Abram, Jacqueline Waldren and Donald V. L. Macleod (eds), *Tourists and Tourism: Identifying with People and Places* (Oxford and New York, 1997), 45.
82 Lagarde, *Voyage dans le Pays basque et aux bains de Biarritz*, 65: 'c'est l'occupation favorite de toute la population. Ce goût se manifeste dès l'enfance, et il serait aussi rare de trouver un petit garçon sans pelote dans la poche de sa veste, qu'un normand sans pomme, ou un petit bambino italien sans chapelet.'
83 *Le Courrier de Bayonne*, 21 August 1853: 'se présenta pour soutenir l'honneur de la France, avec trois jeunes hommes tous vigoureux comme lui. L'amour-propre national était en jeu'.
84 *Le Journal de Saint-Jean-de-Luz*, 8 August 1909: 'une véritable partie de championnat, France contre Espagne'.
85 *Eskualduna*, 4 April 1902.
86 Jouy, *L'Hermite en province*, 145: 'véritable fureur'.
87 Chausenque, *Les Pyrénées*, 191: 'Au milieu de cette foule, parlant un langage inconnu, j'étais aussi étranger qu'au fond de la Russie.'
88 Pierre Loti, *Le Pays basque. Récits et impressions de l'Euskal-Herria* (Bordeaux, 1992), 81: 'On entendit bien çà et là quelques rires bêtes s'échapper de dessous des chapeaux élégants ... des plus vulgaires touristes.'
89 Perret, *Les Pyrénées françaises*, 163.
90 Fabre, *Lettres labourdines*, 225; Perret, *Les Pyrénées françaises*, 161–2.
91 Vigreux, 'Biarritz in 1858', 166; Anonymous, *Une Saison d'été à Biarritz*, 122: 'Ce jour-là le Basque, qui est bon et respectueux de sa nature, y met un peu de malignité; on le lui pardonne, parce qu'on sait que ce jour-là c'est son jour.'
92 Anonymous, *Une Saison d'été à Biarritz*, 121–2: 'les Basques sont rois à Biarritz'.

93 On the practice of the *charivari* in the early nineteenth century, see Sheryl Kroen, *Politics and Theater: The Crisis of Legitimacy in Restoration France* (Berkeley, 2000), 208.
94 Erve Chambers, *Native Tours: The Anthropology of Travel and Tourism* (Long Grove, 2010), 102.
95 Gurrutxaga, *Transformation of National Identity*, 98–9.

Conclusion: a Basque region in a French nation

France in the long nineteenth century was both a 'nationalising state' and a regionalising nation.[1] The two phenomena were simultaneous and symbiotic, and were a reaction to the French Revolution's formulation of a unitary idea of French nationhood in 1789. The invention of the political nation in the 1790s produced two consequences that defined the political debate in France and Europe in the following century. On the one hand, the nation needed to be defined, negotiated and, ultimately, constructed. On the other, pre-existing local identities had to be refashioned in order to fit into the new European political and cultural system of nation-states. Local cultures, then, were not victims of nation-building,[2] but equally they did not simply precede the age of nationalism. The region was a cultural 'imagined community'[3] that was invented in the nineteenth century alongside the nation in order to counter nationalism's inherent claims of cultural and linguistic uniformity and to craft a role for local cultures within the new nation-state. Like the nation, the region was built in phases that, as Miroslav Hroch has posited, started with cultural practitioners and ended in a mass movement.[4] The first half of the nineteenth century corresponded to phase A of region-building, when cultural practitioners engaged in processes of cultural production. The second half of the century witnessed a slow transition to phases B and C, when the population at large became receptive to regional culture and militant regionalists began to instrumentalise it for propagandistic and political purposes.[5] The turn of the twentieth century, which historians have defined as the pinnacle of regionalism in Europe,[6] represented the climax of a process of region-building that started in 1789.

With its ancient language and distinctive culture, the French Basque country was one of those regions of France, alongside Brittany and Flanders among others, that became an ideal testing ground for new ideas of nationhood in the nineteenth century. Conservatives, for one, identified the region as a cradle of such traditional values as piety, monarchy and ancestry. The restored Bourbons believed that a return to these ideals would re-establish law and order in France after the Revolutionary and Napoleonic Wars. After 1830, legitimists, losing ground in the symbolic counterrevolutionary region of the Vendée, regarded the Basque country as their last hope for countering the advance of liberalism and restoring an *ancien-régime* system of government in Europe. Additionally, conservatives at the turn of the twentieth century viewed the Basque country as one of the regions that embodied the values of *la terre et les morts* that came to define the far-right monarchist movement Action française in 1899.

The liberal, bourgeois elites that governed France during the July Monarchy and part of the Second Empire, in turn, also showed appreciation for the Basques' simplicity of mores and moral 'authenticity' but regarded them primarily as a counterexample to the alleged corruption and immorality of the aristocracy.[7] At the same time, they deplored the Basques' lack of interest in progress and 'modernity' and identified the Basque country and Brittany as examples of ahistorical nations that, like the peoples of the colonies, had no place in the 'modern' world and were doomed to be swallowed by bigger, historical nations. Finally, republicans shared with liberals a progressive view of history, which they believed began with the French Revolution and ended with the achievement of France's predestined unity under a republican government. The principle of unity was the defining feature of republicans' idea of France and, after the proclamation of the Third Republic in 1870, they regarded the attachment to local languages and religion of the Basques, the Bretons and the Flemish as remnants of counterrevolutionary thought and, hence, as dangerous instances of anti-patriotic and anti-French sentiments. Concurrently, though, republicans accepted regional diversity to be an essential aspect of the nation. They envisaged the local community as a school of democratic values and the *petite patrie* as a 'local metaphor' for the *grande patrie*.[8] In this regard, François Ploux has contended that the first decades of the Third Republic were the golden age of the *petites patries*.[9]

Basque elites' response to such an appropriation of Basque culture was simultaneously proactive and reactive. On the one hand, their own interpretation of 'Basqueness' was the result of the position they hoped to obtain and play within France. Across the nineteenth century, Basque elites interpreted the same tropes of identity differently according to their ideological stance and whether or not they wished to support the regime in power. At the beginning of the Third Republic, for instance, two rival newspapers, the conservative *Eskualduna* and the pro-republican *Le Réveil basque*, emphasised the historical myths of Basque liberty and independence to support opposite political commitments: *Eskualduna* to prove the Basques' preservation of traditional values vis-à-vis republican France, and *Le Réveil basque* to associate Basque liberty and equality with the classic ideals of the French Revolutionary and republican tradition.[10]

Basque elites' employment of folklore was equally fluid, insofar as they used it both as a defence of Basque cultural exceptionalism within France and as a touristic source of revenue directed primarily at French visitors. Basque 'staged authenticity'[11] for tourist consumption perpetuated cultural stereotypes that standardised Basque identity and contributed to an idea of France as the sum of its regions. In this respect, Basque identity was reactive to France's politically and culturally changing circumstances and was malleable enough to accommodate the needs of those who wished to use it. On the other hand, local notables emphasised the uniqueness of Basque culture in order to foster the wellbeing of local communities. During the Revolutionary and Napoleonic Wars, for instance, administrative and military personnel defended Basque soldiers' proneness to desertion by making use of such tropes of identity as their attachment to liberty and susceptibility to the *mal du pays*. Local and national authorities 'flagged' Basque-specific qualities and metonymic stereotypes that they believed would both shield the Basques from aggressive state centralisation and smooth their process of integration into France. In its use of local culture vis-à-vis the nation, the Basque region shared similarities with Alsace. There, according to Elizabeth Vlossak, the creation of an Alsatian identity was contingent on the forging of French and German national identities. As such, it was fluid and was responsible for the homogenisation of a diverse range of pre-existing local identities.[12] Thus, the flexible, recurrent and often 'banal' employment of the *petite patrie* in the national discourse contributed to the emergence of self-aware regional cultural communities in the long nineteenth century.[13]

The invention of the Basque region was a transnational phenomenon. While historians have shown that it was customary for nineteenth-century European cultural practitioners to operate simultaneously at the national and international level,[14] Basque culture complicated such a relationship because it extended across the boundaries of France and Spain. The *ancien-régime* French Basque *pays* of Labourd, Basse-Navarre and Soule shared cultural and linguistic traits with the Spanish Basque provinces of Guipúzcoa, Álava, Vizcaya and Navarra, which local and international scholars worked to identify, define, protect and mobilise throughout the nineteenth century. French and Spanish Basque *savants'* mutual influence produced paradoxical results. For one thing, it increased the Basques' self-consciousness of their shared cultural identity and strengthened the cultural unity of the seven Basque provinces. At times when local elites perceived the pressure of state centralisation as a threat to Basque tradition, the Basque country's transnational identity was a powerful tool of political mobilisation. At the same time, Basque elites regarded local culture as a vehicle towards nation-building, national patriotism and the integration of the Basque provinces into France and Spain. Although the lines between culture and politics were blurred, French and Spanish Basque militants in the nineteenth century always fell into the category of regionalists, not of nationalists.

As scholars have recently pointed out with reference to the Spanish Basque country, then, the construction of the French Basque region in the long nineteenth century was not a teleological prelude to the advent of independentist nationalism.[15] It was a period of negotiation between different understandings of Basque and French identity, which laid the foundation for the relationship between France and the Basque country in the twentieth century. Especially significant was the invention of a transnational Basque linguistic and literary tradition in the nineteenth century. It was part of a scholarly effort to equip the Basque country with a historical and cultural repertoire that would strengthen its position within the French nation-state and consequently avoid the slow disappearance of Basque culture and, especially, language. Comparative philological works, for example, reinforced the myth of Basque Iberianism, the theory according to which the biblical ancestors of the Basques were the first population of Spain and Euskara the first language of the whole Iberian Peninsula. Basque literary œuvres, on their part, strengthened the myth of Basque Cantabrianism, the belief that throughout history the Basques had never been conquered. Both myths aimed to prove the purity of the Basque nation, as well as its antiquity, which Basque elites hoped awarded the Basque country a high and safe position in the hierarchy of 'modern' nations. Antoine d'Abbadie's invention of the *fêtes basques* in 1853 similarly intended to popularise Basque culture as an element of French culture but also to protect it from the French state's cultural and linguistic centralisation. Such dichotomy was inescapably uneasy. On the one hand, Basque tradition was to an extent meant for visitors' consumption, which protected it from disappearance but also attributed to it a folkloric character that deprived it of its vibrancy and spontaneity. On the other hand, as both the French and Spanish Basques battled centralisation at the end of the nineteenth century, the lines between apolitical and militant cultural events became increasingly blurred.

Classic histories of the French Basque country have neglected the importance of the nineteenth century in the definition of both a French Basque cultural identity and its relationship with the French nation-state. Historians have depicted French Basque 'modern' history as a tale of strife between the French state and the Basques that started with the loss of their liberties and attack on their faith during the French Revolution, continued with the secularising policies of the Third Republic, and ended in the troubled twentieth century.[16] Such teleological interpretation of French Basque history presents a distorted understanding of the interplay between ideas of region and nation in the nineteenth century. First, region-building was always, to an extent, a political phenomenon without for this reason being a precursor of separatism. Local *savants* may not always possess openly political goals, but their wish to emphasise and protect local culture within the nation-state, their request for state funding and promotion, and their understanding of culture as a means of improving the welfare of local communities had a political, or at least civic, character. In its civic use of culture, the Basque case shared similarities with Normandy. There, François Guillet has argued, local *savants* studied, cultivated and publicised local culture in order to both protect it from national homogenisation and favour their region's integration into 'modern' France.[17] Given the inherent political meaning of the 'modern' nation, then, culture was rarely completely depoliticised.[18]

Additionally, while historians have argued that regions differ from nations in that they do not possess strong myths of origin,[19] Basque elites developed a strong mythical, literary and historical tradition, and even defined the Basque country as a nation. However, they conceptualised the latter as part of French culture and of the French nation, not as a counterculture or a separate nation to the French. The use of the word 'nation', in this respect, did not have separatist undertones but was a way for such ancient *ethnies* as the Basques, the Bretons and the Provençaux to be recognised for their cultural historicity within France.[20] The French, moreover, used the word *patrie* to define both the Basque region and the French nation. Political elites regarded the region as a *petite patrie*, or small motherland, and France as the *grande patrie*, or big motherland. While the *grande patrie* was the sum of a shared past, territory and cultural values, *and* of its citizens' will to be joined together and strive for national greatness, the *petite patrie* lacked such civic commitment but, at a cultural level, operated like the bigger nation and, as such, could foster national patriotism. In this regard, despite the republican myth's pervasive claim of national unity, France's fostering of its *petites patries* was not dissimilar to federal Germany's use of local *Heimaten* as boosters of national patriotism.[21]

Finally, by overlooking the nineteenth century, historians of the French Basque country have strangely corroborated the republican myth's contention that France started coming into being as a nation in 1789 and achieved completion during the Third Republic. Such teleology fails to recognise the period between 1814 and 1870, when France was mostly not a republic, as crucial for the symbiotic growth of regional and national identities in France. The negotiations between the local and the national across the nineteenth century were essential for the idea of unity-in-diversity that came to define France in the twentieth century and created strong political, socio-economic and cultural ties between France and the Basque country that tamed future nationalistic tendencies.

The tale of Basque region-building in the age of French nationalism, then, is revealing of the oxymoron between Jacobin centralisation and omnipresent regionalism that has defined the dominant idea of

France since 1789. The paradox continues to be impossible to overcome both at the national and at the local level. On the one hand, the nation as a territorially defined community of citizens sharing the same culture is a mirage that will never be fully achieved, and such failure will constantly defy the messianic role of *la République une et indivisible*. In this respect, the French Revolution as the inventor of the myth of national unity is not over and will never be so. On the other hand, regional cultures will never sit comfortably within the unitary nation. Integration into the nation-state cannot be political and economic without being, to an extent, cultural too. Yet cultural integration raises fears of obliteration, and the moment when programmes are set in place to revive or protect local cultures, these become standardised, folkloric and somewhat unserious vis-à-vis the gravitas of *la grande nation*. The inherent incompatibility between the region and the nation, as a result, creates tensions that the state is forced to keep in balance to avoid outbursts that could expose the fragility of the national myth.

Notes

1 Rogers Brubaker, *Nationalism Reframed: Nationhood and the National Question in the New Europe* (Cambridge, 2000), 79.
2 On the classic historiography that argues that nation-building destroyed local identities, see Weber, *Peasants into Frenchmen*. On a classic counterargument, see Ford, *Creating the Nation in Provincial France*.
3 Anderson, *Imagined Communities*.
4 Hroch, *Social Preconditions of National Revival in Europe*, 22–3.
5 Leerssen, 'Introduction', 20–1.
6 See, for example, Wright, *The Regionalist Movement in France*.
7 Leerssen, *National Thought in Europe*, 102–3.
8 Confino, *The Nation as a Local Metaphor*.
9 Ploux, *Une Mémoire de papier*, 15.
10 *Eskualduna*, 15 March 1887; *Le Réveil basque*, 8 August 1886.
11 MacCannell, 'Staged Authenticity'.
12 Vlossak, *Marianne or Germania?*, 15, 19, 23 and 25.
13 On the notions of 'banal nationalism' and of 'flagging the homeland', see Michael Billig, *Banal Nationalism* (London, 2012), 98 and 102.
14 Manias, *Race, Science, and the Nation*; Swenson, *The Rise of Heritage*; Storm, *The Culture of Regionalism*.

15 Agirreazkuenaga, *The Making of the Basque Question*; Molina Aparicio, 'La disputada cronología de la nacionalidad'; Molina Aparicio, 'España no era tan diferente'.
16 See, especially, Jacob, *Hills of Conflict*; James E. Jacob, 'The French Revolution and the Basques of France', in William A. Douglass (ed.), *Basque Politics: A Case Study in Ethnic Nationalism* (Reno, 1985), 51–102. For local studies, see Etcheverry, 'Les Basques et l'unité nationale sous la Révolution'; Isidoro de Fagoaga, 'Dominique Garat, le défenseur du Biltzar', *Bulletin de la Société des sciences, lettres et arts de Bayonne*, 123–5 (1970–71), 153–202, 209–52, 77–125; Maïté Lafourcade, 'Les Fors et les droits de l'homme', *Lapurdum*, 8 (2003), 329–48; Castaingts-Beretervide, *La Terreur et la déportation des Basques du Labourd*.
17 Guillet, *Naissance de la Normandie*, passim.
18 On the distinction between a political and a cultural region, see Joost Augusteijn and Eric Storm, 'Introduction: Region and State', in Joost Augusteijn and Eric Storm (eds), *Region and State in Nineteenth-Century Europe: Nation-Building, Regional Identities and Separatism* (London, 2012), 3.
19 Núñez, 'Historiographical Approaches to Sub-national Identities in Europe', 21.
20 On the notion of *ethnie*, see Smith, *The Ethnic Origins of Nations*.
21 Applegate, *A Nation of Provincials*; Confino, *The Nation as a Local Metaphor*.

Bibliography

Primary manuscript sources
Archives nationales de France, Paris, France (A.N.)

Série D (Missions des représentants du peuple et comités des assemblées révolutionnaires)
  Sous-série D/IVbis (Comité de division): D/IVbis/52, D/IVbis/71
  Sous-série D/XL (Comité des pétitions, dépêches et correspondances): D/XL/15
Série F (Versements des ministères et des administrations qui en dépendent)
  Sous-série F/1bII (Personnel administratif, série départementale): F/1bII/Basses-Pyrénées/9, F/1bII/Basses-Pyrénées/10
  Sous-série F/1cIII (Esprit public et élections): F/1cIII/Basses-Pyrénées/7, F/1cIII/Basses-Pyrénées/8, F/1cIII/Basses-Pyrénées/10, F/1cIII/Basses-Pyrénées/11
  Sous-série F/1cV (Conseils généraux, série départementale): F/1cV/Basses-Pyrénées/1, F/1cV/Basses-Pyrénées/2
  Sous-série F/1cVII (Conseils d'arrondissement, série départementale): F/1cVII/46
  Sous-série F/7 (Ministère de l'Intérieur, police intérieure): F/7/3822, F/7/9171, F/7/9689
  Sous-série F/9 (Affaires militaires): F/9/236, F/9/312, F/9/325
  Sous-série F/17 (Instruction publique): F/17/9251, F/17/9306/1, F/17/9375
  Sous-série F/19 (Cultes): F/19/461, F/19/5502, F/19/5784

Archives départementales des Pyrénées-Atlantiques, Pau, France (A.D. Pau)

Série C (Administration provinciale, archives antérieures à 1789): C/1540, C/1601, C/1621
Série J (Archives privées): 1/J/897/4, 1/J/897/5

Bibliography

Série M (Administration générale et économie, archives de 1800 à 1940)
Sous-série 1M (Administration générale du département): 1/M/52

*Archives départementales des Pyrénées-Atlantiques,
Pôle de Bayonne et du Pays basque, Bayonne, France (A.D.)*

Série E dépôt (Archives communales)
Sous-série BB (Administration communale, archives antérieures à 1789):
E dépôt/Ustaritz/BB8, E dépôt/Bayonne/BB64
Sous-série 1D (Conseil municipal, archives de 1800 à 1940): E dépôt/
Biarritz/1D5, E dépôt/Biarritz/1D6
Sous-série 2D (Actes de l'administration municipale, archives de 1800 à
1940): E dépôt/Bayonne/2D9, E dépôt/Came/2D5, E dépôt/Came/2D6,
E dépôt/Came/2D10
Sous-série 1R (Instruction publique, archives de 1800 à 1940): E dépôt/
Bidart/1R1
Sous-série 3R (Sport et tourisme, archives de 1800 à 1940): E dépôt/
Saint-Jean-de-Luz/3R1

Service Historique de la Défense, Vincennes, France (S.H.D.)

Série B (Révolution)
Sous-série B/4 (Armée de la subdivision sud, 1792–1895): B/4/112
Série K (Documents entrés par voie extraordinaire)
Sous-série KX (Troupes spéciales): KX/11

Newspapers

Ariel
L'Avenir des Pyrénées et des Landes
Le Courrier de Bayonne
Eskualduna
L'Europe
La Gazette de France
La Gazette du Languedoc
Le Journal de Saint-Jean-de-Luz
Le Légitimiste
Le Messager de Bayonne
La Mode
Le Petit Courrier de Biarritz
La Quotidienne
Le Rénovateur

Le Réveil basque
La Sentinelle des Pyrénées

Primary printed sources

Affre, P.-R., *Manuel du baigneur, ou Notice médicale sur les bains de mer de Biarritz (Basses-Pyrénées)* (Paris, 1856).

Anonymous, *Une Saison d'été à Biarritz. Biarritz autrefois, Biarritz aujourd'hui* (Bayonne, 1859).

Araquistain, Juan V., *Tradiciones Vasco-Cántabras* (Tolosa, 1866).

Aulard, F.-A. (ed.), *Recueil des actes du Comité de Salut Public avec la correspondance officielle des représentants en mission et le registre du conseil exécutif provisoire. 10 août 1794–20 septembre 1794*, Volume 6 (Paris, 1904).

Aulard, F.-A. (ed.), *Recueil des actes du Comité de Salut Public avec la correspondance officielle des représentants en mission et le registre du conseil exécutif provisoire. 9 février 1794–15 mars 1794*, Volume 11 (Paris, 1897).

Barère, Bertrand, 'Rapport du Comité de Salut Public sur les idiomes', in Michel de Certeau, Dominique Julia and Jacques Revel, *Une Politique de la langue. La Révolution française et les patois: l'enquête de Grégoire* (Paris, 2002), 321–31.

Basterreche, Léon, *Dénonciation des crimes de Monestier, de Puy-de-Dôme, aux membres composant les comités de gouvernement* (Bayonne, [1795]).

Baudrimont, Alexandre, *Histoire des basques ou escualdunais primitifs* (Paris, 1854).

Bernadou, M., 'Compte rendu des fêtes de la tradition basque à Saint-Jean-de-Luz', in Gustave Boucher (ed.), *La Tradition au Pays basque* (Paris, 1899), 11–77.

Bladé, Jean-François, *Dissertation sur les chants héroïques des Basques* (Paris, 1866).

Bladé, Jean-François, *Études sur l'origine des basques* (Paris, 1869).

Buchez, P.-J.-B. and P.-C. Roux (eds), *Histoire parlementaire de la Révolution française, ou Journal des Assemblées Nationales depuis 1789 jusqu'en 1815*, Volume 4 (Paris, 1834).

Burrow, George Henry, *The Bible in Spain* (Champaign, [1843] 1996).

Campión, Arturo, 'Amaya ó los bascos en el siglo VIII. Estudio crítico', *Revista Euskara*, 3 (1880), 54–64, 74–86, 115–22, 145–54.

Campión, Arturo, *Orreaga (Roncesvalles). Balada escrita en el dialecto guipuzcoano* (Pamplona, 1880).

Caumery and Joseph Pinchon, *Bécassine au Pays basque* (Paris, 1925).

Chaho, Augustin, *Paroles d'un Bizkaïen aux libéraux de la reine Christine* (Paris, 1834).

Chaho, Augustin, *De l'agonie du parti révolutionnaire en France. Lettre à Monsieur Jacques Laffitte* (Paris, 1838).

Chaho, Augustin, *La Légende d'Aïtor*, Hector Iglesias ed. (Saint-Denis, [1845] 2017).

Chaho, Augustin, *Histoire primitive des Euskariens-Basques* (Madrid and Bayonne, 1847).

Chaho, Augustin, *Biarritz entre les Pyrénées et l'océan. Itinéraire pittoresque*, Volume 2 (Bayonne, 1855).

Chaho, Augustin, *Voyage en Navarre pendant l'insurrection des Basques (1830–1835)* (Bayonne, 1865).

Chaho, Augustin, 'La leyenda de Aitor', *Revista Euskara*, 1 (1878), 220–30, 241–9 and 281–92.

Comisión de fiestas euskaras, 'Elizondoco Bestac/Fiestas euskaras de Elizondo', *Revista Euskara*, 2 (1879), 153–7.

D'Abbadie, Antoine and Augustin Chaho, *Études grammaticales sur la langue euskarienne* (Paris, 1836).

D'Abbadie d'Arrast, Marie, *Causeries sur le Pays basque. La femme et l'enfant* (Paris, 1909).

Darrigol, Jean-Pierre, *Dissertation critique et apologétique sur la langue basque par un ecclésiastique du diocèse de Bayonne* (Bayonne, 1827).

Dasconaguerre, J.-B., *Les Échos du Pas de Roland* (Paris, 1867).

De Arrese y Beitia, Felipe, 'Ama Euskeriari azken agurrak', *Revista Euskara*, 2 (1879), 238–43.

De Astarloa, Pablo Pedro, *Apología de la lengua bascongada, ó ensayo crítico filosófico de su perfeccion y antigüedad* (Madrid, 1803).

De Chausenque, Vincent, *Les Pyrénées, ou Voyages pédestres dans toutes les régions de ces montagnes depuis l'océan jusqu'à la Méditerranée*, Volume 1 (Agen, 1854).

De Custine, Robert, *Les Bourbons de Goritz et les Bourbons d'Espagne* (Paris, 1839).

De Erro y Azpiroz, Juan Bautista, *Alphabet de la langue primitive de l'Espagne et explication de ses plus anciens monumens, en inscriptions et médailles; suivi de la critique de cet ouvrage*, Éloi Johanneau trans. (Paris, 1808).

De Fourcaud, Louis, 'Discours prononcé à Saint-Jean-de-Luz à l'occasion de l'ouverture du Congrès de la tradition basque', in Gustave Boucher (ed.), *La Tradition au Pays basque* (Paris, 1899), 3–7.

De Galarza, Arellano et al., 'Fiestas euskaras de Bilbao', *Revista Euskara*, 5 (1882), 117–48.

De Goizueta, José María, *Leyendas vascongadas* (Madrid, 1851).

De Iparraguirre, José Maria, 'Gernikako Arbola', *Revista Euskara*, 2 (1879), 18–19.

De Jouy, Étienne, *L'Hermite en province, ou observations sur les mœurs et les usages français au commencement du XIXe siècle*, Volume 1 (Paris, 1819).

De Lagarde, Prosper, *Voyage dans le Pays basque et aux bains de Biaritz* (Paris, 1835).

De Lancre, Pierre, *Tableau de l'inconstance des mauvais anges et démons, où il est amplement traicté de sorciers et de la sorcellerie* (Paris, 1613).

De Larramendi, Manuel, *Diccionario trilingüe del castellano, bascuence y latin* (San Sebastián, [1745] 1853).

De Lavigne, Germond, *Autour de Biarritz. Promenades à Bayonne, à la frontière et dans le Pays basque* (Paris, 1856).

De Polverel, Étienne, *Tableau de la constitution du royaume de Navarre, et de ses rapports avec la France* (Paris, 1789).

De Quatrefages, Armand, *Souvenirs d'un naturaliste*, Volume 2 (Paris, 1854).

De Saint-Léger, A. and E. Delbet, 'Paysan du Labourd (Basses-Pyrénées, France)', in Frédéric Le Play (ed.), *Les Ouvriers des deux mondes*, Volume 1 (Paris, 1857), 161–220.

D'Iharce de Bidassouet, Pierre, *Histoire des cantabres ou des premiers colons de toute l'Europe avec celle des basques, leurs descendants directs* (Paris, 1825).

Du Mège, Alexandre, *Statistique générale des départements pyrénéens, ou des provinces de Guienne et de Languedoc*, Volume 2 (Paris, 1829).

Engels, Friedrich, 'Der magyarische Kampf', in Karl Marx and Friedrich Engels, *Werke*, Volume 6 (Berlin, 1959), 165–73.

Fabre, M. H.-L., *Lettres labourdines ou lettres sur la partie du Pays basque appelée le Labourd* (Bayonne, 1869).

Fauriel, Claude, *Histoire de la Gaule méridionale sous la domination des conquérants Germains*, Volume 2 (Paris, 1836).

Filon, Augustin, *Souvenirs sur l'impératrice Eugénie* (Paris, 1920).

Gambetta, Léon, 'Discours prononcés le 1er octobre 1872 à La Roche et à Annecy', in *Discours et plaidoyers politiques de M. Gambetta*, Volume 3, Joseph Reinach ed. (Paris, 1881), 154–86.

Garat, Dominique-Joseph, 'Analyse de l'entendement', in *Séances des Écoles Normales, recueillies par des sténographes, et revues par les professeurs*, Volume 2 (Paris, 1795), 3–40.

Garat, Dominique-Joseph, *Mémoire sur la Hollande* (Paris, 1805).

Garat, Dominique-Joseph, 'Lettre de D. J. Garat à Napoléon 1er', Jean Casenave ed., *Lapurdum*, 11 ([1811] 2006), 131–2.

Garat, Dominique-Joseph, 'Recherches sur le peuple primitif de l'Espagne; sur les révolutions de cette péninsule; sur les Basques espagnols et françois.

Rapport établi en 1811 pour Napoléon Ier', Jean Casenave ed., *Lapurdum*, 11 ([1811] 2006), 75–123.

[Garay de Monglave, Eugène], 'Canto de Altobiscar', Hermilio Olóriz ed., *Revista Euskara*, 1 (1878), 28–32.

Gautier, Théophile, *Voyage en Espagne* (Paris, 1859).

Grégoire, Henri, 'Rapport sur la nécessité et les moyens d'anéantir les patois et d'universaliser l'usage de la langue française', in Michel de Certeau, Dominique Julia and Jacques Revel, *Une Politique de la langue. La Révolution française et les patois: l'enquête de Grégoire* (Paris, 2002), 331–51.

Haristoy, Pierre, *Les Paroisses du Pays basque pendant la période révolutionnaire*, Volume 1 (Pau, 1895).

Hugo, Victor, *Voyage vers les Pyrénées*, Francis Claudon ed. (Paris, [1845] 2001).

Loti, Pierre, *Le Pays basque. Récits et impressions de l'Euskal-Herria* (Bordeaux, 1992).

Malthus, Thomas, *First Essay on Population* (London, [1798] 1926).

Manterola, José, *Cancionero vasco. Poesías en lengua euskara*, Volume 1 (San Sebastián, 1877).

Mazure, Adolphe, *Histoire du Béarn et du Pays basque* (Pau, 1839).

Michel, Francisque, *Le Pays basque. Sa population, sa langue, ses mœurs, sa littérature et sa musique* (Paris, 1857).

Michel, Francisque, 'Basque Popular Poetry', *The Gentleman's Magazine*, 5 (1858), 381–3.

Michelet, Jules, *Le Peuple* (Paris, 1846).

Montaran, Marie Constance Albertine, *Mes Pensées en voyage: excursions dans les Pyrénées* (Paris, 1868).

Morel, Félix, *Bayonne, vues historiques et descriptives* (Bayonne, 1836).

Navarro Villoslada, Francisco, *Amaya o los vascos en el siglo VIII*, Volume 3 (Madrid, 1879).

Obanos, Estéban et al., 'Asociacion Euskara de Navarra. Programa', *Revista Euskara*, 1 (1878), 3–5.

Olivier, G., 'Chants populaires', *Dictionnaire de la conversation et de la lecture*, Volume 13 (Paris, 1834), 14–29.

Olóriz, Hermilio, 'El romance en Euskaria', *Revista Euskara*, 1 (1878), 99–105.

Paris, Gaston, 'Discours prononcé à la Sorbonne le 24 mars 1895', in *La Tradition en Poitou et en Charentes: art populaire, ethnographie, folk-lore, hagiographie, histoire. Société d'ethnographie nationale et d'art populaire, Congrès de Niort* (Paris, 1897), iii–vii.

Perret, Paul, *Les Pyrénées françaises: le Pays basque et la Basse-Navarre*, Volume 2 (Paris and Poitiers, 1882).

Petit, Charles, 'Antoine d'Abbadie', in Gustave Boucher (ed.), *La Tradition au Pays basque* (Paris, 1899), 539–60.

Planté, Adrien, 'Les Basques, ont-ils une histoire?', in Gustave Boucher (ed.), *La Tradition au Pays basque* (Paris, 1899), 111–37.

Reclus, Élisée, 'Les Basques. Un peuple qui s'en va', *Revue des Deux Mondes*, 68:2 (1867), 313–40.

Renan, Ernest, *Qu'est-ce qu'une Nation?*, Philippe Forest ed. (Paris, [1882] 1991).

Roergas de Serviez, Emmanuel-Gervais, *Statistique du département des Basses-Pyrénées* (Paris, 1801).

Rousseau, Jean-Jacques, 'Discours sur l'origine de l'inégalité parmi les hommes', in *Œuvres complètes de J.-J. Rousseau*, Volume 6, Louis Barré ed. (Paris, [1754] 1856–7), 230–94.

Sallaberry, J.-D.-J., *Chants populaires du Pays basque* (Bayonne, 1870).

Sanadon, Jean-Baptiste, *Essai sur la noblesse des basques: pour servir d'introduction à l'histoire générale de ces peuples* (Pau, 1785).

Santesteban, José António, *Colección de aires vascongados para canto y piano* (San Sebastián, 1878).

Spach, Louis, 'Chants populaires', *Encyclopédie des gens du monde*, Volume 5 (1835), 416–19.

Stuart Costello, Louisa, *Bearn and the Pyrenees: A Legendary Tour to the Country of Henri Quatre*, Volume 2 (London, 1844).

Taine, Hippolyte, *Voyage aux Pyrénées* (Paris, 1860).

Van Eys, Willem, *Essai de grammaire de la langue basque* (Amsterdam, 1867).

Vigreux, Alfred, 'Biarritz in 1858', *L'Illustration. Journal universel*, 32:2 (1858), 165–6.

Vinson, Julien, *Les Basques et le Pays basque: mœurs, langage et histoire* (Paris, 1882).

Vinson, Julien, *Le Folk-lore du Pays basque* (Paris, 1883).

Vocaltha, *Zumalacarreguy et l'Espagne, ou Précis des évènemens militaires qui se sont passés dans les provinces basques depuis 1831* (Nancy, 1835).

Von Humboldt, Wilhelm, *Die Vasken, oder Bemerkungen auf einer Reise durch Biscaya und das französische Basquenland im Frühling des Jahrs 1801, nebst Untersuchungen über die Vaskische Sprache und Nation, und einer kurzen Darstellung ihrer Grammatik und ihres Wörtervorraths* (Berlin, [1801] 1920).

Von Humboldt, Wilhelm, 'Berichtungen und Zusätze zum ersten Abschnitte des zweyten Bandes des Mithridates über die Cantabrische oder Baskische Sprache', in Johann Christoph Adelung, *Mithridates oder allgemeine Sprachenkunde mit dem Vater Unser als Sprachprobe in bey nahe fünf hundert Sprachen und Mundarten* (Berlin, 1817), 275–360.

Von Humboldt, Wilhelm, *Recherches sur les habitants primitifs de l'Espagne, à l'aide de la langue basque*, M. A. Marrast trans. (Paris, [1821] 1866).

Webster, Wentworth, *Basque Legends* (London, 1877).
Webster, Wentworth, 'Les Pastorales basques', in Gustave Boucher (ed.), *La Tradition au Pays basque* (Paris, 1899), 244–58.
Weld, Charles Richard, *The Pyrenees, West and East* (London, 1859).
Wellesley, Arthur, *The Dispatches of Field Marshal the Duke of Wellington during his Various Campaigns in India, Denmark, Portugal, Spain, the Low Countries, and France*, Volume 7, Colonel Gurwood, C.B., K.C.T.S. ed. (London, 1845).
Yturbide (ed.), 'Cahiers de doléances de Bayonne et du Pays du Labourt aux États Généraux de 1789', *Bulletin de la Société des sciences, lettres et arts de Bayonne* (1909), 5–32, 65–84, 129–54, 193–220.

Secondary sources

Aaslestad, Katherine B., *Place and Politics: Local Identity, Civic Culture, and German Nationalism in North Germany During the Revolutionary Era* (Leiden and Boston, 2005).
Abram, Simone, 'Performing for Tourists in Rural France', in Simone Abram, Jacqueline Waldren and Donald V. L. Macleod (eds), *Tourists and Tourism: Identifying with People and Places* (Oxford and New York, 1997), 29–50.
Agirreazkuenaga, Joseba, *The Making of the Basque Question: Experiencing Self-Government, 1793–1877* (Reno, 2011).
Agnew, John, 'The Territorial Trap: The Geographical Assumptions of International Relations Theory', *Review of International Political Economy*, 1:1 (1994), 53–80.
Ahedo Gurrutxaga, Igor, *The Transformation of National Identity in the Basque Country of France, 1789–2006*, Cameron J. Watson trans. (Reno, 2008).
Anderson, Benedict, *Imagined Communities: Reflections on the Origin and Spread of Nationalism* (London and New York, 1983).
Andreu Miralles, Xavier, *El descubrimiento de España. Mito romántico e identidad nacional* (Barcelona, 2016).
Applegate, Celia, *A Nation of Provincials: The German Idea of Heimat* (Berkeley, 1990).
Aragón Ruano, Álvaro, 'French Basque and Béarnais Trade Diaspora from the Spanish Basque Country During the Eighteenth Century', *Atlantic Studies*, 16:4 (2019), 452–81.
Aranzadi, Juan, *Milenarismo vasco: Edad de Oro, etnia y nativismo* (Madrid, 2000).
Augusteijn, Joost and Eric Storm, 'Introduction: Region and State', in Joost Augusteijn and Eric Storm (eds), *Region and State in Nineteenth-Century*

Europe: Nation-Building, Regional Identities and Separatism (London, 2012), 1–9.

Augusteijn, Joost and Eric Storm (eds), *Region and State in Nineteenth-Century Europe: Nation-Building, Regional Identities and Separatism* (London, 2012).

Bann, Stephen, *The Clothing of Clio: A Study of the Representation of History in Nineteenth-Century Britain and France* (Cambridge, 1984).

Bann, Stephen, 'History as Romance and History as Atonement: Nineteenth-Century Images from Britain and France', in Stefan Berger, Chris Lorenz and Billie Melman, *Popularizing National Pasts: 1800 to the Present* (New York and London, 2012), 58–74.

Banti, Alberto Mario, *La nazione del Risorgimento: parentela, santità e onore alle origini dell'Italia unita* (Turin, 2000).

Banti, Alberto Mario, 'Conclusions: Performative Effects and "Deep Images" in National Discourse', in Laurence Cole (ed.), *Different Paths to the Nation: Regional and National Identities in Central Europe and Italy, 1830–1870* (London, 2007), 220–9.

Barnard, Frederick M., *Herder on Nationality, Humanity, and History* (Montreal, 2003).

Bauman, Richard and Charles L. Briggs, *Voices of Modernity: Language Ideologies and the Politics of Inequality* (Cambridge, 2003).

Baycroft, Timothy, *Culture, Identity and Nationalism: French Flanders in the Nineteenth and Twentieth Centuries* (Woodbridge, 2004).

Baycroft, Timothy, 'France: Ethnicity and the Revolutionary Tradition', in Timothy Baycroft and Mark Hewitson (eds), *What Is a Nation? Europe 1789–1914* (Oxford, 2006), 28–41.

Baycroft, Timothy, *France* (London, 2008).

Bell, David A., *The Cult of the Nation in France: Inventing Nationalism, 1680–1800* (Cambridge, MA, 2003).

Benes, Tuska, *In Babel's Shadow: Language, Philology, and the Nation in Nineteenth-Century Germany* (Detroit, 2008).

Berger, Stefan, 'National Histories and the Promotion of Nationalism in Historiography – the Pitfalls of "Methodological Nationalism"', in Stefan Berger and Eric Storm (eds), *Writing the History of Nationalism* (London, 2019), 19–40.

Bergès, Louis, *Résister à la conscription, 1798–1814. Le cas des départements aquitains* (Paris, 2002).

Biard, Michel, *Les Lilliputiens de la centralisation. Des intendants aux préfets, les hésitations d'un 'modèle français'* (Seyssel, 2007).

Billig, Michael, *Banal Nationalism* (London, 2012).

Blanchard, Laëtitia, 'Violence politique et légitimisme pendant la première guerre carliste: une occasion manquée', *Amnis*, 17 (2018).

Blanchard Rubio, Laëtitia, 'Les Provinces basques et la Navarre en guerre vue par les français, 1833–1839' (PhD thesis, Université Paris 3, 1999).

Blanchard Rubio, Laëtitia, 'Impressions de guerre: images et imaginaires de la première guerre carliste (1833–1840)', *Cahiers de la Méditerranée*, 83 (2011), 147–62.

Blanchard Rubio, Laëtitia, 'La Première guerre carliste ou la guerre de la dernière chance: la communauté légitimiste face à son destin', *Amnis*, 10 (2011).

Blanchard Rubio, Laëtitia, 'La Mémoire du conflit carliste et ses enjeux: entre usage politique et mise en ordre du passé', *Amnis*, 18 (2019).

Boivin, Nicole and Michael D. Frachetti, 'Introduction: Archaeology and the "People Without History"', in Nicole Boivin and Michael D. Frachetti (eds), *Globalization in Prehistory: Contact, Exchange, and the 'People Without History'* (Cambridge, 2018), 1–14.

Bortone, Pietro, *Language and Nationality: Social Inferences, Cultural Differences, and Linguistic Misconceptions* (London, 2022).

Broers, Michael, *Europe Under Napoleon, 1799–1815* (London, 1996).

Broers, Michael, 'Cultural Imperialism in a European Context? Political Culture and Cultural Politics in Napoleonic Italy', *Past and Present*, 170 (2001), 152–80.

Broers, Michael, 'Napoleon, Charlemagne and Lotharingia: Acculturation and the Boundaries of Napoleonic Europe', *Historical Journal*, 44:1 (2001), 135–54.

Broers, Michael, *The Napoleonic Empire in Italy, 1796–1814: Cultural Imperialism in a European Context?* (London, 2004).

Broers, Michael, *Napoleon's Other War: Bandits, Rebels and their Pursuers in the Age of Revolutions* (Witney, 2010).

Brophy, James M., 'Which Political Nation? Soft Borders and Popular Nationhood in the Rhineland, 1800–1850', in Maarten van Ginderachter and Marnix Beyen (eds), *Nationhood from Below: Europe in the Long Nineteenth Century* (London and New York, 2012), 162–89.

Brubaker, Rogers, *Citizenship and Nationhood in France and Germany* (Cambridge, MA, 1992).

Brubaker, Rogers, *Nationalism Reframed: Nationhood and the National Question in the New Europe* (Cambridge, 2000).

Burns, William, 'Industrial Revolution', in Christopher John Murray (ed.), *Encyclopedia of the Romantic Era, 1760–1850*, Volume 1 (New York and London, 2004), 558–9.

Canal, Jordi, *El Carlismo. Dos siglos de contrarrevolución en España* (Madrid, 2000).

Castaingts-Beretervide, Mayi, *La Terreur et la déportation des Basques du Labourd, 1794* (Sare, 1994).

Chabal, Émile, *A Divided Republic: Nation, State and Citizenship in Contemporary France* (Cambridge, 2015).

Chakrabarty, Dipesh, *Provincializing Europe: Postcolonial Thought and Historical Difference* (Princeton, 2009).

Chambers, Erve, *Native Tours: The Anthropology of Travel and Tourism* (Long Grove, 2010).

Chanet, Jean-François, *L'École républicaine et les petites patries* (Paris, 1996).

Charbonnel, Jean, *Les Légitimistes. De Chateaubriand à de Gaulle* (Paris, 2006).

Chauvirey, Marie-France, *La Vie quotidienne au Pays basque sous le Second Empire* (Paris, 1975).

Confino, Alon, *The Nation as a Local Metaphor: Württemberg, Imperial Germany, and National Memory, 1871–1918* (Chapel Hill, 1997).

Corbin, Alain, *Le Territoire du vide. L'Occident et le désir de rivage (1750–1840)* (Paris, 1988).

Corbin, Alain, *Le Monde retrouvé de Louis-François Pinagot. Sur les traces d'un inconnu, 1798–1876* (Paris, 1998).

Coverdale, John F., *The Basque Phase of Spain's First Carlist War* (Princeton, 1984).

Craiutu, Aurelian, *Liberalism under Siege: The Political Thought of the French Doctrinaires* (Oxford, 2003).

Crook, Malcom, *Napoleon Comes to Power: Democracy and Dictatorship in Revolutionary France, 1795–1804* (Cardiff, 1998).

D'Andurain de Maytie, 'Les Élections législatives de 1824 dans l'arrondissement de Mauléon', *Bulletin de la Société des sciences, lettres et arts de Bayonne*, 137–8 (1981–82), 355–63.

D'Auria, Matthew, *The Shaping of French National Identity: Narrating the Nation's Past, 1715–1830* (Cambridge, 2020).

De Certeau, Michel, Dominique Julia and Jacques Revel, *Une Politique de la langue. La Révolution française et les patois: l'enquête de Grégoire* (Paris, 2002).

Decroix, Arnaud, *Question fiscale et réforme financière en France (1749–1789). Logique de la transparence et recherche de la confiance publique* (Aix-en-Provence, 2006).

De Fagoaga, Isidoro, 'Dominique Garat, le défenseur du Biltzar', *Bulletin de la Société des sciences, lettres et arts de Bayonne*, 123–5 (1970–71), 153–202, 209–52, 77–125.

De la Granja Sainz, José Luis, 'La invención de la historia. Nación, mitos e historia en el pensamiento del fundador del nacionalismo vasco', in Justo G. Beramendi, Ramón Máiz and Xosé M. Núñez (eds), *Nationalism in Europe: Past and Present*, Volume 2 (Santiago de Compostela, 1994), 97–140.

Bibliography

Deluermoz, Quentin, *Le Crépuscule des révolutions, 1848–1871* (Paris, 2012).

Desan, Suzanne, *Reclaiming the Sacred: Lay Religion and Popular Politics in Revolutionary France* (Ithaca, 1990).

Desplat, Christian, 'Crise et projets économiques à Bayonne et en Labourd à la fin du XVIIIe siècle', *Bulletin de la Société des sciences, lettres et arts de Bayonne*, 137–8 (1981–82), 263–77.

De Syon, Guillaume, 'French Romanticism: Its Literary Legacy', in Christopher John Murray (ed.), *Encyclopedia of the Romantic Era, 1760–1850*, Volume 1 (New York and London, 2004), 385–6.

De Tocqueville, Alexis, *L'Ancien Régime et la Révolution* (Paris, 1856).

Ellingson, Ter, *The Myth of the Noble Savage* (Berkeley, 2001).

Esdaile, Charles J., *The Wars of Napoleon* (London and New York, 2019).

Etcheverry, Michel, 'Les Basques et l'unité nationale sous la Révolution', *Bulletin de la Société des sciences, lettres et arts de Bayonne*, 11 (January–June, 1933), 75–97.

Fellerer, Jan, 'Theories of Language', in Paul Hamilton (ed.), *The Oxford Handbook of European Romanticism* (Oxford, 2016).

Fitzsimmons, Michael P., 'Privilege and Polity in France, 1786–1791', *American Historical Review*, 92:2 (1987), 269–96.

Fleming, K. E., 'Philhellenism', in Christopher John Murray (ed.), *Encyclopedia of the Romantic Era, 1760–1850*, Volume 2 (New York and London, 2004), 872–3.

Force, Pierre, *Wealth and Disaster: Atlantic Migrations from a Pyrenean Town in the Eighteenth and Nineteenth Centuries* (Baltimore, 2016).

Ford, Caroline, *Creating the Nation in Provincial France: Religion and Political Identity in Brittany* (Princeton, 1993).

Forrest, Alan, *The French Revolution and the Poor* (Oxford, 1981).

Forrest, Alan, 'Conscription and Crime in Rural France during the Directory and the Consulate', in Gwynne Lewis and Colin Lucas (eds), *Beyond the Terror: Essays in French Regional and Social History* (Cambridge, 1983), 92–120.

Forrest, Alan, *Conscripts and Deserters: The Army and French Society During the Revolution and Empire* (Oxford, 1989).

Forrest, Alan, *The Revolution in Provincial France: Aquitaine, 1789–1799* (Oxford, 1996).

Forrest, Alan, *The Legacy of the French Revolutionary Wars: The Nation-in-Arms in French Republican Memory* (Cambridge, 2009).

Forrest, Alan, 'Reimagining Space and Power', in Peter McPhee (ed.), *A Companion to the French Revolution* (Chichester, 2012), 91–106.

Frick McKean, Philip, 'Towards a Theoretical Analysis of Tourism: Economic Dualism and Cultural Involution in Bali', in Valene L. Smith (ed.), *Hosts and Guests: The Anthropology of Tourism* (Philadelphia, 1977), 93–107.

Furet, François and Jacques Ozouf, *Lire et écrire: l'alphabétisation des français de Calvin à Jules Ferry* (Paris, 1977).

Garner, Alice, *A Shifting Shore: Locals, Outsiders, and the Transformation of a French Fishing Town, 1823–2000* (Ithaca, 2004).

Garzia, Joxerra, Jon Sarasua and Andoni Egaña, *The Art of Bertsolaritza: Improvised Basque Verse Singing* (San Sebastián, 2001).

Gates, David, *The Spanish Ulcer: A History of the Peninsular War* (London, 1986).

Gellner, Ernest, *Nations and Nationalism* (Oxford, 1983).

Gemie, Sharif, *Brittany, 1750–1950: The Invisible Nation* (Cardiff, 2007).

Gengembre, Gerard, *La Contre-révolution ou l'histoire désespérante* (Paris, 1989).

Gerson, Stéphane, 'Parisian Litterateurs, Provincial Journeys and the Construction of National Unity in Post-Revolutionary France', *Past and Present*, 151 (1996), 141–73.

Gerson, Stéphane, *The Pride of Place: Local Memories and Political Culture in Nineteenth-Century France* (Ithaca, 2003).

Gildea, Robert, *Education in Provincial France, 1800–1914: A Study of Three Departments* (Oxford, 1983).

Gildea, Robert, *The Past in French History* (New Haven and London, 1994).

Girardet, Raoul, *Mythes et mythologies politiques* (Paris, 1986).

Godechot, Jacques, *La Contre-révolution: doctrine et action, 1789–1804* (Paris, 1961).

Godechot, Jacques, 'Les Variations de la politique française à l'égard des pays occupés, 1792–1815', in *Occupants-occupés, 1792–1815. Actes du colloque qui s'est tenu à Bruxelles, les 29 et 30 janvier 1968* (Brussels, 1969), 15–33.

Goedert, Nathalie, 'La Corse et l'exception administrative: les premiers pas de l'administration préfectorale', *La Revue administrative*, 54:320 (2001), 229–52.

Goldstein Sepinwall, Alyssa, *The Abbé Grégoire and the French Revolution* (Berkeley, 2005).

Goyheneche, Eugène, 'Un Ancêtre du nationalisme basque. Augustin Chaho et la guerre carliste', *Euskal Herria (1789–1850). Actes du colloque international d'Études Basques* (Bayonne, 1978), 229–59.

Goyhenetche, Jean, 'Deux cas historiographiques des guerres de la Convention: l'évacuation des communes du Labourd et l'exécution de Madeleine Larralde', in Jean-Baptiste Orpustan (ed.), *La Révolution française dans l'histoire et la littérature basques du XIXe siècle* (Saint-Étienne-de-Baïgorry, 1994), 163–88.

Goyhenetche, Manex, *Histoire générale du Pays basque. Évolution politique et institutionnelle du XVIe au XVIIIe siècle*, Volume 2 (San Sebastián and Bayonne, 2000).

Goyhenetche, Manex, *Histoire générale du Pays basque. La Révolution de 1789*, Volume 4 (San Sebastián and Bayonne, 2002).

Grab, Alexander, 'Army, State, and Society: Conscription and Desertion in Napoleonic Italy (1802–1814)', *Journal of Modern History*, 67:1 (1995), 25–54.

Greenfield, Jerome, *The Making of a Fiscal-Military State in Post-Revolutionary France* (Cambridge, 2022).

Grémion, Pierre, *Le Pouvoir périphérique. Bureaucrates et notables dans le système politique français* (Paris, 1976).

Gueniffey, Patrice, *Histoires de la Révolution et de l'Empire* (Paris, 2011).

Guillet, François, *Naissance de la Normandie. Genèse et épanouissement d'une image régionale en France, 1750–1850* (Caen, 2000).

Halty, Dominique, *Épisodes des guerres napoléoniennes au Pays basque* (Pau, 1998).

Hargenvilliers, A.-A., *Compte général de la conscription*, Gustave Vallée ed. (Paris, 1937).

Haritschelhar, Jean, 'The Eighteenth and Nineteenth Centuries: Bridges across Borders', in Mari Jose Olaziregi (ed.), *Basque Literary History* (Reno, 2012), 109–33.

Harp, Stephen L., *Learning to Be Loyal: Primary Schooling as Nation-Building in Alsace and Lorraine, 1850–1940* (DeKalb, 1998).

Harris, Ruth, *Lourdes: Body and Spirit in the Secular Age* (London, 1999).

Haywood, Ian, *The Making of History: A Study of the Literary Forgeries of James MacPherson and Thomas Chatterton in Relation to Eighteenth-Century Ideas of History and Fiction* (London and Toronto, 1986).

Hazareesingh, Sudhir, *From Subject to Citizen: The Second Empire and the Emergence of Modern French Democracy* (Princeton, 2016).

Heiberg, Marianne, *The Making of the Basque Nation* (Cambridge, 1989).

Heitmann, Klaus, *Das Rumänenbild im deutschen Sprachraum, 1775–1918* (Cologne, 1985).

Herman, Arthur, *The Idea of Decline in Western History* (New York, 1997).

Hobsbawm, Eric, 'Introduction: Inventing Traditions', in Eric Hobsbawm and Terence Ranger (eds), *The Invention of Tradition* (Cambridge, 1983), 1–14.

Hobsbawm, E. J., *Nations and Nationalism Since 1780: Programme, Myth, Reality* (Cambridge, 1990).

Hopkin, David, 'Regionalism and Folklore', in Xosé M. Núñez Seixas and Eric Storm (eds), *Identity Construction and Movements from 1890 to the Present Day* (London, 2018), 43–64.

Hourmat, Pierre, 'L'Enseignement primaire dans les Basses-Pyrénées au temps de la Monarchie Constitutionnelle 1815–1848 (suite)', *Bulletin de la Société des sciences, lettres et arts de Bayonne*, 127 (1972), 1–102.

Hroch, Miroslav, *Social Preconditions of National Revival in Europe: A Comparative Analysis of the Social Composition of Patriotic Groups Among the Smaller European Nations* (New York, 2000).

Ilacqua, Talitha, 'An Open Border for Two Bordered States: Basque Disputes and the Remaking of the Franco-Spanish Frontier', in Anna Ross and Christos Aliprantis (eds), *State Formation and Administration in Europe, 1830–1870* (Oxford, forthcoming).

Israel, Jonathan, *Revolutionary Ideas: An Intellectual History of the French Revolution from* The Rights of Man *to Robespierre* (Oxford and Princeton, 2014).

Jacob, James E., 'The French Revolution and the Basques of France', in William A. Douglass (ed.), *Basque Politics: A Case Study in Ethnic Nationalism* (Reno, 1985), 51–102.

Jacob, James E., *Hills of Conflict: Basque Nationalism in France* (Reno, 1994).

Jaume, Lucien, *L'Individu effacé ou le paradoxe du libéralisme français* (Paris, 1997).

Jeismann, Michael, 'Nation, Identity, and Enmity: Towards a Theory of Political Identification', in Timothy Baycroft and Mark Hewitson (eds), *What Is a Nation? Europe 1789–1914* (Oxford, 2006), 17–27.

Jennings, Jeremy, *Revolution and the Republic: A History of Political Thought in France since the Eighteenth Century* (Oxford, 2011).

Jones, Chris, 'Middle Ages', in Christopher John Murray (ed.), *Encyclopedia of the Romantic Era, 1760–1850*, Volume 2 (New York and London, 2004), 743–4.

Jourdan, Annie, *Nouvelle Histoire de la Révolution* (Paris, 2018).

Juaristi, Jon, '*El Cantar de Beotibar, ¿un romance noticiero vasco?*', *Anuario del Seminario de filología vasca 'Julio De Urquijo'*, 20:3 (1986), 845–56.

Juaristi, Jon, *El linaje de Aitor: La invención de la tradición vasca* (Madrid, 1987).

Juaristi, Jon, *El bucle melancólico: historias de nacionalistas vascos* (Madrid, 2000).

Judson, Pieter M., *The Habsburg Empire: A New History* (Cambridge, MA, 2016).

Kale, Steven D., *Legitimism and the Reconstruction of French Society, 1852–1883* (Baton Rouge, 1992).

Karila-Cohen, Pierre, *L'État des esprits. L'invention de l'enquête politique en France (1814–1848)* (Rennes, 2008).

Kaufman, Asher, *Reviving Phoenicia: The Search for Identity in Lebanon* (London, 2014).

Kedward, Rod, *La Vie en Bleu: France and the French Since 1900* (London, 2005).

Kibbee, Douglas A., '"The People" and their Language in 19th-Century French Linguistic Thought', in Sheila Embleton, John E. Joseph and Hans-Josef Niederehe (eds), *The Emergence of the Modern Language Sciences: Studies on the Transition from Historical-Comparative to Structural Linguistics in Honour of E. F. K. Koerner. Volume 1: Historiographical Perspectives* (Amsterdam, 1999), 111–26.

Kwass, Michael, *Privilege and the Politics of Taxation in Eighteenth-Century France: Liberté, Égalité, Fiscalité* (Cambridge, 2000).

Kwass, Michael, *Contraband: Louis Mandrin and the Making of a Global Underground* (Cambridge, MA, 2014).

Kroen, Sheryl, *Politics and Theater: The Crisis of Legitimacy in Restoration France* (Berkeley, 2000).

Laborde, Jean, 'L'Impératrice Eugénie à Bayonne et à Biarritz (suite et fin)', *Bulletin de la Société des sciences, lettres et arts de Bayonne*, 75 (1956), 1–20.

Labouche, 'Le Chef de brigade Harispe et les chasseurs basques', *Bulletin de la Société des sciences, lettres et arts de Pau*, 22 (1892–93), 53–219.

Lafourcade, Maïté, 'Les Fors et les droits de l'homme', *Lapurdum*, 8 (2003), 329–48.

Laharie, Claude, *La Révolution dans les Basses-Pyrénées* (Pau, 1989).

Lawrence, Mark, *Spain's First Carlist War, 1833–1840* (London, 2014).

Leerssen, Joep, 'Introduction', in Joep Leerssen (ed.), *Encyclopedia of Romantic Nationalism in Europe*, Volume 1 (Amsterdam, 2018), 18–44.

Leerssen, Joep, *National Thought in Europe: A Cultural History* (Amsterdam, 2018).

Lefebvre, Georges, *Napoléon* (Paris, 1953).

Lefebvre, Georges, *The French Revolution from its Origins to 1793*, Elizabeth Moss Evanson trans. (London, 1962).

Lefebvre, Georges, *Les Paysans du Nord pendant la Révolution française* (Paris, 1972).

Lentz, Thierry, *Nouvelle Histoire du Premier Empire. Napoléon et la conquête de l'Europe, 1804–1810*, Volume 1 (Paris, 2002).

Lentz, Thierry, *Nouvelle Histoire du Premier Empire. L'effondrement du système napoléonien, 1810–1814*, Volume 2 (Paris, 2004).

Le Play, Frédéric, *L'Organisation de la famille selon le vrai modèle signalé par l'histoire de toutes les races et de tous les temps* (Tours, 1884).

Lethuillier, Jean-Pierre, 'Costumes régionaux, objets d'histoire', in Jean-Pierre Lethuillier (ed.), *Les Costumes régionaux entre mémoire et histoire* (Rennes, 2009), 7–26.

Lévêque, Pierre, *Histoire des forces politiques en France, 1789–1880*, Volume 1 (Paris, 1992).

Levi, Margaret, 'The Institution of Conscription', *Social Science History*, 20:1 (1996), 133–67.

Lignereux, Aurélien, *La France rébellionnaire. Les résistances à la gendarmerie (1800–1859)* (Rennes, 2008).

Limouzy, Jacques, *Émile Combes. Le fondateur spirituel de la laïcité. Du séminaire de Castres à la loi de 1905* (Toulouse, 2019).

López Antón, José Javier, *Escritores carlistas en la cultura vasca* (Pamplona, 1999).

Luc, Jean-Noël, Jean-François Condette and Yves Verneuil, *Histoire de l'enseignement en France, XIXe–XXIe siècles* (Malakoff, 2020).

Luis, Jean-Philippe, 'France and Spain: A Common Territory of Anti-Revolution (End of the 18th Century–1800)', in Matthijs Lok, Friedemann Pestel and Juliette Reboul (eds), *Cosmopolitan Conservatisms: Countering Revolution in Transnational Networks, Ideas and Movements (c. 1770–1930)* (Leiden, 2021), 261–82.

MacCannell, Dean, 'Staged Authenticity: Arrangements of Social Space in Tourist Settings', *American Journal of Sociology*, 79:3 (1973), 589–603.

Macdonald, Sharon, 'A People's Story: Heritage, Identity and Authenticity', in Chris Rojek and John Urry (eds), *Touring Cultures: Transformations of Travel and Theory* (London and New York, 1997), 155–75.

Madariaga Orbea, Juan, *Anthology of Apologists and Detractors of the Basque Language* (Reno, 2006).

Maier, Charles S., 'Consigning the Twentieth Century to History: Alternative Narratives for the Modern Era', *American Historical Review*, 105:3 (2000), 807–31.

Manfredini, Julie, *Les Syndicats d'initiative. Naissance de l'identité touristique en France* (Tours, 2017).

Manias, Chris, *Race, Science, and the Nation: Reconstructing the Ancient Past in Britain, France and Germany* (New York and London, 2013).

Maoz, Darya, 'The Mutual Gaze', *Annals of Tourism Research*, 33:1 (2006), 221–39.

Maron, Eugène, 'Notice sur la vie de Garat', in Dominique-Joseph Garat, *Mémoires de Garat* (Paris, 1862), i–xlvi.

Martel, Philippe, 'Le Félibrige', in Pierre Nora (ed.), *Les Lieux de mémoire. Les France 2*, Volume 3 (Paris, 1997), 567–611.

Martone, Eric, 'The Last Vendée: The Duchesse de Berry, Legitimist Propaganda, and Alexandre Dumas', in Eric Martone (ed.), *Royalists, Radicals and les Misérables: France in 1832* (Newcastle upon Tyne, 2013), 13–73.

Masson, Jean-Louis, *Provinces, départements, régions: l'organisation administrative de la France d'hier à demain* (Paris, 1984).

McCain, Stewart, *The Language Question under Napoleon* (Basingstoke, 2018).

Bibliography

McPhee, Peter, *Liberty or Death: The French Revolution* (New Haven, 2016).

Mihail, Benoît, *Le Passé flamand de la France et sa redécouverte de l'époque romantique au régime de Vichy* (Charleroi, 2006).

Molina Aparicio, Fernando, 'La disputada cronología de la nacionalidad. Fuerismo, identidad vasca y nación en el siglo XIX', *Historia contemporánea*, 30 (2005), 219–45.

Molina Aparicio, Fernando, 'España no era tan diferente. Regionalismo y identidad nacional en el País Vasco (1868–1898)', *Ayer*, 64 (2006), 179–200.

Moravia, Sergio, *Il pensiero degli Idéologues: scienza e filosofia in Francia (1780–1815)* (Florence, 1974).

Morel-Borotra, Natalie, 'Le Chant et l'identification culturelle des Basques (1800–1950)', *Lapurdum*, 5 (2000), 351–81.

Morgan, Nigel and Annette Pritchard, *Tourism Promotion and Power: Creating Images, Creating Identities* (Chichester, 1998).

Nisbet, Robert, *History of the Idea of Progress* (New York, 1980).

Nora, Pierre, 'Entre Mémoire et histoire. La problématique des lieux', in Pierre Nora (ed.), *Les Lieux de mémoire. La République*, Volume 1 (Paris, 1984), xvii–xlii.

Núñez, Xosé-Manoel, 'Historiographical Approaches to Sub-National Identities in Europe: A Reappraisal and Some Suggestions', in Joost Augusteijn and Eric Storm (eds), *Region and State in Nineteenth-Century Europe: Nation-Building, Regional Identities and Separatism* (London, 2012), 13–35.

Núñez Seixas, Xosé M. and Eric Storm, 'Introduction: Region, Nation and History', in Xosé M. Núñez Seixas and Eric Storm (eds), *Regionalism and Modern Europe: Identity Construction and Movements from 1890 to the Present Day* (London, 2019), 1–23.

Núñez Seixas, Xosé M. and Eric Storm (eds), *Regionalism and Modern Europe: Identity Construction and Movements from 1890 to the Present Day* (London, 2019).

Oişteanu, Andrei, *Inventing the Jews: Antisemitic Stereotypes in Romanian and Other Central-East European Cultures* (Lincoln and London, 2009).

Orpustan, Jean-Baptiste (ed.), *La Révolution française dans l'histoire et la littérature basques du XIXe siècle* (Saint-Étienne-de-Baïgorry, 1994), 279–93.

Ozouf, Mona, *L'École, l'Église et la République, 1871–1914* (Paris, 1963).

Ozouf, Mona, 'Esprit public', in François Furet and Mona Ozouf (eds), *Dictionnaire critique de la Révolution française* (Paris, 1988), 711–19.

Ozouf, Mona, *Composition française. Retour sur une enfance bretonne* (Paris, 2009).

Ozouf, Mona, *De Révolution en République. Les chemins de la France* (Paris, 2015).

Ozouf-Marignier, Marie-Vic, 'De l'Universalisme aux intérêts locaux: le débat sur la formation des départements en France (1789–1790)', *Annales: Économies, Sociétés, Civilisations*, 41:6 (1986), 1193–213.

Ozouf-Marignier, Marie-Vic, *La Formation des départements: la représentation du territoire français à la fin du dix-huitième siècle* (Paris, 1992).

Parsis-Barubé, Odile, *La Province antiquaire. L'invention de l'histoire locale en France (1800–1870)* (Paris, 2011).

Patriarca, Silvana, 'Indolence and Regeneration: Tropes and Tensions of Risorgimento Nationalism', *American Historical Review*, 110:2 (2005), 380–408.

Pauquet, Alain, '*Le Phare de Bayonne* et *La Sentinelle des Pyrénées*: regards croisés de deux journaux français sur l'actualité espagnole de 1838', *Cahiers de civilisation espagnole contemporaine*, 29 (2022).

Pitchford, Susan, *Identity Tourism: Imaging and Imagining the Nation* (Bingley, 2008).

Ploux, François, *Une Mémoire de papier. Les historiens de village et le culte des petites patries rurales (1830–1930)* (Rennes, 2011).

Price, Munro, *The Perilous Crown: France Between Revolutions, 1814–1848* (London, 2007).

Price, Munro, *Napoleon: The End of Glory* (Oxford, 2014).

Prost, Antoine, *Histoire de l'enseignement en France, 1800–1967* (Paris, 1968).

Quinn, Josephine, *In Search of the Phoenicians* (Princeton, 2017).

Ritzer, George and Allan Liska, '"McDisneyization" and "Post-Tourism": Complementary Perspectives on Contemporary Tourism', in Chris Rojek and John Urry (eds), *Touring Cultures: Transformations of Travel and Theory* (London and New York, 1997), 96–109.

Roessel, David, *In Byron's Shadow: Modern Greece in the English and American Imagination* (Oxford, 2002).

Rosanvallon, Pierre, *Le Moment Guizot* (Paris, 1985).

Rosenbaum, Adam T., *Bavarian Tourism and the Modern World, 1800–1950* (Cambridge, 2016).

Rothman, Hal, *Devil's Bargain: Tourism in the Twentieth-Century American West* (Lawrence, 1998).

Rudé, George, 'The Crisis of 1775 and the Traditions of Popular Protest', in Isser Woloch (ed.), *The Peasantry in the Old Regime* (New York, 1970), 82–7.

Rulof, Bernard, *Popular Legitimism and the Monarchy in France: Mass Politics Without Parties, 1830–1880* (New York, 2020).

Sacx, M., *Bayonne et le Pays basque. Témoins de l'histoire* (Bayonne, 1968).

Sahlins, Peter, *Boundaries: The Making of France and Spain in the Pyrenees* (Berkeley, 1991).
Said, Edward W., *Orientalism* (New York, 1978).
Schechter, Ronald, *Obstinate Hebrews: Representations of Jews in France, 1715–1815* (Oakland, 2003).
Shapiro, Gilbert, 'What Were the Grievances of France in 1789? The Most Common Demands in the *Cahiers de Doléances*', in Gilbert Shapiro and John Markoff, *Revolutionary Demands: A Content Analysis of the Cahiers de Doléances of 1789* (Stanford, 1998), 253–79.
Smith, Anthony D., *Myths and Memories of the Nation* (Oxford, 1999).
Smith, Anthony D., *The Ethnic Origins of Nations* (Hoboken, 1999).
Staum, Martin S., *Minerva's Message: Stabilizing the French Revolution* (Montreal, 1996).
Storm, Eric, *The Culture of Regionalism: Art, Architecture and International Exhibitions in France, Germany and Spain, 1890–1939* (Manchester, 2010).
Storm, Eric, 'Tourism and the Construction of Regional Identities', in Xosé M. Núñez Seixas and Eric Storm (eds), *Regionalism and Modern Europe: Identity Construction and Movements from 1890 to the Present Day* (London, 2018), 99–118.
Storm, Eric and Joep Leerssen, 'Introduction', in Joep Leerssen and Eric Storm (eds), *World Fairs and the Global Moulding of National Identities* (Leiden and Boston, 2022), 1–30.
Swenson, Astrid, 'The Law's Delay? Preservation Legislation in France, Germany and England, 1870–1914', in Melanie Hall (ed.), *Towards World Heritage: International Origins of the Preservation Movement, 1870–1930* (Farnham, 2011), 139–54.
Swenson, Astrid, *The Rise of Heritage: Preserving the Past in France, Germany and England, 1789–1914* (Cambridge, 2013).
Tackett, Timothy, *Priest and Parish in Eighteenth-Century France: A Social and Political Study of the Curés in a Diocese of Dauphiné, 1750–1791* (Princeton, 1977).
Tackett, Timothy, *Religion, Revolution, and Regional Culture in Eighteenth-Century France* (Princeton, 1986).
Thiesse, Anne-Marie, *Écrire la France. Le mouvement littéraire régionaliste de langue française entre la Belle Époque et la Libération* (Paris, 1991).
Thiesse, Anne-Marie, *Ils Apprenaient la France. L'exaltation des régions dans le discours patriotique* (Paris, 1997).
Thiesse, Anne-Marie, *La Création des identités nationales. Europe XVIIIe–XXe siècle* (Paris, 1999).
Todd, David, *L'Identité économique de la France. Libre-échange et protectionnisme, 1814–1851* (Paris, 2008).

Tombs, Robert, *France 1814–1914* (London and New York, 1996).
Tort, Olivier, *La Droite française. Aux origines de ses divisions (1814–1830)* (Paris, 2013).
Totoricagüena, Gloria P., *Identity, Culture, and Politics in the Basque Diaspora* (Reno, 2015).
Tozzi, Christopher, 'Soldiers of the *Pays*: Localism and Nationalism in the Revolutionary Era Army', in Philip Whalen and Patrick Young (eds), *Place and Locality in Modern France* (London and New York, 2014), 161–70.
Tozzi, Christopher J., *Nationalizing France's Army: Foreign, Black, and Jewish Troops in the French Military, 1715–1831* (Charlottesville and London, 2016).
Truesdell, Matthew, *Spectacular Politics: Louis-Napoleon Bonaparte and the* Fête Impériale, *1849–1870* (Oxford, 1997).
Tulard, Jean, *Napoleon: The Myth of the Saviour*, Teresa Waugh trans. (London, 1984).
Turner, Frank M., *European Intellectual History from Rousseau to Nietzsche*, Richard A. Lofthouse ed. (New Haven and London, 2016).
Turner, Louis and John Ash, *The Golden Hordes: International Tourism and the Pleasure Periphery* (London, 1975).
Umbach, Maiken, 'Nation and Region: Regionalism in Modern European Nation-States', in Timothy Baycroft and Mark Hewitson (eds), *What Is a Nation? Europe 1789–1914* (Oxford, 2006), 63–80.
Urbain, Jean-Didier, *Sur la Plage. Mœurs et coutumes balnéaires (XIXe–XXe siècles)* (Paris, 1996).
Urry, John, *The Tourist Gaze* (Los Angeles and London, 2001).
Van der Leeuw, Barbara, 'Regionalismo y nacionalismo en el siglo XIX: la batalla de los conceptos (País Vasco, Flandes y Frisia)', *Rubrica contemporánea*, 6:11 (2017), 44–64.
Vincent, Johan, *L'Intrusion balnéaire. Les populations littorales bretonnes et vendéennes face au tourisme (1800–1945)* (Rennes, 2007).
Vlossak, Elizabeth, *Marianne or Germania? Nationalizing Women in Alsace, 1870–1946* (Oxford, 2010).
Wagner, Peter, *Modernity: Understanding the Present* (Cambridge and Malden, 2012).
Wallon, Armand, *La Vie quotidienne dans les villes d'eaux, 1850–1914* (Paris, 1981).
Weber, Eugen, *Peasants into Frenchmen: The Modernization of Rural France, 1870–1914* (Stanford, 1976).
Weil, Patrick, *Être français. Les quatre piliers de la nationalité* (La Tour-d'Aigues, 2011).
Winock, Michel, 'L'Héritage contre-révolutionnaire', in Michel Winock (ed.), *Histoire de l'extrême droite en France* (Paris, 1993), 17–49.

Wolf, Eric R., *Europe and the People Without History* (Berkeley, 1982).
Wolff, Larry, *Inventing Eastern Europe: The Map of Civilisation on the Mind of the Enlightenment* (Stanford, 1994).
Woloch, Isser, 'Napoleonic Conscription: State Power and Civil Society', *Past and Present*, 111 (1986), 101–29.
Woloch, Isser, *The New Regime: Transformations of the French Civic Order, 1789–1820s* (New York and London, 1994).
Woodworth, Paddy, *The Basque Country: A Cultural History* (Oxford, 2008).
Woolf, Stuart, 'French Civilization and Ethnicity in the Napoleonic Empire', *Past and Present*, 124 (1989), 96–120.
Wright, Beth S., *Painting and History During the French Restoration: Abandoned by the Past* (Cambridge, 1997).
Wright, Julian, *The Regionalist Movement in France, 1890–1914: Jean Charles-Brun and French Political Thought* (Oxford, 2003).
Wright, Vincent, 'The Basses-Pyrénées from 1848 to 1870: A Study of Departmental Politics' (PhD thesis, University of London, 1965).
Young, Patrick, *Enacting Brittany: Tourism and Culture in Provincial France, 1871–1939* (Farnham, 2012).
Yvert, Benoît, *La Restauration. Les idées et les hommes* (Paris, 2013).
Zabaltza, Xabier, *Augustin Chaho, precursor incomprendido – un précurseur incompris, 1811–1858* (Vitoria-Gasteiz, 2011).
Zantedeschi, Francesca, *The Antiquarians of the Nation: Monuments and Language in Nineteenth-Century Roussillon* (Leiden, 2019).
Zuelow, Eric G. E., *Making Ireland Irish: Tourism and National Identity since the Irish Civil War* (Syracuse, 2009).

Index

Abarcarer Cantua 123
Action française 160, 168, 225
Adéma, Gratien, *curé* 118, 128, 131, 134
Affre, P.-R. 185
Aïtor (mythical founder of the Basques) 125, 141n.32
    legend of 124–6
Álava 5, 102, 133, 227
Alsace 8, 11, 55, 226
ancien régime 2, 3, 9, 17–22, 25, 26–7, 29–30, 31, 32–3, 40, 42, 46, 47, 53, 63–4, 65, 67, 71, 82, 99, 148, 151, 159, 225, 227
    fermiers 20–1
    franc-aleu 23
    intendant 21, 26, 30
    pays d'élection 13n.11, 19
    pays d'état 3, 13n.11, 19, 22, 25
    syndic 21, 27
Arana y Goiri, Sabino 6, 10, 81, 119
Araquistain, Juan de 129
Arcachon 202, 204, 205
Ariel 124, 129, 141n.32
Arrese y Beitia, Felipe de 132–3
    Ama Euskeriari azken agurrak 133
Asociación Euskara de Navarra 128, 131

Astarloa, Pablo Pedro de 92, 93, 96, 100
    Apología de la lengua bascongada 92, 96
Aubert du Bayet, Jean-Baptiste Annibal 45–6
L'Avenir des Pyrénées et des Landes 189, 191, 206, 213

Barère, Bertrand 150, 152, 168
    Rapport du Comité de Salut Public sur les idiomes 150
Barrès, Maurice 10, 135, 137
Basque Cantabrianism 40, 67, 78–9, 121, 133, 165, 166–7, 180, 228
Basque Iberianism 89, 91, 92, 93, 95, 97, 99, 101, 102, 107, 133, 227
Basse-Navarre 3, 17, 19, 22–4, 25, 27, 28, 29, 30, 31, 33, 41, 42, 124, 150, 227
    Estates of Navarre 23–4, 30
    kingdom of Navarre 23, 24–5, 121
Basses-Pyrénées (*département*) 18, 29, 31, 33, 43, 47, 48, 49, 52, 76, 81, 152, 153, 154, 155, 157, 158, 159, 161, 166, 191, 199, 200
Baudrimont, Alexandre 106

Bayonne 20, 27, 28, 51, 52, 53, 73, 75, 81, 150, 156, 178, 185, 201, 203, 204, 210
arrondissement of 31, 73, 157
district of 31
sub-prefect of 48, 147, 154
Béarn 18, 19, 28, 29, 30, 31, 53, 72, 118, 154, 158, 182, 212
Beauchesne, Alcide de 68
Bécassine au Pays basque 1
Béhobie 212
Belgium 200
Belzunce, Henri de, marquis 75, 76
Berdoly, Martial-Henri 166
bertsolaritza 7, 129, 130, 131, 132, 133, 163
Biarritz 8, 181, 182, 183, 184, 185, 186, 191, 199, 200–5, 206, 207–9, 210, 215–16
Bidassouet, Pierre d'Iharce de, abbé 53, 99–103, 104, 106, 107, 108, 111
Histoire des cantabres 53, 99–100, 103
Bilbao 43, 66, 70, 132
Bladé, Jean-François 107, 122–3
Études sur l'origine des basques 107
Blair, Hugh 123
A Critical Dissertation on the Poems of Ossian 123
Boisaumarié, Pierre 200
Bonaparte, Louis-Lucien 124, 131
Bonaparte, Louis-Napoleon *see* Napoleon III
Bonaparte, Napoleon *see* Napoleon I
Botrel, Théodore 165
Boucher, Gustave 134, 135, 137
Boulainvilliers, Henri de 21, 23
Boulogne 183

Brittany 1, 10, 24, 26, 152, 157, 158, 163, 165, 167, 206, 212, 225
Breton constitution 26
Breton language 134, 136, 150, 158, 167
Breton leisure societies 206
Breton population 10, 26, 129, 148, 158, 159, 165, 167, 189, 225, 229
Breton regionalist movement 10
Estates of Brittany 24
Burrow, George Henry 141n.29

cacolet 210–11
cahiers de doléances 26, 27, 30, 34n.13, 40, 42
Cambo 20, 187, 205, 215–16
Campión, Arturo 120, 123, 126
Orreaga 123
Cantar de Beotibar 121
Canto de Lelo 121–2
Canto de los Cantabres see Canto de Lelo
Carlism 63–4, 65, 68, 71, 76, 77, 78, 81
Carlist Wars 190, 199
First Carlist War (1833–40) 53, 54, 63–4, 65, 67, 73, 74, 76, 77, 78, 79, 80, 81, 103, 190, 191, 203
Carlists 63, 65, 69, 71, 74, 79, 80
cristinos 64, 68, 77, 79
Second Carlist War (1846–49) 190
Third Carlist War (1872–76) 191
Carlos de Borbón, known as Don Carlos 63–4, 65, 67, 68, 69, 70, 71, 75, 77–8, 181
as Carlos or Charles V 65, 71, 72, 75
Carnot, Lazare 52
Carnot-Feulin, Claude-Marie 53
Castellane-Novejean, Boniface de 47

Chaho, Augustin 53, 63, 76–81,
    82, 103–6, 109, 111, 120,
    124–6, 129–30, 141n.32
  Chant d'Annibal 124, 125
  Histoire primitive des
    Euskariens-Basques
    141n.32
  Légende d'Aïtor 124, 126
  Paroles d'un Bizkaïen aux
    libéraux de la reine
    Christine 77, 78
  Voyage en Navarre pendant
    l'insurrection des Basques
    77, 80, 81, 111, 141n.32
  see also Aïtor
Chambre d'Amour 210–11
chanson de geste 122, 123, 129,
    137
Chanson de Roland 122
charivari 216
Charles X 65, 100
Charles-Brun, Jean 135
chasseurs basques 40–1, 42, 43,
    44, 46, 47–8, 49–50, 51,
    52, 53, 54, 55, 160, 166,
    180
Chausenque, Vincent de 178, 190,
    215
Ciboure 20, 151
Civil Constitution of the Clergy
    99, 150–1
Combes, Émile 159, 161, 164
Combe-Sieyès, Georges 52
Comité de salut public 44, 148, 153
Congress of Basque Tradition 118,
    133, 134, 136
conscription 44, 47, 49, 50, 51,
    55, 153, 155, 156, 180
  desertion 9, 44, 45, 46, 47, 49,
    50, 55, 60n.48, 95, 155,
    166, 180, 211, 226
  levée en masse of 1793 47
  Loi Jourdan of 1798 44, 47,
    155
contraband 9, 74, 75, 180
  during the First Carlist War 74
  in popular folklore 9, 75, 180

corrida 1
Corsica 50, 152
Courrier de Bayonne, Le 214
Crónica de Vizcaya 40
Custine, Robert de 74, 75, 76

d'Abbadie, Antoine 8, 129, 130–1,
    162, 212, 228
d'Abbadie d'Arrast, Marie 188,
    212
d'Antin d'Ars, Pierre 154
d'Argout, Antoine Maurice
    Apollinaire 52–3
Darrigol, Jean-Pierre 103, 107
  Dissertation critique et
    apologétique sur la langue
    basque 103
Dasconaguerre, Jean-Baptiste 76
d'Auribeau, Louis Guillome 156
Declaration of the Rights of Man
    and of the Citizen 65,
    152, 159, 168, 190
Deffès, Jules 165
d'Elissagaray, Renaud 160
Dessolle, Jean Gabriel 154
d'Hiriart, Pierre Eustache 27, 28
Dieppe 183, 184, 200, 205
Dumay, Charles 165–6
Duvoisin, Jean-Pierre 131

Eaux-Bonnes 182, 212
Elizondo 133
Engels, Friedrich 189
Enlightened see Enlightenment
Enlightenment 63, 71, 82, 168,
    177, 179, 185, 190, 191
Erro y Azpiroz, Juan Bautista de
    92–3, 101
  Alfabeto de la lengua primitiva
    de España 92
Eskualduna 127–8, 132, 134, 135,
    160, 161, 162, 163,
    165–6, 167, 206, 213,
    226
espadrilles 1, 212
Estates-General 94
  summoning of 23, 27, 30

Index

Étretat 183
Eugénie de Montijo, empress of France 203
L'Europe 67
Euskara (Basque language) 3, 5, 6, 22, 29–30, 79, 89–90, 91–4, 95–100, 101–2, 103–11, 128, 130, 131, 133–4, 136, 147–9, 150, 151, 153, 154, 155, 157–8, 159, 162, 163, 164, 165, 167–8, 188, 216, 217, 228
Eys, Willem van 106

Fabre, Louis-Marie-Hyacinthe 178, 179, 183, 186, 187, 191
fandango 206
Fauriel, Claude 79, 122
  Histoire de la Gaule méridionale 122
Félibrige 128, 130
Fernando VII of Spain 64
fêtes basques 130–1, 134, 198, 206, 212–13, 228
fiestas euskaras 132, 133
First Empire (1804–14/15) 55, 94, 95, 97, 98, 200
First Republic (1792–1804) 45, 54, 98, 148, 149, 150, 152, 158, 159, 161–3, 168
First World War (1914–18) 11
Flanders 12n.2, 119, 158, 161, 163, 225
Flemish language 136, 158, 159
Flemish population 148, 158, 225
fors 3, 5, 22, 23, 24, 25, 82, 90, 108
  abolition of 3, 5, 25, 82, 90
Fourcaud, Louis de 133, 136–8
Francière, Georges 160, 164
Frisia 12n.2
fueros 5, 22, 63–5, 67, 68, 71, 72–3, 77, 79–80, 81–2, 90, 91, 120, 123, 128, 132, 133, 189, 190–1
  abolition of 5, 123, 128, 132, 133, 189, 191
fuerismo 119
fuerista movement 81
fueristas 5, 6, 79, 120, 121, 122, 123, 125, 129, 132, 135, 190

Gambetta, Léon 137
Garat, Dominique 30
Garat, Dominique-Joseph 27, 29, 30, 94–9, 100, 106, 111, 122
  'Nouvelle Phénicie' 94, 95, 98
  Recherches sur le people primitif de l'Espagne 94–5, 98
Garay de Monglave, Eugène 122
  Chant d'Altabiscar (Altabizarko Kantua) 122, 123
Gazette de France, La 68, 71
Gazette du Languedoc, La 73
Germany 90, 108, 111, 127, 128, 138, 229
German language 28, 30, 90, 150
Gilbert, Ambroise 164
Goizueta, José María de 129
Goyenèche, Albert 120
grande patrie 11, 41, 119, 135, 136, 137, 139, 159–60, 191, 218, 225, 229
Grand Sanhedrin 98
Grand Tour 179
Great Britain 98, 127, 138, 198
  British navy 95
Greece 5, 178
  ancient Greece 178
  ancient Greek epic literature 123
  philhellenes 5, 192
Grégoire, Henri, *abbé* 148, 150, 152, 168
  Rapport Grégoire 148

Guéthary 201, 206, 208
Guipúzcoa 5, 102, 121, 133, 182, 227

Habsburg Empire 4
Harispe, Jean Isidore 43, 50, 52–3, 53–4, 160, 166, 180
Haristoy, Pierre, *abbé* 131, 162
   Les Paroisses du Pays basque pendant la période révolutionnaire 131, 162
Harriet (*chef de brigade*) 46
Harriet, Maurice, *abbé* 131
Harriet, Pierre (*procureur du roi*) 20, 21
Heimaten 11, 229
Hendaye 201, 206, 207, 212
Herder, Johann Gottfried 79
Holland 98
Hondarribia 43, 212
Hugo, Victor 182, 184, 189
Humboldt, Wilhelm von 4, 93, 101, 107, 108, 121, 189
   journey to the Basque country 4, 93
   Prüfung der Untersuchungen über die Urbewohner Hispaniens vermittelst der vaskischen Sprache 93, 107–8

idéologue 94, 96
Inchauspé, Emmanuel, *abbé* 124, 131
Iparraguirre, José María de 132
   Guernicaco Arbola 132
Irún 43, 182, 183, 214
Isabel II of Spain 64, 66, 74
Italy 46, 124, 178
   ancient Rome 124, 178
Itxassou 44, 151, 154, 213

jeu de paume see pelota
Joannateguy (Dominican priest) 131

Journal de Saint-Jean-de-Luz, Le 206, 214
Jouy, Étienne de 98–9, 180
   L'Hermite en province 98
July Monarchy (1830–48) 65, 72, 81, 103, 225

Labourd 3, 17, 19, 20–1, 22, 25, 27, 28, 30, 31, 33, 40, 41, 42, 77, 80, 94, 102, 108, 153, 227
   Bilçar 19, 21, 27
Lagarde, Prosper de 178, 180, 188, 210, 212, 214
Laity, Armand 204
Lancre, Pierre de 210
   Tableau de l'inconstance des mauvais anges et démons 210
Landes 28, 154
Larralde, Madeleine 162–3
Larramendi, Manuel de 91–2, 94, 96, 100, 106
   Diccionario trilingue des castellano, bascuence y latin 91, 96
Lavigne, Germond de 181
Legislative Assembly (1791–92) 42
legitimism 63, 64, 65, 66, 70, 71, 72, 77
legitimists 63–4, 65–76, 77, 78, 79, 81, 82, 190, 225
Légitimiste, Le 71
Le Tréport 183, 184
L'Hôpital, de (state official) 21
Lorraine 28
Loti, Pierre 8, 215
Louis XIII 19, 24
Louis XIV 22
Louis XVI 23, 24, 30, 72, 151
Louis Antoine, duc d'Angoulême 66
Louis-Philippe 64, 65, 66, 74, 75

Macaye, Ganix de 75–6, 181
McPherson, James 123
   Ossian cycle 123

makhila 131, 212
Malthus, Thomas 177, 182
Manterola, José 129
María Cristina of Spain 64, 65, 66, 69, 70, 74, 77, 78, 191
María Teresa de Braganza, known as the princess of Beira 75–6, 181
'matrix language' 91–3, 94, 167
langue mère 100
Mauléon 73
  arrondissement of 31, 73
  district of 31
  sub-prefect of 155
Maurras, Charles 10
Maury, Jean-Sifrein, *abbé* 24
Mège, Alexandre du 104
  Statistique générale des départements pyrénéens 104
Messager de Bayonne, Le 203
Michel, Francisque 107, 122, 123–4, 127, 128, 129, 141n.29, 181
  Le Pays basque 107
Michelet, Jules 190
  Le Peuple 190
Mistral, Frédéric 128, 130
Mode, La 68, 70
Moncey, Bon-Andrien Jeannot de 45–6
Monestier, Pierre-Laurent 43
Montalivet, Jean-Pierre Bachasson, comte de 49
Montaran, Marie 182
Morel, Félix 179, 180, 186, 201
Murat, Joachim 47

Napoleon I 11, 31, 41, 46, 47, 48, 51, 55, 67, 94–5, 97, 98, 166, 180, 211
Napoleon III 8, 9, 11, 109, 187, 201, 203, 204
  in Biarritz 8, 203, 204

Napoleonic Wars 40, 46, 49, 52, 53, 54, 95, 180, 181, 198, 209, 225, 226
  Armée d'Espagne 48
  Peninsular War (1808–14) 41, 46, 51, 75
National Assembly (1789–91) 3, 17, 18, 24, 25, 27, 28, 29, 30, 40, 152
National Convention (1792–95) 148, 152
Navarra 5, 43, 70, 71, 72, 81, 99, 125, 133, 227
Normandy 33, 200, 228

Olivier, G. 127
Olóriz, Hermilio de 121, 123
One Hundred Days (1815) 41, 51, 52
O'Shea, Henry 205
Ostend 184, 200, 205

Paris, Gaston 136
Pasajes 182
pastorales 110, 129
patois 30, 96, 148, 158, 159, 167
Pau 31, 199
Paul, Henri 159
pelota 1, 9, 179, 206, 211, 213, 214, 215
Perret, Paul 183, 186, 208, 212
Petit Courrier de Biarritz, Le 205, 207, 208
petite patrie 9, 11, 41, 119, 135, 136, 137, 139, 159–60, 217, 225, 226, 229
philology 4, 30, 89–90, 91, 93, 98, 100, 103, 111, 166
Pinet, Jacques 43
Planté, Adrien 118, 138
'Les Basques, ont-ils une histoire?' 118, 138
Plombières 203
Polverel, Étienne de 23, 24

primary schooling 98, 135, 152–3, 156, 159, 160, 163, 168
instituteurs 109, 149, 152, 154, 157, 158, 164
Loi Ferry of 1882 149, 163
Loi Guizot of 1833 157
Lois Ferry of 1881–82 158, 163, 165
primitive monotheism 79, 89, 91, 93, 106
primogenital inheritance law 25
Provence 72, 128, 130

Quatrefages, Armand de 178, 208, 211
Quinet, Edgar 79
Quotidienne, La 72

Reclus, Élisée 106–10, 111
'Les Basques. Un peuple qui s'en va' 107
Renan, Ernest 137
Rénovateur, Le 72
représentants en mission 43, 44, 148, 150, 153, 162, 168
Restoration (1814/15–30) 31, 98–9
restored Bourbons 9, 74, 225
Réveil basque, Le 149, 166, 226
Revista Euskara 121, 126, 128
Revolution of 1789 2, 3, 7, 10, 11, 17–19, 23, 25, 26, 29–30, 33, 41, 42, 47, 53, 63–4, 68, 71–2, 78, 82, 94, 96, 97–8, 99, 102, 110, 119, 147–9, 150–3, 154, 155, 157, 159, 162, 163, 168, 190, 217, 224, 225, 228, 230
abolition of privileges (4 August 1789) 3, 17, 25, 33
creation of the *départements* (January 1790) 18, 26–30, 33
Comité de constitution 26, 27–8, 30, 33

Revolutionary army 41, 42, 166
Revolutionary Wars 40, 42, 47, 49, 52, 53, 54, 55, 180, 225, 226
Armée des Pyrénées 42
Armée des Pyrénées Occidentales 49
Armée du Midi 42
War of the Pyrenees (1793–95) 41, 43, 44, 50, 55
Rhine (region) 52, 55, 101, 152
Riger, V. 208
Romantic *see* Romanticism
Romanticism 4, 6, 75–6, 79, 91, 93, 106, 111, 118, 120, 124, 125, 126, 129, 177, 179, 182, 183, 184, 185, 199, 201, 202, 203, 209, 210, 211, 212
Roncesvalles 122, 123
battle of 122
Rostand, Edmond 205
Rousseau, Jean-Jacques 176, 185–6, 187
Discours sur l'origine de l'inégalité parmi les hommes 186
Russia 198, 215

Saint-Jean-de-Luz 1, 20, 52, 118, 120, 130, 133, 136, 163, 201, 206, 213, 214, 215
Saint-Jean-Pied-de-Port 42, 52, 75
Saint-Palais 28, 214
district of 31
Saint-Sauveur 203
Salic Law 64, 66
Sallaberry, Jean-Dominique-Julien 129
Sanadon, Jean-Baptiste 22, 150
San Sebastián 43, 122, 132, 199
Sanskrit 79, 99, 103, 104–5, 106
Santesteban, José António 129
Sare 21, 51, 154, 162
Schlegel, Friedrich 106

Scott, Walter 125, 126
Second Empire (1852–70) 8, 10,
   31, 76, 109–10, 182, 184,
   185, 187, 191, 198, 203,
   204, 225
Second Republic (1848–52) 54, 81
Sentinelle des Pyrénées, La 76,
   179, 201
Serviez, Emmanuel de 165–6
Soule 3, 17, 19, 22, 25, 27, 28,
   31, 33, 41, 42, 63, 76,
   81, 129, 227
Soult, Jean-de-Dieu 48, 52
Spach, Louis 127
Spain 5, 6, 20, 21, 22, 26, 41, 42,
   43, 46, 47, 48, 51, 52,
   53, 64, 65, 66, 67, 68,
   70, 71, 73, 74, 75, 79,
   82, 89, 90, 91–4, 95, 98,
   99, 101–2, 108, 119, 120,
   125, 126, 127, 128, 129,
   131, 132, 135, 150, 153,
   158, 162, 166, 178, 181,
   189, 190–1, 198–9, 207,
   211, 212, 214, 227, 228
Spanish Basque country 5, 10,
   12n.2, 64, 68, 71, 81, 90,
   91, 131–2, 133, 227
Stuart Costello, Louisa 180, 181,
   211

Taine, Hippolyte 182
Terray, Joseph Marie 21
Terror (1793–94) 29, 44, 99, 148,
   153–4, 158, 162, 163
Third Republic (1870–1940) 4, 8,
   10, 11, 31, 82, 112, 135,
   137, 149, 158, 159,
   160–3, 166, 167, 168,
   187, 188, 190, 198, 217,
   225, 226, 228, 229
Towiański, Andrzej 79
Tragia, Joaquín de 92
   *Diccionario geográfico-histórico
   de España* 92

Trouville 183, 205
Tubal (mythical founder of the
   Basques) 22, 89, 93,
   125

United States 199
Urrugne 52, 131, 206, 213, 214
Ursprache (original Indo-European
   language) 94, 106

Vanssay, Charles-Achille de 49–50,
   55
Vendée 65, 68, 150, 225
   Spanish Vendée 69
Vichy 203
Vigreux, Alfred 201
Villoslada, Francisco Navarro 125,
   126
   *Amaya o los vascos en el siglo
   VIII* 125, 126
Vinson, Julien 8, 129, 188, 189,
   190
Vioménil, Charles du Houx 53
Vitoria 43, 125
Vizcaya 5, 67, 68, 102, 121, 126,
   133, 227
Vocaltha (French legitimist
   volunteer) 67, 68, 70
Voltaire, François-Marie Arouet
   179

Webster, Wentworth 8, 128, 129
Weld, Charles Richard 182, 186,
   204
Wellesley, Arthur 48, 51
women
   as bearers of traditional values
   178–9, 186
   as leaders of local uprisings 20,
   21

Zumalacárregui, Tomás de 53–4,
   68, 69, 70, 71, 77, 79,
   80, 111
   as El Cid of Navarra 70

EU authorised representative for GPSR:
Easy Access System Europe, Mustamäe tee 50,
10621 Tallinn, Estonia
gpsr.requests@easproject.com

www.ingramcontent.com/pod-product-compliance
Lightning Source LLC
Chambersburg PA
CBHW051606230426
43668CB00013B/2007